# SUNDAY

## WEEKLY LEADER GUIDE

*Sundays, Feast Days & Solemnities*

*Year B*

# SUNDAY WEEKLY LEADER GUIDE

*Sundays, Feast Days & Solemnities*
*Year B*

*In Canada*
NOVALIS

*In England*
T. SHAND PUBLICATIONS, Ltd.

*In the United States*
T  R  E  E  H  A  U  S

TREEHAUS COMMUNICATIONS, INC., P.O. BOX 249, LOVELAND, OHIO 45140

*Acknowledgment*
Sr. Paule Freeburg, D.C. and Christopher Walker
wish to express their gratitude to the Daughters
of Charity in Belgium for their hospitality while
working on the *SUNDAY* project.


[ ] Text that appears in brackets may be omitted by the reader.

*United States Publisher*
TREEHAUS COMMUNICATIONS, INC.
P.O. Box 249
Loveland, Ohio 45140
*Website:* www.treehaus1.com
*E-mail:* treehaus@treehaus1.com


Typographical design by Treehaus in Century Schoolbook.
No part of this publication may be reproduced, stored in a
retrieval system, or transmitted in any form or by any means
without prior permission in writing from Treehaus Communications, Inc.

*The Sunday Leader Guide* includes the adapted Scripture texts
from *The Sunday Book of Readings/The Lectionary Adapted for Children*
which has been endorsed for liturgical use in Canada by
The Episcopal Commission for Liturgy,
Canadian Conference of Catholic Bishops.

*Printed and bound in the United States.*
*Fourth Revised Edition: 1996.*

Music © 1990 by Christopher Walker (Sole Agent: Oregon Catholic Press).
Duplication in whole or part prohibited.

ISBN 0-929496-58-2

© 1990, 1992, 1994, 1996, 2002, 2005 Forum Katecheticum

# Contents

\* *For parishes with a children's catechumenate, and in keeping with the* Order for the Christian Initiation of Adults, *the readings for the 3rd, 4th, and 5th Sundays of Lent/Year A may be used in place of the readings selected for those Sundays in Year B.*

\*\* *In keeping with the* Directory For Masses With Children *(Paragraph 43), some of the readings assigned to the day have been changed when they appear "unsuited to the capacity of children." Changes have been made in the following occasions: Christmas, Easter, Body and Blood of Christ, 12th Sunday in Ordinary Time, Transfiguration of the Lord, All Souls, Dedication of St. John Lateran.*

# The Seasons of Advent
## and
## Christmas

# FIRST SUNDAY OF ADVENT

## YEAR B

### PRAYER OF THE DAY:

God,
you love us so much
that you want to be among us
and share your life with us.
Make us ready
to welcome you
by following your ways
and living at peace
with one another.
We ask you to do this
through Christ, our Lord.

### FOCUS OF THE READINGS:

Our God is coming! Stay awake! Be ready!

Culturally, we are accustomed to thinking of all of Advent as preparation for the birth of Jesus. But liturgically, we find a quite different emphasis. Only on the Fourth Sunday of Advent do we focus on the birth of Jesus, the Messiah. The first Sunday reminds us of the coming of Christ at the end of time. The second and third Sundays focus on the acceptance of Christ in our lives today, through baptism. It is this tension between the present and the future that gives meaning to the fourth Sunday and, indeed, to our celebration of the historical birth at Christmas.

Our first reading today tells us that, in spite of God's continued love and care, the chosen people have sinned—they have wandered away from their covenant relationship with their creator. They cry out again for redemption.

### FIRST READING: *Isaiah 63:16-17, 19; 64:2-7*

*This is a reading from the prophet Isaiah.*

You, O God, are our Creator.
You have always been our redeemer,
our Savior.
Why do you let us wander from your ways
and allow our hearts to turn away from you?

Oh, how we wish you would open the heavens
and come down to us.
You have already done mighty things for us—
things beyond our hopes and dreams.
No one has ever heard or seen any God but you
doing such things.
You do wonderful things
for those who trust in you.

[You want to find us doing what is right,
following your ways.
But you are angry with us
because we are sinful.
We have all done what is wrong.
We are weak, and we live in sinful ways.

We don't pay any attention to you
or pray to you.
And yet, you are our Creator.
We are the clay and you are the potter.
We have all been made by your hand.]

*The Word of the Lord.*

[ ] Reader may omit text that appears in brackets.

### RESPONSE: *Psalm 80*

RESPONSE:
Come and stay with us O Lord. Ho-ly is your name.

VERSES: to Response
1. God in heav-en, shine on us. You who are might-y, save __ us.
2. Come our Sav-ior, stay with us. Come__ and bring us back to you.

## GOSPEL ACCLAMATION:

"Stay a-wake, be read-y. You do not know the hour when the Lord is com-ing. Stay a-wake, be read-y." The Lord is com-ing soon! Al-le-lu-ia, al-le-lu-ia! "The Lord is com-ing soon."

GOSPEL: *Mark 13:33-37*

*This is a reading from the Gospel of Mark.*

Jesus said to his disciples,

"Always be ready!
Stay awake.
You do not know
when the special time will come.
Think about someone going on a long trip.
Before leaving, the owner of the house
puts the servants in charge of everything
and gives each one a special task.
One servant is told
to guard the door very carefully.

"Pay attention!
You do not know
when the owner of the house is coming back.
It may be in the evening,
at midnight or early in the morning.
Do not let the owner come home suddenly
and find you asleep.
What I am saying to you,
I say to everyone:
Pay attention! Be ready!"

*The Gospel of the Lord.*

The Gospel focuses on the coming of Christ at the end of time and our need to be prepared. It was the constant warning of the early church—Christ will come again, but we do not know the time. Like the early Christians, we are called to love in such a way that we are always ready to greet the Lord at his coming. We too are urged to "stay awake, be ready!"

## REFLECTING ON THE READINGS WITH CHILDREN:

*NOTE: As a basic principle, it is important to have the children express what they heard in the readings. One need not do this by asking, "What did you hear?" each time you gather. But once you set up that style of reflection, the children will naturally learn to participate by sharing what they have heard.*

Give the children time to share what they have heard. Then help them see that we usually prepare for events because we know when they are expected. For example, we prepare for Christmas now because we know that Christmas is celebrated on December 25th. We prepare for a birthday party because we know the date of the birthday. But Jesus tells us in today's Gospel that we do not know the date when he will return, and so we must always be prepared for that great event. We must be ready to meet him when he comes.

How do you think we can be ready? What does Jesus mean, "be ready"? What would you want to be doing when Jesus comes? Would you want to be at war or fighting someone? Spend some time, if possible, on the image presented in the first reading: "We are the clay and you are the potter."

The children should leave today's liturgy believing that we are waiting for a day of joy and peace and that there are things we can do (on their level) to be ready for it. They should also be aware that even though we are not always perfect, God loves us and is always our creator—the God who made us, the redeemer—and is with us to help us live as Jesus tells us to live.

## SECOND SUNDAY OF ADVENT

## YEAR B

### PRAYER OF THE DAY:

Forgiving God,
help us prepare
for your coming
by being sorry for
what we have done wrong.
Fill us with your power
so that we may know you
and love you more and more,
and let all the world
live in peace.
We ask you to do this
through our friend
and brother,
Jesus Christ,
who lives forever.

### FOCUS OF THE READINGS:

Our God is coming! Prepare the way! Change your lives!

The people of Israel were in exile in Babylon. In their understanding, this was the punishment for their sin. Our reading focuses on their liberation from their exile. It speaks of the "herald of good news" who will be the voice proclaiming, "Your God is coming, in power and justice, to save you. Prepare the way!" Isaiah uses symbolic language—every valley and mountain shall be level. This image tells us that, with the coming of our God, justice will reign, and all will be equal. Our Gospel passage introduces John the Baptist whose role is to announce the beginning of the public ministry of Jesus. To prepare the way for the one who will baptize in the Holy Spirit, John the Baptist calls us to repent and change our lives. He calls us to conversion—now!

### FIRST READING: *Isaiah 40:1-5, 9-10*

*This is a reading from the prophet Isaiah.*

Our God says:

"Give comfort to my people.
  Speak tenderly to the people of Jerusalem
  and tell them that their punishment is over."

A voice proclaims:

"Prepare the way for the coming of our God!
  In the desert,
  make a straight path for our God!
Every valley will be filled in.
Every mountain and hill will be made small.
The rough and rugged land
  will be made smooth.
Then the glory of God
  will be seen by all the people,
  for our God has spoken!"

Our God says,

"Go up on a high mountain,
  O herald of good news,
  and say to the people,

  'Here is your God!
  Our God is coming in power
  to rule with strength
  and to bring reward and justice to all.' "

*The Word of the Lord.*

### RESPONSE: *Psalm 85*

RESPONSE:
Come and stay with us O Lord. Ho - ly is your name.

VERSES:
to Response

1. For all your peo-ple you bring peace. Now— sal - va - tion comes for us.
2. You come with jus-tice; be with us. As you have prom-ised: Save— us.

## GOSPEL ACCLAMATION:

Change your lives, he's com-ing. The one who will bap-tize with the Ho-ly Spir-it. Change your lives, he's com-ing. The Lord is com-ing soon! Al-le-lu-ia, a-le-lu-ia! "The Lord is com-ing soon."

## GOSPEL: *Mark 1:1-8*

*This is a reading from the Gospel of Mark.*

This is the beginning
of the Gospel of Jesus Christ, the Son of God.
Isaiah, the prophet, wrote,

"I am sending my messenger
 to prepare the way for you.
 He will proclaim,

 'Prepare the way for the coming of God!
 Make a straight path for our God!' "

And so, John the Baptizer came,
telling everyone to change their lives and be baptized
so their sins would be forgiven.

Many people around Jerusalem
went to the desert to see John.
They confessed their sins
and were baptized in the Jordan River.

John wore clothes made from the hair of camels,
and he wore a leather belt around his waist.
He ate locusts and wild honey.

When he preached, he always said,

"Someone else is coming after me.
 He is more powerful than I am.
 I am not even worthy to undo his sandals.
 I am baptizing you in water,
 but he will baptize you in the Holy Spirit."

*The Gospel of the Lord.*

## REFLECTING ON THE READINGS WITH CHILDREN:

What did you hear?

Help the children come to know John the Baptist and his role in salvation history. What was his message? What is the "good news" that he announced? What did he say about Jesus?

Help the children see that we are called now, during Advent, to change our lives in order to prepare to celebrate the Lord's coming. How can we change our lives? It is important that the children focus on their own lives rather than on changes needed in the world at large. Children are not responsible for the problems of the world and have very little to do with the solutions to them. They should see that what they can do in their families, schools, neighborhoods, and so forth, is important. Help the children see that, because they have been baptized in the Holy Spirit, they too are heralds of good news for others. God has promised a time when people will know justice and all will be treated equally. ("Every valley will be filled in. Every mountain and hill will be made small. The rough and rugged land will be made smooth.") How can we help that come to be? How can we help bring about justice around us? Help the children see that God calls us to treat all persons politely. Children will readily see the possibilities of this in their own lives.

Finally, assure the children of God's great love for us. Even when we have sinned, God sends words of comfort. God always comes to us with mercy and good news.

## THIRD SUNDAY OF ADVENT

### YEAR B

### PRAYER OF THE DAY:

Give us strength;
build up our courage,
mighty God,
because we are sometimes
weak and afraid.
You sent Jesus
to make the sick better
and to be a friend of the poor.
May we believe in him
and be happy
that you always support us.
We pray to you
through Jesus, our Lord.

### FOCUS OF THE READINGS:

Good news for the poor! Christ, our Light, is among us!

Our first reading focuses on justice. The One sent by God is anointed by the Spirit for mission, and his mission is to the poor, the oppressed, the brokenhearted. He will bring justice to the world and the poor will be exalted—bedecked with the jewels of salvation.

The Gospel reading focuses on Christ the Light. Again we hear from John the Baptist who is the witness to the Light. John calls us to see the Light who is already in our midst. That Light is Christ, and he is the God who comes to save.

### FIRST READING: *Isaiah 61:1-2, 10-11*

*This is a reading from the prophet Isaiah.*

The spirit of God is upon me.
God has anointed me
and sent me to bring good news to the poor,
to comfort those whose hearts are broken,
to proclaim freedom
to those who are being held captive
and to those who are oppressed by others,
and to announce a time of blessing
and justice from our God.

My heart is happy and filled with joy,
for God has given me the clothes of salvation.
God has put on me a robe of justice.
I am like a bridegroom wearing a crown
or a bride wearing her jewels.
And now, our God will bring justice
and glory to all the nations.

*The Word of the Lord.*

### RESPONSE: *Luke 1:46-55*

God, my heart de-lights in you. Ho-ly is your name.____

VERSES:
to Response

1. You keep_ your prom-ise al - ways; help-ing your peo - ple all their days.
2. You care for your ser-vant; all will see. Now_ your good-ness bless-es me.

### GOSPEL ACCLAMATION:

Change your lives, he's com-ing. The one who is the light of the world is com-ing. Change your lives, he's com-ing. The reign of God is near, al-le-lu-ia, al-le-lu-ia, the reign of God is near.

GOSPEL: *John 1:6-8, 28, 19-27*

*This is a reading from the Gospel of John.*

There was a man sent by God—
a man whose name was John.
He came as a witness
to tell the world about the light
so that everyone would believe.
John was not the light
but only a witness
to tell others about the light.
John was baptizing people
near the Jordan River. One day the Pharisees
sent priests and levites to ask John,

  "Who are you?"

He told them very clearly,

  "I am not the Messiah."

Then they asked him,

  "Are you a prophet?"

John said,

  "No, I am not."

Finally, they said to him,

  "Tell us who you are
    so we can give some answer
    to those who sent us.
    What do you say about yourself?"

John told them,

  "I am the one the prophet Isaiah wrote about.
  I am 'the voice in the desert, proclaiming,
  'Make a straight path for our God!' "

Then they asked John,

  "If you are not the Messiah
    and not the prophet, why do you baptize?"

John answered,

  "I baptize with water.
    But the one I am telling you about
    is with you now,
    but you do not recognize him.
    I am not even worthy to untie his sandal."

*The Gospel of the Lord.*

## REFLECTING ON THE READINGS WITH CHILDREN:

Begin by giving the children an opportunity to reflect on what they heard.

The children were introduced to John the Baptist in last Sunday's Gospel. There he was presented as the one who calls us to change our lives. This week, help the children understand the meaning of a "witness." Spend some time on this. Allow the children time to verbalize their understanding of the word. They may be familiar with witnesses on T.V. programs. Perhaps some have personal family experiences of witnessing an accident. Help them understand that a witness is one who has seen and then speaks out. How was John the Baptist a witness to Jesus? How can we be witnesses to Jesus? As always, it is important that the children focus on ways of witnessing that are truly possible at their age rather than on generalities or projects beyond the sphere of their lives. The Gospel will impact their lives only if it is related to their real lives.

Like the prophet in *Isaiah*, Jesus came to "bring good news to the poor, to comfort those whose hearts are broken. . . ." Explore with them the meaning of this today. Who are the poor, the brokenhearted, and so forth? Can we be a witness to Jesus by helping the poor, comforting those who are sad, and so forth?

Above all, this Third Sunday of Advent, proclaim the joy that we have because God loves us and sent Jesus for us.

# FOURTH SUNDAY OF ADVENT

## YEAR B

### PRAYER OF THE DAY:

God,
you chose ordinary people,
common people,
to make a home for Jesus.
We want to make a home
for him in our hearts;
give us the love to do this,
and let him be our brother,
forever and ever.

### FOCUS OF THE READINGS:

God's love is faithful! Mary will give birth to a son. Holy is his name!

Our first reading focuses on the promise made to David—a member of his family would be a great king whose kingdom would last forever. This reading is filled with the fidelity of God: "I called you. . . .I have always been with you. . . .I promise to be with you forever. . . .He will be like a son to me. . . .I will never take my love away from him."

That promise is fulfilled in the Annunciation. By the power of the Spirit, Mary will give birth to a child, and "he will be called the Son of God, . . .and he will be the ruler of the family of David."

In both of these readings we see the power of God at work in human beings—God's faithful love made real in history.

### FIRST READING: *2 Samuel 7:8-16*

*This is a reading
from the second book of Samuel.*

God said to King David,

"I am the one who found you
  while you were taking care of your sheep
  in the pasture.
I called you to be a leader of my people.
I have been with you wherever you went.
I have destroyed all your enemies.
I will make you famous
  like the great people of the earth.
I will build a house for you,
and I will be with you
and your family forever.
I will give my people
a special place to live in peace without fear.
And when you die,
I will make a member of your family
a great king.
He will be like a son to me,
and I will never take my love away from him.
I will make your family strong,
and your kingdom will last forever."

*The Word of the Lord.*

### RESPONSE: *Psalm 89*

RESPONSE:
God, my heart de-lights in you. Ho - ly is your name. ____

VERSES: *to Response*
1. I sing, your love is won-der-ful. You are al-ways faith - ful.
2. You said to Da-vid long a - go: You will al-ways bless__ him.

## GOSPEL ACCLAMATION:

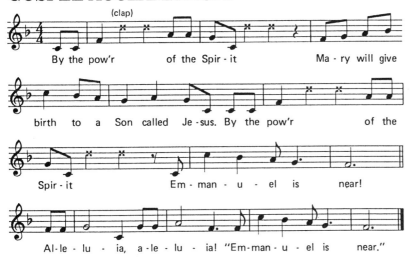

(clap)
By the pow'r of the Spir-it Ma-ry will give
birth to a Son called Je-sus. By the pow'r of the
Spir-it Em-man-u-el is near!
Al-le-lu-ia, a-le-lu-ia! "Em-man-u-el is near."

## GOSPEL: *Luke 1:26-38*

### *This is a reading from the Gospel of Luke.*

The angel Gabriel was sent from God
to the town of Nazareth in Galilee.
The angel went to a young virgin
who was engaged to Joseph, from the family of David.
The virgin's name was Mary.
The angel said to her,
  "Rejoice, Mary, you have been blessed by God.
   The Lord is with you, and you are filled with grace."

Mary was very confused and disturbed
by what the angel said,
and she wondered what it could mean.
The angel said to her,
  "Don't be afraid, Mary. God has chosen you.
   You are going to give birth to a baby.
   You will give him the name, Jesus.
   He will be great, and he will be called the Son of God.
   He will be the ruler of the family of David,
   and his kingdom will never end."

Mary said to the angel,
  "How can this happen, since I do not have a husband?"
The angel answered her,
  "The power of God will make it possible.
   The Holy Spirit will come to you,
   and this Holy Child will be called the Son of God.
   And your cousin, Elizabeth, is also going to have a baby
   even though she seems too old,
   for nothing is impossible with God."
And Mary said,
  "I am the servant of the Lord.
   Let what you have said be done."
And the angel left her.

### *The Gospel of the Lord.*

## REFLECTING ON THE READINGS WITH CHILDREN:

Advent is a season of hope—hope in the fulfillment of God's promise made long ago, hope in a better world because Jesus was born, hope in eternal life when Jesus comes in glory. All of the readings during Advent have given us hope. Help the children see that God's promises never fail and that God loves us and is always faithful.

The Fourth Sunday of Advent, in all three cycles, focuses on the relationship between the creative power of the Holy Spirit and the human agent, Mary, in the role of salvation. Today is a day for reflecting with the children on the role of Mary. Help the children see Mary as a human person, a woman who lived an ordinary life. If we create an image of Mary which gives the impression that she is somehow different from the rest of humanity, we strip her fiat—her freely-given response to God in faith—of its true meaning. We also deny ourselves and the children the model for growing in the reality that we, like Mary, are called to total faith in God and that, as human beings like Mary, we can do that. Help the children understand that, like Mary, we can bring Christ to others. Help them see and admire in Mary her active, free, and obedient response to God. It is in this way that the children will see in Mary a model that they can not only look up to, but can indeed imitate. Help them see that in doing this we are also truly the servant of the Lord, and that when we say, "Let it be done to me as you have said," we also make Christ present in our world.

You might make the Annunciation real by asking the children questions such as:

- Where did Mary live?
- Who was she going to marry?
- How did the angel Gabriel greet Mary?
- Why was Mary confused?
- What did Gabriel tell Mary?
- Why was Mary's answer to the angel so special?

Help the children see that Mary said "yes" even though she didn't understand everything God was asking through the angel.

# CHRISTMAS DAY

## YEAR B

### PRAYER OF THE DAY:

God in heaven,
you never forget we need you,
and that is why
you sent your Son, Jesus,
to be born as a baby
like one of us.
We thank you
for such a tremendous gift
and praise Jesus,
who is mighty God
and Prince of Peace,
now and forever.

*Note: In keeping with the* Directory for Masses With Children *(paragraph 43), the authors have elected to use the readings for Midnight Mass instead of those for Christmas Day Mass because they seem better suited "to the capacity of children."*

### FOCUS OF THE READINGS:

The Gospel for the Christmas Day celebration is taken from the prologue of John's Gospel (1:1-18). This magnificent hymn of the Incarnation is perhaps one of the most beautiful passages in all of scripture. However, its language, at once poetic and highly theological, is scarcely understood by children. We have, therefore, chosen to use the nativity story in *Luke* which is proclaimed at the Mass of Midnight and Dawn.

### FIRST READING: *Isaiah 9:1-2, 5-7*

*This is a reading from the prophet Isaiah.*

The people who were in darkness
have seen a great light.
You, God, have filled them with great joy.
For a child is born to us; a son is given to us.
He is called:

> Wonderful Counselor,
> the Mighty God,
> the One Who Lives Forever,
> the Prince of Peace.

His kingdom will be great.
He will rule with justice and peace, now and forever.
The love of our God will make this happen!

*The Word of the Lord.*

### RESPONSE: *Psalm 96*

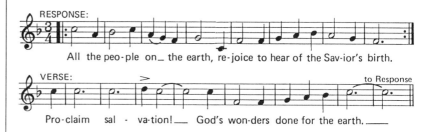

### GOSPEL ACCLAMATION:

### GOSPEL: *Luke 2:1-20*

*This is a reading from the Gospel of Luke.*

When Caesar Augustus, the ruler of Rome,
passed a law that everyone in the world
should be enrolled,
all the people went to be registered in the towns
where they were born.

Joseph and Mary went from the town of Nazareth
to the City of David, which is called Bethlehem,
because Joseph was born to the family of David.
While they were there,
the time came for Mary's child to be born,
and she gave birth to her first-born son.
She wrapped him in swaddling clothes
and laid him in a manger
because there was no room for them in the inn.

At that time,
there were shepherds in the fields
watching over their sheep during the night.
An angel of God appeared to them,
and the glory of God surrounded them
with a great light. And they were frightened.

The angel said to them,

"Do not be afraid.
I have come to bring you good news—
news of great joy to be shared by all the people.
Today, in the City of Bethlehem,
a Savior has been born for you, Christ the Lord!
And this will be a sign for you—
you will find a child wrapped in swaddling clothes
and lying in a manger."

Suddenly, all the angels of heaven
were praising God and singing,

"Glory to God in heaven,
and peace to all people on earth."

The shepherds said to one another,

"Let us go over to Bethlehem
and see this wonderful thing God has told us about."

They hurried to Bethlehem
and found Mary and Joseph
and saw the baby lying in the manger.
When they saw the child,
they repeated what the angel had said about him.

Everyone was amazed
at what the shepherds told them.
And Mary thought about all these things
and kept them in her heart.

The shepherds returned to their fields,
thanking and praising God
for all they had heard and seen.

*The Gospel of the Lord.*

While it, too, is highly theological
(Please see "Introduction to the
Infancy Narratives," p. 163.), it is
written in a language children can
understand and enjoy. They may
miss many of the theological
references, but they will surely
understand the joy and excitement
which accompanies our salvation.
They will understand the great love
God has for us as expressed in this
event. And this, we suggest, is the
focus of the readings: God's great
love for the world—God's great gift
to the world. Into a world of
darkness and sin, a child is born,
bringing light and peace. The Gospel
proclaims, "Do not be afraid. I bring
you good news. A Savior has been
born for you."

*Rejoice, all people on earth!*
*Today a Savior is born for you,*
*Christ the Lord!*

REFLECTING ON THE READINGS
WITH CHILDREN:

We suggest that, on this day, the
children participate in a
dramatization of the Christmas story,
allowing the rich symbols to speak
for themselves. The drama on the
following pages is one example.

## Gospel Drama for Christmas Season

Gospel: *Luke 2:1-20*

Children always enjoy acting out the Christmas story. It should be prepared before Christmas. Children will be needed for the roles of:

| | |
|---|---|
| Mary | Shepherds |
| Joseph | Youngest child to bring child Jesus |
| Angels | Narrator (older child) |

Props required: A crib or manger. A candle for each child. A doll.

*Narrator*: In those days, Caesar Augustus, the ruler of Rome, passed a law that everyone in the world should be counted. And so, all the people went to the town where they were born to give their names. Joseph and Mary went from the town of Nazareth to the city of David, which is called Bethlehem, because Joseph was born into the family of David.

*Action: Mary and Joseph travel to Bethlehem. Under her cloak, Mary hides a doll wrapped in swaddling clothes.*
*Or: Standing off-stage, the youngest child holds the doll.*

*Narrator*: While they were there, the time came for Mary's child to be born. She gave birth to her first-born son and wrapped him in swaddling clothes and laid him in a manger because there was no room for them in the inn.

*Action: Mary carries the doll under her cloak and places it in the manger.*
*Or: The youngest child brings the doll and gives it to Mary and remains at her side.*

*Narrator*: At that time, shepherds who lived in the fields were watching over their sheep at night. An angel of God appeared to them, and the glory of the Lord surrounded them like a great light. And they were frightened.

*Action: An angel approaches the shepherds.*

*Angel*: Do not be afraid, I come to bring you Good News, news of great joy to be shared by all the people. Today, in the City of Bethlehem, a Savior has been born for you. This Savior is Christ the Lord! And here is a sign for you: you will find a child wrapped in swaddling clothes and lying in a manger.

*Narrator*: Suddenly, all the angels of heaven were praising God and singing:

*Angels:* Glory to God in heaven, and peace to all people on earth. (*A few children join in the singing of the Gloria.*)

*Narrator:* Let us join our voices to the voices of the angels and sing: "Glory to God in heaven, and peace to all people on earth."

*All:* (*Sing a Gloria taken from the Christmas carols repertoire.*)

*Narrator:* The shepherds said to one another:

*One Shepherd:* Let us go over to Bethlehem and see this wonderful thing God has told us about.

*Narrator:* They hurried to Bethlehem and found Mary and Joseph and saw the baby lying in the manger. When they saw Jesus, they repeated what the angel had said about him, and they knelt down and adored Jesus, their Lord and Savior.

*Action: Three shepherds kneel and sing a song.*

*All:* (*Continue singing "Glory to God."*)

*Action: The shepherds slowly leave.*

*Narrator:* The shepherds returned to their fields, thanking and praising God because of all that they had heard and seen. They told the Good News to many. Everyone who heard what they saw were amazed at what the shepherds told them. And Mary thought about all these things and kept them in her heart.

*Minister of the Word*: Today we are happy to hear again the Good News which the shepherds have told to so many. Let us take our lighted candles and bring them to the crib. Today we come to see and worship this child, our Lord and Savior, who was born from Mary in Bethlehem, many years ago.

*Action: Lighted lamps or candles are given to everyone. The children form a procession and bring the lights to the crib where they are carefully placed in sandboxes. The leader may invite the children to kneel before the child Jesus. A Christmas song or a gloria acclamation may be sung. After some time all return to their places and the celebration continues with the profession of faith.*

# HOLY FAMILY

## YEAR B

### PRAYER OF THE DAY:

God,
you care for us
and protect us
like a mother and father.
Teach us to be
kind and patient,
honest and gentle,
and, most of all,
at peace with the people
with whom we live.
This is our prayer to you,
through Jesus Christ,
our Lord.

### FOCUS OF THE READINGS:

Our readings focus on the importance and holiness of family life. By holiness we mean that the family truly reflects and participates in the creative activity of God.

In the first reading, Paul gives us the Christian principles that both animate and characterize the family life of baptized Christians. We are to live in mutuality, each respecting and loving the other. We are to help each other grow by being kind, forgiving, gentle, honest, peacemaking and, most of all, by our love for one another. Christian families live this way because they are chosen and loved by God.

The Gospel recounts the day that Mary and Joseph present Jesus in the temple. There, in the temple, he is recognized by both Simeon and Anna as the fulfillment of God's promise. He is the Savior of the Israelites and the Gentiles as well. But the Gospel also forewarns that this Savior will suffer and will be a sign of contradiction among his own people.

## FIRST READING: *Colossians 3:12-21*

*This is a reading
from Paul's letter to the Colossians.*

Brothers and sisters,
You are God's chosen people,
holy and well loved.
Therefore, be kind and patient
with one another.

Be honest and gentle
with one another.
Forgive each other
as God has forgiven you.
And most of all, love one another.

Let the peace of Christ be in your hearts.
And always be thankful.
Let the word of Christ,
which is so wonderful, live in you.

Help each other to grow and to become better.
Everything you say or do,
do it in the name of the Lord Jesus.
And always give thanks to God through Jesus.

Wives and husbands,
love one another and take care of each other,
because this is what God asks of you.
Children, obey your parents
because this is what God asks of you.
Parents,
be patient and gentle with your children
so they will be encouraged.

*The Word of the Lord.*

## RESPONSE: *Psalm 96*

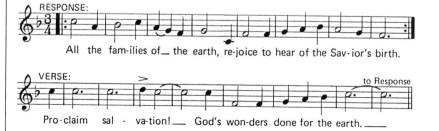

RESPONSE:
All the fam-ilies of_ the earth, re-joice to hear of the Sav-ior's birth.

VERSE:
Pro-claim sal - va-tion!_ God's won-ders done for the earth. ___

14

## GOSPEL ACCLAMATION:

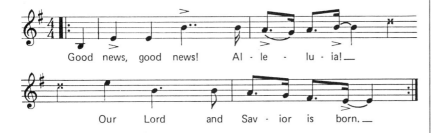

Good news, good news! Al - le - lu - ia! —

Our Lord and Sav - ior is born. —

## GOSPEL: *Luke 2:22-25, 27-36, 38-40*

*This is a reading from the Gospel of Luke.*

Mary and Joseph brought Jesus
to the temple in Jerusalem
to present him to God
and to make an offering of two turtledoves.
That same day,
a man named Simeon came to the temple.
He was a good and holy man
and was waiting for the Messiah to come.
When Simeon saw the child, Jesus,
he took him in his arms and praised God and said,

 "Now, God, you have kept your promise.
 I have seen the Savior.
 He is the light of the Gentiles
 and the glory of your people Israel."

Jesus' mother and father were amazed
at what Simeon said about him.
Then Simeon blessed them
and said to Mary, Jesus' mother,

 "This child will be a sign
 for all the people of Israel.
 Some people will accept him and be saved.
 Others will reject him.
 And in your heart
 you will suffer because of this."

There was also a holy woman,
a prophetess named Anna,
who was in the temple.
When she saw the child,
she, too, began to praise God.
And she talked about him to everyone
who was waiting for the Messiah to come.

Mary and Joseph went back to Nazareth.
And the child, Jesus, grew in size and strength.
He was filled with the wisdom and grace of God.

*The Gospel of the Lord.*

## REFLECTING ON THE READINGS WITH CHILDREN:

Help the children see that it is mutuality that makes for peaceful and loving family life. In this environment each one can grow, as Jesus did—physically, mentally and spiritually. One example might be growth of a plant. It needs sun, rain, good soil, and so forth. Rain alone will not produce growth. Each one is needed for good growth. Discuss with the children how family members share God-given talents to help bring about a peaceful family life. The children should see their value to the family group which personalizes this feast. Help the children to see that we live this way because God loves us and because we are baptized Christians.

Concerning the Gospel text, though not directly related to the first reading, explain to the children that it was customary to take the first child (son) to the temple to be consecrated to God. Since this rite was specific to the first male child only, we will not want to compare it to Christian baptism. This was a Jewish ceremony which included a rite of purification and the offering of a sacrifice. In this case, the offering was two turtledoves, the offering of the poor.

Two points might be emphasized in today's Gospel:

1. Simeon, the holy man, recognized Jesus as the Light and Savior of the world. *He is our Light and our Savior.* Help the children understand what this means in our everyday lives.

 • How is Jesus our Light?
 • How is Jesus our Savior?

Remind the children that we often use a candle as a symbol of Christ:

 • Easter candle,
 • a baptismal candle,
 • an altar candle,
 • a sanctuary lamp.

2. Anna, the prophetess, "talked about him to everyone who was waiting for the Messiah." Many people today are waiting for a sign of hope, for help, for light, for salvation. Can we talk to them about Jesus? *Can we, like Anna, tell others the Good News of Jesus?*

# MARY, MOTHER OF GOD

## YEAR B

### PRAYER OF THE DAY:

Loving God,
through the power
of your Spirit,
you have made
Mary the mother
of your only Son, Jesus.
In the name of Mary,
we proclaim your glory.
In the name
of Jesus, our Savior,
we rejoice in the gift
of your Spirit,
and we bless your name,
forever and ever.

### FOCUS OF THE READINGS:

The focus of both of our readings is the significance of "the name." In the first reading from the book of *Numbers*, we have the well-known blessing of the Jewish people. But the meaning of the blessing comes from the last line, "When they bless... *in my name*, I will bless them." In other words, when we bless in God's name, it is actually God who is blessing. The name stood for the whole person. To say, "in God's name," is to say in or with all that God is and all that God does. To bless in God's name is to make God totally present.

The Gospel reading for today recounts the circumcision and naming of Jesus. It is interesting that this feast has been called in the past both the Feast of the Circumcision and the Feast of the Holy Name. At the presentation, Jesus was given the name foretold by

### FIRST READING: *Numbers 6:22-27*

*This is a reading from the book of Numbers.*

God said to Moses,

"Tell Aaron and all the priests of Israel that, when they bless the people, they must say,

'May God bless you and keep you.
May God's face shine on you.
May God be kind to you and give you peace.'

"When they bless the people like this, in my name, I will bless them."

*The Word of the Lord.*

### RESPONSE: *Numbers 6:24-26*

RESPONSE:
May God bless and keep you, may God's face shine on you:
May God be kind to you and give you peace.

## GOSPEL ACCLAMATION:

The an - gel said to Ma - ry: "You shall call him Je - sus."
Al - le - lu - ia! "Ma - ry, you shall call him Je - sus."

## GOSPEL: *Luke 2:16-21*

*This is a reading from the Gospel of Luke.*

When the shepherds went to Bethlehem
where Jesus was born,
they found Joseph and Mary,
and they saw the baby lying in the manger.
When they saw the child,
they repeated what the angel had said
about him.

Everyone who heard it was amazed
at what the shepherds told them.
And Mary thought about all these things
and kept them in her heart.
The shepherds went back to their fields,
thanking and praising God
for all they had heard and seen.

When the baby was eight days old,
he was circumcised,
and Mary and Joseph gave him the name Jesus,
which was the name
the angel Gabriel told Mary to call him.

*The Gospel of the Lord.*

the angel at the Annunciation—
Jesus, the name which means
"Savior." Because the whole person
is represented by the name, scripture
tells us that "at the name of Jesus,
every knee should bend," and "those
who call upon the name of the Lord
will be saved." When Mary proclaims
in the Magnificat, "Holy is God's
name!" she proclaims that all God is
and all God does is holy! Today's
feast celebrates the naming of Jesus.
This feast proclaims that Jesus is the
Savior!

*He is God's blessing and peace!*
*You shall call him Jesus!*

REFLECTING ON THE READINGS
WITH CHILDREN:

You might ask the children if they
know why they received their name
or if they know what their name
means. It would be interesting to
share with them the meaning of
some common names. There are
several little books available that give
brief meanings.

Explain to the children that, in
the past, people's names often stood
for who they were and what they did.
For example, people who made bread
often had the name "Baker." The
name "Smith" comes from families
who were blacksmiths, and so forth.
In the Old Testament, people often
had names that indicated their
mission in life or some significant
event in their life. The name
"Moses" means "I drew you out of
the water!" Moses was saved from
drowning when he was a baby. He
became the leader of his people.

This introduction to the
significance of names will lead
naturally to a discussion of today's
Gospel which recounts the naming of
Jesus. Jesus was given this name
because it means "Savior."

# EPIPHANY

## YEAR B

### PRAYER OF THE DAY:

God,
you love all people
and want them
to know Jesus, your Son.
Make us know him better
and, by the way we live,
may others get to know him
through us.
We ask you this
through Jesus,
who lives with you,
forever and ever.

### FOCUS OF THE READINGS:

The birth of the Christ is the manifestation (epiphany) of God in the world. In Christ, salvation has come for everyone, Jew and gentile alike.

Our first reading tells us that the light has come, a light to guide us all. In *this* light, the glory of God shines forth. This light is the Epiphany of God. The Gospel tells us that this light shone in the east and brought visitors from afar to see this manifestation of God's love. Christ is the one to whom all people will come, bringing gifts fit for a king. He is the "newborn King of the Jews" and, indeed, of all the earth. He reveals God's unconditional love for all people.

*God's love is made known
to all the world!
Let all nations rejoice!*

### FIRST READING: *Isaiah 60:1-6*

*This is a reading from the prophet Isaiah.*

People of Jerusalem, arise! Stand up!
Your light has come!
The glory of God shines on you!
And the rulers of nations
will come to your shining light.

Look all around you and see;
people are gathering and coming to you.
They will come from far away,
bringing gifts of gold and frankincense,
and singing the praises of God.

*The Word of the Lord.*

### RESPONSE: *Psalm 96*

RESPONSE:
All the na-tions of the earth, re-joice to hear of the Sav-ior's birth!

VERSE:
Pro-claim sal-va-tion! God's won-ders done for the earth.

### GOSPEL ACCLAMATION:

Good news, good news! Al-le-lu-ia!

The world will know of his love!

18

## GOSPEL: *Matthew 2:1-12*

*This is a reading from the Gospel of Matthew.*

When Jesus was born in Bethlehem of Judaea,
the magi came from the east.
When they arrived in Jerusalem,
they asked the people,

> "Where is the newborn King of the Jews?
> We have seen his star in the east,
> and we have come to worship him."

When they said this,
King Herod and all the people of Jerusalem
became very disturbed.
Herod gathered the leaders
of the Jewish people and asked them
where the Messiah was supposed to be born.
They told him,

> "In Bethlehem of Judaea."

Then Herod asked the magi
to tell him the exact time
they had seen the star in the east.
When they told him, Herod said,

> "Go to Bethlehem
> and find out all you can about this child.
> When you have found him,
> come back and tell me
> so that I may go, too, and worship him."

And so they left for Bethlehem.
The star, which they had seen in the east,
went ahead of them,
and it stopped over the place where Jesus was.

When they went in,
they found the child with Mary, his mother.
And they were filled with joy.
They knelt down and worshipped Jesus,
and they gave him gifts of gold,
frankincense and myrrh.

That night, God told the magi in a dream
not to go back to Herod.
So they went back to their own country
by another way.

*The Gospel of the Lord.*

REFLECTING ON THE READINGS
WITH CHILDREN:

Children will not grasp the
profound theological signs in these
readings. However, they will
experience the joy and wonder at
such an event.

Again we offer you a drama in
which the children may participate.
These presentations require a little
preparation but should not become a
major production. If the children are
not participating in the dramatization,
lead them in reflections on the signs
Matthew presents and on God's love
for all people of every race, nationality
and belief. These reflections could
begin with "What did you hear?"

19

# Gospel Drama For Epiphany

Gospel: *Matthew 2:1-12*

*The Story of the Magi*

Children will be required for the roles of:

| | |
|---|---|
| Narrator | Herod |
| Magi (3) | Jesus |
| Child holding a star | Mary |
| | Joseph |

Props required:
    Star
    Gifts

*Narrator:* This is the Good News from the Gospel of Matthew.

*Action: Mary, Joseph and the child Jesus take their place on one side. A child holding a star leads the magi to Herod who is seated on the other side.*

*Narrator:* When Jesus was born in Bethlehem of Judaea, while Herod was king, magi from the east came one day to Jerusalem. They asked:

*Magi:* Where is the newborn King of the Jews? We have seen his star in the east, and we have come to worship him.

*Action: Herod's friends at the back of the stage murmur to one another: "Where is the Messiah? Where was he born?"*

*Narrator:* When they said this, King Herod and all the people of Jerusalem became very disturbed. Herod gathered the leaders of the Jewish people and asked them where the Messiah was to be born. They said:

*All:* In Bethlehem of Judaea.

*Narrator:* Then Herod asked the magi to tell him the exact time they had seen the star. Then he sent the magi to Bethlehem, and he told them:

*Herod:* Find out all you can about this child. When you have found him, come back and tell me so that I, too, may go and worship him.

*Narrator:* And so they set out for Bethlehem. The star, which they had seen in the east, went ahead of them, and it stopped over the place where Jesus was.

*Action: The magi kneel before the child and give their gifts. All kneel before the child and sing an epiphany song which is familiar to the children.*

# BAPTISM OF THE LORD

## YEAR B

### PRAYER OF THE DAY:

God in heaven,
you sent down your power
and your Spirit on Jesus
to be the light of the world.
Lead us by that same light
so that we may see
where we have done wrong
and find the way
to be happy with you,
forever and ever.

### FOCUS OF THE READINGS:

The first reading describes the mission of the servant who is chosen by God to bring justice and truth to the world and to make God known to the people. At his baptism, Jesus is revealed as the Son of God and is anointed with the Spirit. Coupled with our first reading, the Baptism of the Lord also reveals Jesus as the servant described by Isaiah. He is anointed for the mission. His mission is to bring justice, to be a light to the nations, to be a healer and a liberator. In this liturgy, the church holds before us the power and the challenge of our own baptism—we are children of God, anointed with the Spirit, and the mission of Jesus is *our* mission.

### REFLECTING ON THE READINGS WITH CHILDREN:

In reflecting on the Baptism of the Lord with children, we encounter a particular difficulty. The baptism of Jesus was like most experiences in the early church—an adult experience. While the essential truth of gratuitous grace was certainly recognized, baptism was intimately linked with conversion and a life of service.

### FIRST READING: *Isaiah 42:1, 6-7*

*This is a reading from the prophet Isaiah.*

Our God says,
  "This is my servant, my chosen one.
   I give him my strength and my spirit
   to bring justice to all the people.
   And I say to him,

     'I, your God, have called you.
      I have taken you by your hand.
      I have sent you
      as my covenant to the people,
      as a light for the world.
      I have sent you
      to open the eyes of the blind,
      to free those in prison,
      and to give light
      to those who live in darkness.' "

*The Word of the Lord.*

### RESPONSE: *Psalm 146*

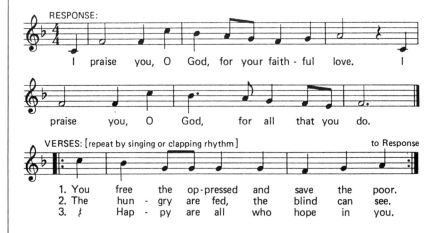

RESPONSE:
I praise you, O God, for your faith-ful love. I praise you, O God, for all that you do.

VERSES: [repeat by singing or clapping rhythm]                    to Response

1. You    free   the   op-pressed   and   save   the   poor.
2. The    hun -  gry   are   fed,    the   blind  can   see.
3.    Hap - py   are   all    who   hope   in   you.

## GOSPEL ACCLAMATION:

A voice from heav-en said,____ "This is my be-lov-ed Son."____

____ Al - le - lu - ia. Al - le - lu - ia.____ Al - le - lu - ia. Al - le - lu -

ia.____ Al - le - lu - ia. Al - le - lu - ia. Al - le - lu - ia.

## GOSPEL: *Mark 1:7-11*

*This is a reading from the Gospel of Mark.*

When John the Baptist preached,
he always said,

"Someone else is coming after me
who is more powerful than I am.
I am not even worthy
to undo his sandal straps.
I am baptizing you in water,
but he will baptize you in the Holy Spirit."

During that time, Jesus came from Nazareth
and was baptized by John.
As soon as Jesus came out of the water,
he saw the Spirit
coming on him in the form of a dove.

Then a voice from heaven said,

"You are my beloved Son;
I am very pleased with you."

*The Gospel of the Lord.*

The baptism of Jesus is the inauguration of his public life, a life of service. Our baptism, like that of Jesus, calls us to the service described in our reading from *Isaiah*. This connection is more difficult to see and reflect on in light of infant baptism, which is the case of most of the children with whom we are ministering. And so, we hope in this reflection to plant a seed of this truth which the children will gradually come to understand and live more fully.

*After the Gospel*, ask the children what they heard. Help them to recall: water, Spirit, "You are my Son." Ask them if they have been present for a baptism or if their parents have told them about their own baptism. Help them to recall what happens at a Christian baptism. Draw from them comments about the following:

- Water.
- Spirit ("I baptize you in the name of the Father, and the Son, and the Holy Spirit").
- We receive the Holy Spirit at our baptism, as Jesus did.
- We are sons and daughters of God.

Ask the children to recall the message of the first reading. You may want to read it again. How is this reading like the Gospel story on the Baptism of Jesus? Consider the following:

- "Spirit."
- "With whom I am well pleased."

What did God ask the servant to do? (Bring justice, heal people, free people.) Did Jesus do these things after his baptism? Can you recall any stories about that?

God said to the servant, "I have sent you as a light to the people."

Remind the children that we receive a lighted candle when we are baptized. Because we are baptized and receive the Holy Spirit, we are like Jesus. We can be a light for other people. We are like Jesus; we can serve other people.

- How can we be a light for people in our homes, classrooms, neighborhoods?
- How can we help people, as Jesus did, in our homes, classrooms, neighborhoods? (As always, it is important that this reflect their age.)

Conclude by inviting the children to ask their parents to share with them pictures and memories of their baptisms.

# The Season of Lent

# FIRST SUNDAY OF LENT

## YEAR B

## PRAYER OF THE DAY:

Protect us, our God,
from all the evil
that would attract us
away from your love.
May we be loyal to you
and worship you
above all the things
which you have made.
We ask you to do this
through Christ, our Lord.

### SEASON OF LENT

All of the readings of Lent focus on our brokenness and God's fidelity. Some of the readings focus on the redemption yet to come, others on our need to renew our acceptance of that redemption. All of them, in the context of liturgy, call us to examine our lives, acknowledge our sin, and trust in the love and saving power of our faithful God. All of them invite us to renew our baptismal promises at the Paschal Vigil.

### FOCUS OF THE READINGS:

We live in a world of broken promises.

Our readings for this first Sunday focus on the fidelity of God and our share in that fidelity through baptism. Our first reading is the conclusion of the story of the flood. The rainbow, a sign of "the covenant made with all living creatures," reminds us that God is always faithful. In the Gospel, Mark recalls Jesus' baptism and reminds us that even baptism does not exempt us from the temptation of straying from the covenant. Jesus meets the test and emerges victorious. His victorious proclamation is a call to us to renew our own fidelity to the covenant and to our baptismal promises, by changing our lives and believing in the Gospel.

## FIRST READING: *Genesis 9:8-15*

*This is a reading from the book of Genesis.*

God said to Noah and his children:

"I am making a covenant with you,
and with your children for all time,
and with every living creature on earth.
This is my covenant with you
that will last forever:
I promise that never again
will a flood destroy the earth
and all living creatures.
As a sign of this covenant,
I am putting my rainbow in the sky.
When I bring clouds over the earth,
and a rainbow appears in the sky,
I will remember the covenant
I have made with you,
and with all living creatures."

*The Word of the Lord.*

## RESPONSE: *Psalm 89*

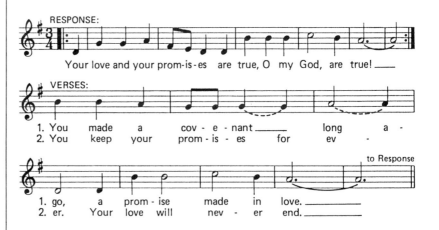

RESPONSE:
Your love and your prom-is-es are true, O my God, are true!

VERSES:
1. You made a cov-e-nant long a-
2. You keep your prom-is-es for ev-

to Response
1. go, a prom-ise made in love.
2. er. Your love will nev-er end.

## GOSPEL ACCLAMATION:

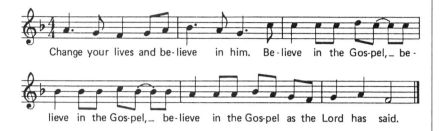

Change your lives and be-lieve in him. Be-lieve in the Gos-pel,_ be-lieve in the Gos-pel,_ be-lieve in the Gos-pel as the Lord has said.

## GOSPEL: *Mark 1:12-15*

*This is a reading from the Gospel of Mark.*

After his baptism,
the Holy Spirit sent Jesus out into the desert.
He stayed there for forty days
and was tempted by Satan
to do what was wrong.
And the angels were with Jesus to help him.
When Jesus returned to Galilee,
he told everyone the Good News of God:

   "The time has come!
   Change your lives
   and believe in the Gospel!"

*The Gospel of the Lord.*

## REFLECTING ON THE READINGS WITH CHILDREN:

*After the first reading*, you may wish to engage the children in the reading by asking questions such as:
- What did God say?
- Why do you think God chose a rainbow as a symbol of the covenant?
- What does God promise in this covenant?
- How do you feel about God's promise?

The Psalm response for today is particularly appropriate. It should be one that the children take to heart and remember.

*After the Gospel*, ask the children:
- What did you hear in today's Gospel?
- What did Jesus ask us to do?

When the children have shared their thoughts, summarize for them. Jesus says, "Change your lives. Believe in me." Jesus asks us to follow him.
- What do you think Jesus wants us to change in our lives?
- How can we show Jesus that we believe in him?

Remind the children that the word "Gospel" means "Good News."
- What is the Good News that Jesus asks us to believe in?

Help the children understand that we change our lives gradually. Jesus too was tempted, and so he knows that sometimes it is hard for us. But he is always there to help us when we try. Remember, God made a covenant with us and is always true to it.

Lent is a special time in the church. It is a time when we think even more about changing our lives and believing more in Jesus. How can we do that? Help the children focus on the reality of their everyday lives. They are not responsible for the sins of the world and cannot change things on a large scale. Help them focus on the small, but real, ways they can try in their own lives.

# SECOND SUNDAY OF LENT

## YEAR B

### PRAYER OF THE DAY:

God in heaven,
you put courage
in the apostles
by giving them a glimpse
of the victory
that would be won
by your Son after his death.
Make us always true to him,
quick to overcome our fear,
and trust in his resurrection.
We ask you to do this
through Jesus Christ,
who lives with you
and the Holy Spirit,
forever and ever.

### FOCUS OF THE READINGS:

We live in a world broken by violence and evil.

Today's first reading assures us that nothing can take us from the love of God. God is on our side, and we have nothing to fear. Nothing that is now and nothing that is to come can separate us from God. Our Psalm response echoes this belief: "And when evil is around me, I have no fear." The Gospel gives us a glimpse of our future glory in the Transfiguration. In the midst of the brokenness in the world, we are called to recognize Christ as the beloved Son of God and to listen to him. With him on our side, we have nothing to fear in this world or the next.

### FIRST READING: *Romans 8:31-39*

*This is a reading
from a letter written by Paul to the Romans.*

If God is on our side, who will be against us?
Surely not God,
who was willing to give up even Jesus
so that we would be saved.
God has saved us through Jesus
and will always bless us.
No one can take that away from us.

Who will keep us away from heaven?
Surely not Christ Jesus,
who died and was raised to life
and is now with God to help us.

I am sure that nothing
will ever take us away from the love of God.
Not death, not anything in life,
nothing now or in the future,
nothing in all of creation
will ever take us away from the love of God
which is in Christ Jesus, our Lord!

*The Word of the Lord.*

### RESPONSE: *Psalm 27*

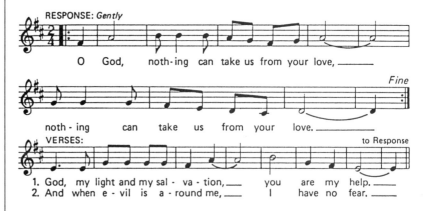

### GOSPEL ACCLAMATION:

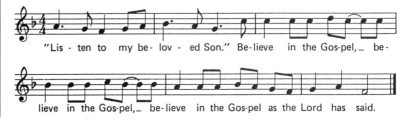

## GOSPEL: *Mark 9:2-10*

*This is a reading from the Gospel of Mark.*

Jesus took Peter, James, and John
up on a high mountain.
While they were there,
a change came over Jesus.
And as they were watching him,
his clothes became a dazzling white—
whiter than anyone could wash them.
Suddenly, they saw Moses and Elijah
talking with Jesus.
Peter spoke up and said to Jesus,

  "Master, it is good for us to be here!
    Let us make three tents:
    one for you, one for Moses,
    and one for Elijah."

Peter really didn't know what to say
because, like James and John,
he was amazed and frightened
by what he was seeing.
Then the shadow of a cloud came over them,
and a voice came from the cloud saying,

  "This is my beloved Son.  Listen to him."

Suddenly, they didn't see
Moses and Elijah anymore.
They only saw Jesus.
As they came down the mountain,
Jesus told them not to tell anyone
what they had seen
until he had risen from the dead.
So they didn't.
But they kept wondering what Jesus meant
when he said that he would rise from the dead.

*The Gospel of the Lord.*

REFLECTING ON THE READINGS
WITH CHILDREN:

If you choose to reflect on the first reading, ask the children if they have played games that have "sides" such as baseball, soccer, and so forth.  What does it mean when someone is "on your side"?  Help the children explore such concepts as loyalty, support, solidarity, etc.  When they have discussed that, ask them:

- What do you think Paul means when he says, "God is on our side"?
- Is there anything that can take God's love away from us?
- Is there anything or anyone who can take us away from God's love?
- How do you feel about what you have discussed?

Explain to the children that all during Lent we are hearing about how much Jesus loves us.  Jesus was even willing to give his life for us.  St. Paul tells us that anyone who loves us that much will surely want us to live with him forever.  So we know that Jesus will always keep us safe.

Sing the Psalm response again.

In your reflections on the Gospel, ask the children to recall what they heard. If they have difficulty recalling, you may wish to help them with questions such as:

- Who did Jesus take with him to the mountain?
- What happened while they were there?
- Who did Peter, James and John see with Jesus?
- What did Peter say?  What did Peter, James and John hear God say?

Ask the children if they have ever seen previews of coming attractions on television or in a theater. Help them understand that previews tell us what the coming attraction is going to be and help us look forward to it.

Help them see that, at the Transfiguration, Jesus was giving a preview of what he will be like after the Resurrection. He was also showing us that we will be like him. We will live with him in glory.  As Jesus was showing this to Peter, James and John, God told them what we must do to live with Jesus forever.

Do you remember what God said to Peter, James and John?  God tells us, too, "This is my beloved Son, listen to him."

Discuss how we listen to Jesus today:

- in the Bible,
- in our parents and others who teach us,
- in the good thoughts we have that encourage us to do the right thing.

# THIRD SUNDAY OF LENT

## YEAR B

### PRAYER OF THE DAY:
God who knows all things,
you made us your children
in the waters of our baptism.
Keep us faithful to you
by obeying your Son, Jesus,
who lives with you,
forever and ever.

### FOCUS OF THE READINGS:
We live in a world broken by self-sufficiency and material greed.

Our first reading, the Ten Commandments, calls us to a just law which recognizes our dependence on God and the rights of our neighbor. The Gospel presents a seemingly harsh Jesus. In the sacred temple, Jesus lashes out against greed and selfishness, focuses our lives on God and the things of God, and reveals himself as the true "temple." Jesus was harsh with those who insisted on the letter of the Law but did not live its meaning. Our hope for salvation is not found in either doggedly following the Law (self-sufficiency) or in material wealth (greed) but in the Resurrection of Christ.

### FIRST READING: *Exodus 20:1-4a, 7-8, 12-17.*

*This is a reading from the book of Exodus.*

God said:

"I am your God.
I brought you away
from the country of Egypt
and freed you from slavery.

"Therefore:

"You shall not believe in any other God
but me.

"You shall not worship images of false gods
or anything that has been made.

"You shall not say the name of God
in a way that is not holy.

"Remember to keep the Sabbath day holy.

"Honor your father and your mother.

"You shall not kill.

"You shall not be unfaithful to your wife
or husband.

"You shall not steal.

"You shall not lie about your neighbor.

"You shall not be jealous
about anything your neighbor owns."

*The Word of the Lord.*

### RESPONSE: *Psalm 19*

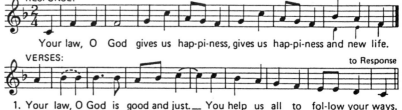

RESPONSE:
Your law, O God gives us hap-pi-ness, gives us hap-pi-ness and new life.

VERSES:
to Response
1. Your law, O God is good and just.__ You help us all to fol-low your ways.
2. Your words__teach us what is right.__Your word, O God gives joy to my life.

## GOSPEL ACCLAMATION:

1. Ev - 'ry-one who be-lieves in him, they will live for ev - er,

1. they will live for ev-er, they will live for ev-er as the Lord has said.

## GOSPEL: *John 2:13-16, 18-22*

*This is a reading from the Gospel of John.*

Jesus went up to Jerusalem
to celebrate the feast of the Passover.
Inside the temple,
he saw people selling cattle
and sheep and pigeons.
And there were others changing money
for the people.
Jesus made a long whip
and chased the cattle and the sheep
out of the temple.
He also knocked over the money tables,
spilling the coins on the ground.
He said to those who were selling pigeons,

"Get them out of here!
Stop using God's house as a marketplace!"

The Jews who were there said to Jesus,

"What gives you the right to do this?
What sign can you give us?"

Jesus answered them,

"Tear down this temple,
and I will raise it up in three days!"

The Jews said,

"It took us forty-six years
to build this temple!
And you think you can raise it up
in three days?"

But the temple Jesus was talking about
was his body.
And later when he was raised from the dead,
his disciples remembered that he said this,
and they believed in him.

*The Gospel of the Lord.*

## REFLECTING ON THE READINGS WITH CHILDREN:

This Gospel text is a difficult one for children. To be sure, it is action-packed and will no doubt have a high interest level! But the meaning of the action — that is, Jesus, the new temple, replaces the old system of worship in the temple in Jerusalem — is not a theme easily grasped by small children who, naturally, have a limited concept of historical time. Since we introduced the season of Lent as a special time to think about our lives and try to change our ways, a reflection on the Ten Commandments may serve us well this Sunday. The "law" appears elsewhere in this cycle, but in each case the Gospel takes priority in the reflections.

*After the first reading*, ask the children what commandment they recall. As each response is given, ask the children for their reflection on that particular commandment. (Do not be concerned with the order of the commandments.)

For example, you shall not lie about your neighbor. You might explore with them how we are all tempted to blame someone else to avoid taking responsibility (or punishment) for our own actions. For a child, this may mean lying about another child in order to gain friends.

The important point in any reflection of this sort is that it be appropriate to their age and behavior. For example, there seems little point in dwelling on the seventh commandment which simply is not relevant to them at this time. Or, with regard to "You shall not kill," children may begin by repeating what they have heard adults say about war or capital punishment. Try to keep it on their level. Can we "kill" others by ignoring them? Does this commandment also tell us to take good care of our bodies so we will stay healthy?

It is important that the children see the Ten Commandments as a positive way we show our love for God and for our neighbor.

# FOURTH SUNDAY OF LENT

## YEAR B

## PRAYER OF THE DAY:

Saving God,
you sent Jesus
to wash away our sins
and help us
to see things your way.
Do not let our hearts go blind
by not loving other people
as much as we love ourselves.
We make this prayer to you
through Jesus, your Son.

## FOCUS OF THE READINGS:

We live in a world broken by a false sense of worth based on the work ethic and personal accomplishment. Our new life in Christ is God's free gift to us.

In our first reading, Paul assures us that our salvation is not a commodity we have earned or worked for. We have been taken out of darkness into the light, freely. We choose to live a life of good deeds—not to earn salvation, but as a fitting thanksgiving because we have been saved. The Gospel reminds us that this free gift was given through the ultimate act of love—the giving of one's life, freely. Christ, lifted up on the cross, is our reminder that we have been saved, gratuitously, by him.

## REFLECTING ON THE READINGS WITH CHILDREN:

The mystery of the cross, the cause of our redemption, will not be easily explained to children. But our readings provide plenty of material for reflection on the love of God that initiates our redemption.

## FIRST READING: *Ephesians 2:4-10*

*This is a reading
from a letter Paul wrote to the Ephesians.*

Because of God's great love for us,
we have a new life with Christ.
Even while we were sinners,
God raised us up with Jesus
and gave us a place in heaven.

It is God's gift that saves us.
We did not work for our salvation
or earn it by doing anything special.
It is God's gift to us.

Through Christ Jesus,
God has made us new
so that we may live our lives doing good.

*The Word of the Lord.*

## RESPONSE: *Psalm 27*

RESPONSE: *Gently*

O God, noth-ing can take us from your love, _____
noth - ing can take us from your love. _____

VERSES:                                              to Response
1. I be-lieve that I will see you. ___ Keep my heart strong. ___
2. And when e - vil is a - round me, ___ I have no fear. _____

## GOSPEL ACCLAMATION:

1. Ev - 'ry-one who be-lieves in him, they will live for ev-er,
2. Ev - 'ry-one who be-lieves in him, Al - le - lu - ia,

1. they will live for ev-er, they will live for ev-er as the Lord has said.
2. al - le - lu-ia, they will live for ev-er as the Lord has said.

## GOSPEL: *John 3:14-21*

*This is a reading from the Gospel of John.*

Jesus said to Nicodemus,

"God's Chosen One must be lifted up
so that everyone who believes in him
will live forever.

"Yes, God loved the world so much that
God sent the only Son of God into the world.
Everyone who believes in him
will live forever.

"God did not send the Son of God
to judge the world, but to save it.
And everyone who believes in him is saved.

"But those who refuse to believe in him
are already being judged.
And this is how they are judged:
when the light came into the world,
they chose to stay in the dark
instead of coming into the light.
They liked to stay in the dark
because the things they are doing
are very evil.
In the dark,
no one can see the evil things they are doing.

"But those who do good things
love to come into the light.
In the light,
everyone can see they do good things
because they believe in God."

*The Gospel of the Lord.*

---

If you choose to reflect on the first reading, ask the children what they remember of the reading. Since this reading is neither story nor dialogue, it may not be easily retained by children. The following questions may help you to recall.

- Do you earn money?
- Do you pay for your food at home?
- Do you pay to have a room in your home?
- Do you buy and pay for your own clothes?
- If you do not do the above deeds, why not?
- Who takes care of these things? Why?

Explain to the children that we do not have to earn God's love. God always loves us and takes care of us. Our parents don't stop loving us and taking care of us even when we do things that are wrong. God doesn't stop loving us and doing things for us even when we sin. Jesus showed how much he loves us by dying for sinners. He did this freely; it was God's gift to all of us. We didn't have to earn it or work for it. Jesus saved us because he loves us.

Ask the children if they help with the things that need to be done at home.

- Do you help your parents?
- Do you clean up your room?
- Do you help with the table for dinner?
- Do you run errands for your parents?
- Why do you help out?

Explain to the children that we do good things for others because they love us and we love them. We don't help at home so that our parents will love us but because they already love us. We do good things for others, like Jesus did, because he loves us and saved us.

NOTE: Unfortunately, not all children live in the loving situation assumed in the above reflections. The catechists will know what image is appropriate in those cases.

*After the Gospel*, ask the children what they heard.

- Do robbers break in when all the lights are on in the house? Why not?
- When do they break in?

Help the children understand that this is what Jesus meant when he said that people who do evil things like to be in the dark, but people who do good things like to come into the light. People who do bad things have to hide. People who do good things don't have to hide.

Jesus is the light of the world. People who are evil stay away from Jesus. But people who do good things like to be with him. They know that he is happy with the things they do.

We never have to be afraid. We know God loves us very much, and he sent Jesus to tell us this. Anyone who believes in Jesus will live forever with him. It is because we are loved so much that we do good things.

33

# FIFTH SUNDAY OF LENT

## YEAR B

### PRAYER OF THE DAY:

God,
who made us
and gives us life,
your Son, Jesus,
came among us
to raise the dead
from their graves
and give us all a life
that will never end.
We love you for this
and pray to you
that we will have that life,
and so live with you,
and Jesus,
and the Holy Spirit,
forever and ever.

### FOCUS OF THE READINGS:

We live in a world broken by exaggerated individualism and personal gain. We have fallen into this trap and have sinned.

Our first reading assures us that although we broke the covenant, God takes us back, forgives our sin, and starts anew with us. We hear the consoling words again, "I will be their God, and they will be my people." The Gospel calls us to live as God's people by dying to our selfishness and living for others. This is our baptismal covenant, and, like Jesus, our true life comes from living with and for others. In him, we too must face the paradox of the cross—we too must die and be raised to new life.

### FIRST READING: *Jeremiah 31:31-34*

*This is a reading from the prophet Jeremiah.*

God said,

"I am going to make a new covenant
with my people.
It will not be like the covenant
I made with their ancestors long ago
when I brought them away from Egypt.
My people broke that covenant.

"But this is the new covenant
I am making with my people now.
I will place my law within their hearts.

"I will be their God,
and they will be my people.

"Everyone, from the smallest to the greatest,
will know me.
I will forgive all the wrong they have done,
and I will forgive all their sin."

*The Word of the Lord.*

### RESPONSE: *Psalm 89*

RESPONSE:
Your love and your prom-is-es are true, O my God, are true!

VERSES:
1. You made a cov - e - nant long a -
2. You keep your prom - is - es for ev -

to Response
1. go, a prom - ise made in love.
2. er. Your love will nev - er end.

## GOSPEL ACCLAMATION:

"Those who give up their lives for me, they will live for ev-er,

they will live for ev-er, they will live for ev-er," as the Lord has said.

## GOSPEL: *John 12:24-25, 32-33*

*This is a reading from the Gospel of John.*

Jesus said to Philip and Andrew,

"You know that if you do not bury
   a grain of wheat,
   it stays just one grain of wheat.
   But if you bury it in the ground,
   it grows and becomes many grains.

"In the same way,
   people who try to hold onto their lives
   will lose them.
   But those who are willing
   to give up their lives
   will live forever.
   And when I am lifted up,
   I will bring all people to me."

When he said this,
Jesus was telling them
how he was going to die.

*The Gospel of the Lord.*

## REFLECTING ON THE READINGS WITH CHILDREN:

If you choose to reflect on the first reading, ask the children what they heard God say about this new covenant.

- Where will it be written? What do you think that means?
- What does God promise in this covenant?

Help the children verbalize: "I will be your God, and you will be my people."

*After the Gospel*, ask the children what they heard. Then ask if they have ever planted a seed or watched someone plant seeds.

- What happens after some time?
- What would happen if you left the seed in the package or on a shelf? Would it grow? Why not?

Ask the children what Jesus said about the grain of wheat. Explain to them that the grain is the seed for the plant.

- What does Jesus mean when he says we must be willing to give up our lives?

   *Note: It is important that the children understand that this is an image. The seed does not actually die, it appears to die. Jesus is not asking us to die physically for others, at least not usually. We are asked to put the wants and needs of others before our own.*

- How is that like the grain of wheat?

35

# PASSION SUNDAY

## YEAR B

## PRAYER OF THE DAY:

Dearest God,
through Jesus you show us
that to love you
we must be humble,
as he was,
and put up with tough times.
When we are proud
of what we have done,
may we thank you
for your gifts to us.
When we are tempted
not to follow Jesus,
may we pray to you
to be strong,
through Jesus, your Son,
who lives with you,
forever and ever.

## FOCUS OF THE READINGS:

We live in a world broken by pride and false identity.

Our first reading is the beautiful hymn of unconditional love, the creed of those who would "think and live like Christ." Jesus, eternal God, humbled himself to be identified with humankind—the humankind that would lead him to his passion. Those who sought their own importance humiliated Jesus and denied his identity—Messiah, beloved Son, Temple of God, Savior of the world. They put him to death but God raised him up and proclaimed his true identity—Jesus Christ is Lord!

## THE PROCESSION WITH PALMS:

Sing ho-san-na, sing ho-san-na, to the King, sing ho-san-na!

## GOSPEL: *Mark 11:1-10*

*This is a reading from the Gospel of Mark.*

When Jesus and his disciples
were on their way to Jerusalem,
they came near the Mount of Olives.
Jesus said to two of his disciples,
  "Go into the village straight ahead of you.
    As soon as you enter it,
    you will find a colt that is tied to a post.
    Untie it and bring it to me.
    If anyone says to you,
      'Why are you doing that?' say,
      'The Lord needs it now,
        but he will bring it back to you.' "
So they went to the village
and found the colt tied to a post near the house.
When they untied it, some of the people said to them,
  "Why are you untying that colt?"
The disciples answered
just as Jesus had told them to,
and the people let them take it.
They brought it to Jesus
and put their coats across its back.
Jesus sat on the colt and rode into Jerusalem.
Many people spread their coats
and palm branches on the road in front of him.
The people sang out,
  "Hosanna!
    Blessed is he who comes in the name of the Lord!
    Hosanna in the highest!"
*The Gospel of the Lord.*

## REFRAIN:

"Bless-ings on the King who comes in the name of the Lord!"____ They came run-ning down the streets so ex-cit-ed were the chil-dren as he came, sing-ing:

FIRST READING: *Philippians 2:5-11*

*This is a reading
from Paul's letter to the Philippians.*

Brothers and sisters,

You must think and live like Christ.
Even though he was always God,
Jesus did not try to hold onto that.
Instead, he became a human being,
just like us.
As a human being,
he lived a humble life.
Jesus obeyed God in everything,
even though it meant he would die on a cross.
Because Jesus obeyed God in everything,
God raised him up
and gave him the name
which is above every other name,
so that at the name of Jesus
everyone should kneel and worship him.
Everyone in heaven, on earth and everywhere
should give glory to God by proclaiming,
"Jesus Christ is Lord!"

*The Word of the Lord.*

RESPONSE: *Psalm 34*

Glo-ri-fy God, glo-ri-fy God, glo-ri-fy God with me. Let us
praise God's ho-ly name. Glo-ri-fy God glo-ri-fy God's ho - ly name!

GOSPEL ACCLAMATION:

Do not fear, Je-sus has con-quered, he is__ ris-en from the dead.

REFLECTING ON THE READINGS
WITH CHILDREN:

We have presented two versions of the
Passion. You may wish to use the shorter
version with younger children. In either
case, we suggest that it be read in parts as
has become customary in many parish
communities.

The experience of Holy Week is more
of a meditation than a theological study.
These reflections should allow the
children to enter into the drama of the
Passion in a way that touches them
personally.

*After the Passion*, ask the children to
recall the scene.

- Who was there? (Jesus, chief priests
  and other leaders, Pilate, a crowd of
  people, soldiers, Simon, the two
  criminals crucified with him.)
- Why did the people take Jesus to
  Pilate? Why did they want Jesus
  crucified?
- How do you think Jesus felt when
  they made fun of him as a king?
- Who was the man Pilate wanted to
  let out of prison?
- How do you think Jesus felt when
  his own people kept shouting,
  "Crucify him, crucify him"?
- Why were the people making fun of
  him on the cross? What did they
  say? How do you think Jesus felt
  when they said these things?
- After Jesus died, what did one of the
  soldiers say? How do you think the
  soldier felt?

If some of the older children have done
the reading, you might ask those who read:

- How did you feel being Jesus?
- How did you feel being Pilate?
- How did you feel being the chief
  priests and leaders?
- How did you feel when you were
  shouting "crucify him"?
- How did you feel being the soldier at
  the end?

# Gospel Drama for Passion Sunday

*Gospel: Mark 15:1-39*

Children will be required for the roles of:

| | | | |
|---|---|---|---|
| Narrator 1 | Pilate | Chief Priests & Leaders (2 or 3 children) | Robbers (2) |
| Narrator 2 | Jesus | Soldiers (2 or 3 children) | Barabbas |
| Narrator 3 | Simon | Crowd (2 or 3 children) | |

Props required: purple robe, crown of thorns, stick, large cross, sign reading: "This is Jesus, King of the Jews."

*Narrator 1:* As soon as it was morning, the chief priests and leaders tied Jesus' hands together and took him to Pontius Pilate. Pilate asked Jesus,

*Pilate:* Are you the King of the Jews?

*Jesus:* You have said so.

*Narrator 1:* During the trial, the chief priests accused Jesus of many things. So Pilate said to him,

*Pilate:* You hear all these things they are saying against you. Don't you have anything to say?

*Narrator 1:* But Jesus didn't say anything, and Pilate wondered why. Now every year at the feast of the Passover, Pilate would free one person from the prison, anyone the people wanted. So Pilate asked them,

*Pilate:* Do you want me to free the King of the Jews?

*Narrator 1:* Pilate knew very well that the chief priests had brought Jesus to him because they were jealous. But the chief priests had already told the people to ask Pilate to free Barabbas instead of Jesus. Barabbas was in prison for committing a murder. Pilate then asked them,

*Pilate:* But what should I do with this man you call the King of the Jews?

*Crowd, Chief Priests, and Leaders (3 or 4 children):* Kill him! Crucify him!

*Pilate:* But why? What has he done wrong?

*Narrator 1:* But they kept shouting louder,

*Crowd, Chief Priests, and Leaders (3 or 4 children):* Crucify him!

*Narrator 2:* Pilate wanted to please the crowd, so he let Barabbas go free. He told the soldiers to whip Jesus, and then he gave Jesus to the people so they could crucify him. The soldiers put a purple robe on Jesus and made a crown of thorns and put it on his head. They knelt in front of Jesus and made fun of him by saying,

*Soldiers  (2 or 3 children):*  Hail, King of the Jews!

*Narrator 2:*  They took a stick and started hitting him on the head with it and spitting at him.  After they made fun of him, they took off the purple robe and led Jesus away to crucify him.  As they were taking him away, they saw a man from Cyrene, named Simon, and they made him carry Jesus' cross.

*Narrator 3:*  When they came to a place called Golgotha, which means "the skull," they crucified Jesus.  They put a sign over his head which said, "The King of the Jews."

*Narrator 2:*  They also crucified two robbers with Jesus, one on his left and one on his right. And while they were hanging there, they made fun of Jesus. People going by made fun of Jesus and laughed at him and said,

*Crowd  (2 or 3 children):*  So you are the one who was going to tear down the temple and raise it up again in three days! Why don't you come down from that cross and save yourself!

*Narrator 2:*  The chief priests and leaders also made fun of him, saying,

*Priests and Leaders  (2 or 3 children):*  He was able to save other people, but he cannot save himself!  If he is the Christ, the King of the Jews, let him come down from that cross!  Then we will believe in him!

*Narrator 3:*  About noon, everything became dark and stayed dark until about three o'clock in the afternoon.  Jesus cried out in a loud voice,

*Jesus:* My God, my God, why have you left me alone?

*Crowd  (2 or 3 children):*  Listen, he is calling for help.  Let's see if God comes to help him.

*Narrator 3:*  Then Jesus cried out again, and he died.

> (PAUSE)

One of the Roman soldiers who was facing Jesus saw him die and said,

*Roman Soldier:*  This man really was the Son of God.

*Narrator 1:*  The Passion of our Lord, Jesus Christ.

# PASSION (PALM) SUNDAY

PASSION: *Mark 15:1-39*

REFRAIN:
    *Leader:*       Jesus has given his life for us.
    *All:*           Jesus has given his life for us.

*The story of the suffering and death of Jesus, from the Gospel of Mark.*

As soon as it was morning, the chief priests and leaders
tied Jesus' hands together and took him to Pontius Pilate.
Pilate asked Jesus,

    "Are you the King of the Jews?"

Jesus said,

    "You have said so."

During the trial, the chief priests accused Jesus of many things.
So Pilate said to him,

    "You hear all these things they are saying against you.
      Don't you have anything to say?"

But Jesus didn't say anything, and Pilate wondered why.
Now every year on the feast of the Passover,
Pilate would free one person from prison,
anyone the people wanted. So Pilate asked them,

    "Do you want me to free the King of the Jews?"

Pilate knew very well that the chief priests
had brought Jesus to him because they were jealous.
But the chief priests had already told the people
to ask Pilate to free Barabbas instead of Jesus.
Barabbas was in prison for committing a murder.
Pilate then asked them,

    "But what should I do with this man
      you call the King of the Jews?"

They shouted back,

    "Kill him! Crucify him!"

40

REFRAIN:

> *Leader:*     Jesus has given his life for us.
> *All:*        Jesus has given his life for us.

Pilate said,

> "But why?  What has he done wrong?"

But they kept shouting louder,

> "Crucify him!"

Pilate wanted to please the crowd, so he let Barabbas go free.
He told the soldiers to whip Jesus,
and then he gave Jesus to the people so they could crucify him.
The soldiers put a purple robe on Jesus
and made a crown of thorns and put it on his head.
And they knelt in front of Jesus and made fun of him by saying,

> "Hail, King of the Jews!"

They took a stick
and started hitting him on the head with it
and spitting at him.
After they made fun of him,
they took off the purple robe
and led Jesus away to crucify him.
As they were taking him away,
they saw a man from Cyrene, named Simon,
and they made him carry Jesus' cross.
When they came to a place called Golgotha,
which means "the skull,"
they crucified Jesus.

They put a sign over his head which said,

> "The King of the Jews."

REFRAIN:

> *Leader:*     Jesus has given his life for us.
> *All:*        Jesus has given his life for us.

They also crucified two robbers with Jesus,
one on his left and one on his right.
And while they were hanging there,
they made fun of Jesus.
People going by made fun of Jesus
and laughed at him and said,

> "So you are the one who was going to tear down the temple
> and raise it up again in three days!
> Why don't you come down from that cross
> and save yourself!"

The chief priests and leaders also made fun of him, saying,

> "He was able to save other people, but he cannot save himself!"
> If he is the Christ, the King of the Jews,
> let him come down from that cross!
> Then we will believe in him!"

About noon, everything became dark
and stayed dark until about three o'clock in the afternoon.
Jesus cried out in a loud voice,

> "My God, my God, why have you left me alone?"

Some of the people who were standing near the cross said,

> "Listen, he is calling for help.
> Let's see if God comes to help him."

Then Jesus cried out again, and he died.

REFRAIN:

> *Leader:*    Jesus has given his life for us.
> *All:*       Jesus has given his life for us.

One of the Roman soldiers who was facing Jesus
saw him die and said,

> "This man really was the Son of God."

*The Passion of our Lord, Jesus Christ.*

# Easter Sunday
## and
## The Season of Easter

# EASTER SUNDAY

## YEAR B

## PRAYER OF THE DAY:

God of us all,
you gather us here today
and help us see
that Jesus lives among us.
Send us your Holy Spirit
to open our hearts and minds
to believe your Son
is really risen from the dead
and also lives with you
and the Holy Spirit,
forever and ever.

*Note: In keeping with the* Directory for Masses With Children *(paragraph 43), the authors have elected to use the first reading from Easter Day Mass and the Gospel from Easter Night Mass because they seem best suited "to the capacity of children."*

### SEASON OF EASTER

All of the readings of Easter focus on the life of the church. The first readings, taken from the *Acts of the Apostles*, tell us of the mission of the church filled with the Spirit. The Gospels tell us that this mission is in union with Christ and reveals Christ. The theme of Easter Season is, "The Risen Lord is our Salvation!"

### FOCUS OF THE READINGS:

The mission of the church is to give witness to the Resurrection. In the reading from *Acts*, Peter gives witness to those who killed Jesus. His witness is based on experience: "We have seen him. We ate and drank with him." His witness is based on the command of Jesus: "He told us to preach to the people." And what he preaches is that "God raised him on the third day!" The witness of the church is that Jesus is alive and among us.

In the Gospel, the women, the first disciples to witness the empty tomb, receive the Good News: "He is risen!" They are filled with fear and confusion. But even in their confusion, they are commissioned to "Go and tell the others." Tell them what? If you are looking for Jesus, the One who was crucified, he is not here in a tomb. He is risen! You will see him, just as he said.

## FIRST READING: *Acts 10:34a, 37-43*

*This is a reading from the Acts of the Apostles.*

Peter said to the people,

"I am sure that you know
what has been told all over Judaea
about Jesus of Nazareth:
that it all began in Galilee
when John was preaching about baptism
and God anointed Jesus
with the Holy Spirit and power;
that Jesus went from place to place
doing good works and healing people from evil,
for God was with him.

"We ourselves saw all that he did
in the land of the Jews and in Jerusalem.

"They killed him by hanging him on a cross.
But God raised him up on the third day.

"And we have seen him.
We ate and drank with him
after he rose from the dead.
He told us to preach to the people
and to tell them that he is the one chosen by God
to be the judge of all people both living and dead.

"All the prophets tell us
that everyone who believes in Jesus
will have their sins forgiven in his name."

*The Word of the Lord.*

## RESPONSE: *Psalm 118*

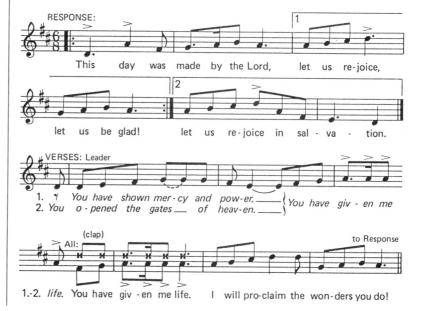

RESPONSE:
This day was made by the Lord, let us re-joice, let us be glad! let us re-joice in sal-va-tion.

VERSES: Leader
1. You have shown mer-cy and pow-er. You have giv-en me
2. You o-pened the gates of heav-en.

(clap) All:

1.-2. *life.* You have giv-en me life. I will pro-claim the won-ders you do!

## GOSPEL ACCLAMATION:

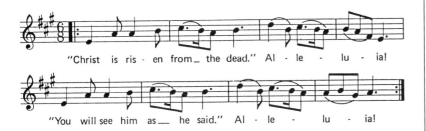

"Christ is ris - en from the dead." Al - le - lu - ia!

"You will see him as he said." Al - le - lu - ia!

## GOSPEL: *Mark 16:1-8*

*This is a reading from the Gospel of Mark.*

On the first day of the week,
when the Sabbath was over,
some of the women
went to the tomb where Jesus was buried.
The women's names were Mary Magdalene,
Salome and Mary, the mother of James.
They brought special oil with sweet spices in it
to put on Jesus' body.
It was very early in the morning,
just after the sun had risen,
and one of the women asked,

"Who will roll away the huge stone
from in front of the tomb for us?"

But when they got there,
they saw that the stone had already been moved.
The women went into the tomb,
and they saw a young man sitting on the right side.
He was wearing a white robe.
The women were frightened.
But the man said,

"Don't be afraid.
You are looking for Jesus,
the one who was crucified.
He has risen! He is not here!
Look, this is the place where he was buried.
Now, go and tell his disciples, and Peter,
that Jesus is going to Galilee.
Say to them,

'You will see him there,
just as he told you.'"

The women ran away from the tomb.
But on the way they did not tell anyone
what happened because they were afraid.

*The Gospel of the Lord.*

And so our Easter readings tell us that the early disciples saw Jesus in sign: eating and drinking with him, and in an empty tomb. With these signs, they were sent out to proclaim that "He is risen! We have seen him!"

## REFLECTING ON THE READINGS WITH CHILDREN:

We are a symbolic people! And often it is in rich symbols that God's self-revelation is available to us. We are accustomed to certain symbols and customs that surround the celebration of Easter, and they are not without meaning. While these symbols and customs will, of course, vary in different parts of the world, they generally have to do with "newness." You might ask the children:

- Why do we wear new Easter clothes?
- Why do we see bunnies and baby chicks on cards, in pictures etc.?
- Why do we have Easter eggs?

These are signs of newness—new life.

Ask the children what their family does to celebrate Easter.

We see signs of new life even in nature:

- new grass,
- new flowers,
- new buds on trees,
- everything is beginning
  to grow new life!

Perhaps some will make a visit to someone today:

- a grandparent,
- an elderly person,
- someone who is alone.

Our visit can bring new life to that person. Why do we celebrate Easter as a time of new life? Ask the children if they remember what the man dressed in white said to the women. You may wish to read the second part of the Gospel again. "He is risen! He is not here" (in the tomb). Jesus really died and was buried in the tomb. But he rose from the dead and lives forever. We will die, too. But, like Jesus, we will rise from death at the end of time, and we will live forever with him. The young man also said,

"Go and tell the others that they will see him, just as he said."

- How do we "see" Jesus today?
- How can we "go and tell others" that he is risen—that he is alive now?

At the end of the reflections, if time permits, you may want to sing the Psalm response again.

# SECOND SUNDAY OF EASTER

## YEAR B

### PRAYER OF THE DAY:

O God,
you want the whole world
to believe in you
and in Jesus
whom you sent to save us.
Show us how to believe,
and teach us
what we should believe.
Though people
may laugh at us for believing,
give us courage
to stand up for you
and live as we should.
We ask you this
through Jesus Christ,
our Lord.

*The Resurrection is the central truth of our faith. Every year the church gives us the story of Thomas on the Sunday after Easter.*

### FOCUS OF THE READINGS:

The mission of the church is to establish and nurture community, giving witness to the peace and forgiveness of the Risen Lord. Our first reading tells us that the early Christians shared everything they had so that no one was poor or in need. Their common belief in Jesus united them in heart and mind. Because of this witness, the disciples were respected when they preached about the Risen Lord.

Jesus' first words to his disciples are of peace and forgiveness, "Peace be with you .... If you forgive the sins of anyone, they are forgiven."

Thomas represents those of us who find it hard to believe that Christ is truly among us and that living in peace and forgiveness is possible. To him Jesus says, "Don't be unbelieving, but believe." The evangelist tells us that he has written this for us, so that we will recognize the signs of the Risen Lord and believe.

### FIRST READING: *Acts 4:32-35*

*This is a reading from the Acts of the Apostles.*

All those who believed in Jesus
were united in heart and mind.
They were a community
and shared everything they had
with one another.

The apostles preached about the Resurrection
of the Lord Jesus with great power,
and God was with them.

No one in the community was poor or in need
because everyone shared.
The people who owned land or houses
sold them
and brought the money to the apostles.
And the apostles
gave everyone what they needed.

*The Word of the Lord.*

### RESPONSE: *Psalm 118*

### GOSPEL ACCLAMATION:

## GOSPEL: *John 20:19-29*

*This is a reading from the Gospel of John.*

On Sunday evening (the same day the women
had been to the tomb of Jesus),
the disciples were gathered in a room upstairs.
They had locked the doors
because they were afraid of the people
who had crucified Jesus.

Then Jesus came and stood in the room and said,

"Peace be with you!"

Then he showed them his hands and his side.
The disciples were filled with joy
when they saw the Lord. Jesus said again,

"Peace be with you. As God has sent me to you,
now I am sending you to others."

Then he breathed on the disciples and said to them,

"Receive the Holy Spirit.
If you forgive the sins of anyone, they are forgiven.
If you do not forgive them, they are not forgiven."

Now, one of the apostles, Thomas, was not there
when Jesus came. So, later, the disciples told him,

"We have seen the Lord!"

But Thomas said,

"I'll never believe it
until I see the marks made by the nails in his hands
and touch the wound in his side."

One week later,
the disciples were in the same room again.
This time, Thomas was with them.
Even though the doors were locked,
Jesus came in and stood among them. He said,

"Peace be with you."

Then he said to Thomas,

"Here, touch the marks on my hands
and feel the wound in my side.
Doubt no longer, but believe."

Thomas said to Jesus,

"My Lord and my God!"

Then Jesus said to Thomas,

"You believe because you see me.
How blessed are people who have not seen me
and still believe!"

*The Gospel of the Lord.*

## REFLECTING ON THE READINGS WITH CHILDREN:

Like the Passion, the theology of the Resurrection is difficult to discuss with children. Let the text speak for itself.

If you choose to reflect on the first reading, ask the children to recall how the Christians lived. Ask them what they think about living that way—sharing everything, no one having more than others. Ask them why they think the Christians lived that way. How did living this way show that they believed in Jesus?

*After the Gospel,* ask the children what they heard. After they have had a chance to share their reflections, ask:

- Where were the apostles? Why?
- Wasn't it normal that they should be there?
- What did Jesus say when he came in? Why?
- Which disciple was not there?
- What did he say when the others told him? Wasn't that a normal way to react?
- What happened one week later?
- What did Jesus say again to the disciples?
- What did he say to Thomas?
- What did Thomas call Jesus?

Help the children understand that when Jesus said, "those who have not seen me," he meant, "seen my body."

Help them understand, also, that it is sometimes difficult to believe in things we haven't seen. Often we come to believe because someone we trust tells us. For example, we believe certain food is good for us because our parents have told us so.

In the same way, people come to believe in Jesus by what we say and do, by seeing Jesus in our lives.

*Note:* If time permits and you wish to include an Easter Creed, you may wish to use what follows.

*Leader:* We believe that Jesus died and that God raised him up.

*All Sing:* This day was made by the Lord; let us rejoice; let us be glad! This day was made by the Lord; let us rejoice in salvation!

*Leader:* We believe he is here with us, in other people, in the Eucharist, in our hearts.

*All Sing:* This day was made by the Lord...

*Leader:* We believe Jesus is our Lord and our God!

*All Sing:* This day was made by the Lord...

# THIRD SUNDAY OF EASTER

## YEAR B

### PRAYER OF THE DAY:

God always true,
after you raised Jesus
from death,
he has been with us,
even though
we cannot see him.
Let us hear his voice
as he speaks to us
secretly in our prayers;
let us feel him near us
when we gather together
in the church.
Stay with us;
keep close to us
through Jesus,
who lives with you,
forever and ever.

### FOCUS OF THE READINGS:

The mission of the church is to call us to constant conversion and invite us to give witness to our faith in the Risen Lord.

Jesus, the Risen Lord, appears and proclaims peace and forgiveness, the good news of the Resurrection. He tells his disciples that all the writings of the Old Testament have pointed to this day, and they are now witnesses to it. And he commands them to go out and call others to "change their lives and believe."

Our first reading finds Peter doing just that—proclaiming the Resurrection to those who killed Jesus. Yet, even to these, he proclaims, "now, change your lives. . . be forgiven."

### FIRST READING: *Acts 3:13-15, 17, 19*

*This is a reading from the Acts of the Apostles.*

Peter said to the people:

"The God of our ancestors—
Abraham, Jacob and Isaac—
has now glorified Jesus.
You took him to Pilate
and accused him of things he didn't do.
And even when Pilate wanted to free him,
you said, "No!"
You asked Pilate to free a murderer
instead of Jesus, who is good and holy.
You killed the One who gives us eternal life!
But God raised him up from the dead,
and we have seen him!

"But I know, my brothers and sisters,
you didn't really understand
what you were doing
when you put Jesus to death.
Your leaders didn't understand either.
But now, be sorry for what you did
and change your lives!
Turn to God so your sins may be forgiven!"

*The Word of the Lord.*

### RESPONSE: *Psalm 118*

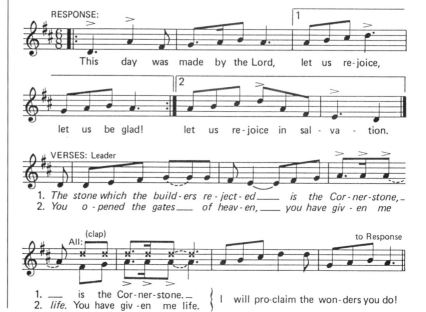

RESPONSE:

This day was made by the Lord, let us re-joice,
let us be glad! let us re-joice in sal-va-tion.

VERSES: Leader

1. *The stone which the build-ers re-ject-ed___ is the Cor-ner-stone,_*
2. *You o-pened the gates___ of heav-en, ___ you have giv-en me*

(clap) All:                                                    to Response

1. ___ is the Cor-ner-stone._
2. *life.* You have giv-en me life.    } I will pro-claim the won-ders you do!

48

# GOSPEL ACCLAMATION:

"Peace be with you," Jesus said. Alleluia!

"I am risen from the dead." Alleluia!

## GOSPEL: *Luke 24:35-48*

*This is a reading from the Gospel of Luke.*

Two disciples
who had met Jesus on the road to Emmaus
came to tell others all that happened.  They told them
how they knew it was Jesus when he broke the bread.
While they were talking about all of this,
suddenly Jesus was there and said to them,

   "Peace be with you!"

They were so frightened
that they thought they were seeing a ghost.
But Jesus said to them,

   "Why are you so frightened and confused?
   Look at my hands and feet.  Touch me.
   A ghost doesn't have a body like I do.
   I am really here!"

Even though the disciples
were filled with joy and wonder,
they still could not believe it.  So Jesus said to them,

   "Do you have anything here to eat?"

They gave him some cooked fish and he ate it.
Then he said to them,

   "Remember all the things that I told you before.
   Everything that was written in the law of Moses
   and in the prophets and psalms
   was really talking about me
   and all that would happen to me."

And Jesus helped the disciples
to understand the Scriptures.  He said to them,

   "It is written that the Christ would suffer and die
   but would rise from the dead on the third day.
   In his name, everyone must be told
   that their sins are forgiven
   when they change their lives and believe.
   You are now witnesses to all of this."

*The Gospel of the Lord.*

REFLECTING ON THE READINGS
WITH CHILDREN:

*After the Gospel*, ask the children
to recall what they heard.  You might
help them with questions such as:

- Who was there?
- What did the two from Emmaus
  tell the others?
- What did Jesus say when he
  came?
- Why were the disciples
  frightened?
- What did Jesus say?
- What did Jesus do?

Ask the children to recall the first
reading (you may wish to reread it).

- What did Peter tell those who
  killed Jesus?

*Summary:* Jesus rose from the
dead to bring us peace and
forgiveness, and he asks us to bring
peace and forgiveness to others.
When we do that, we show that Jesus
is here with us.

How do we feel when we are
forgiven?

How can we bring Jesus' peace
and forgiveness to others?

49

# FOURTH SUNDAY OF EASTER

## YEAR B

### PRAYER OF THE DAY:

Loving Lord,
you sent Jesus
to give us real life,
your life.
Because we belong to you,
help us live as your children
and follow Jesus
by loving others
and caring for those
who need help.
As his sisters and brothers,
may we always
recognize his voice
when he calls us
and leads us to you.
We ask you to do this
through that very same
Jesus, who lives with you,
forever and ever.

### FOCUS OF THE READINGS:

The mission of the church is to shepherd: to preach, to heal, and to give witness with our lives.

Our Gospel presents the Good Shepherd as one who is both gentle and powerful. He leads his flock by the sound of his voice. The Good Shepherd has power to lay down his life, and the power to raise it up again. He is willing to die rather than abandon his sheep.

When the disciples claim the power of the Risen Lord by healing a crippled man, they are put in jail. Peter proclaims that it is by the power of the name of Jesus that the man was healed. It is a sign of the Resurrection. "You crucified him. But God raised him from the dead."

Continued healing and preaching are signs that the Good Shepherd is among us.

### FIRST READING: *Acts 4:8-12*

*This is a reading from the Acts of the Apostles.*

Peter, who was filled with the Holy Spirit, spoke up and said,

"Leaders of the people, you have put us in jail,
and now you want us to explain to you
how this crippled man was healed.
We tell you and all the people of Israel
that this man was healed
by the name of Jesus Christ.

"He is the same Jesus you crucified,
but God raised him from the dead.
And so, he is like a stone
which you builders didn't want.
But this stone
has now become the cornerstone
which holds up the whole building!

"And by the power of the name of Jesus,
this man has been healed.
Jesus is the Savior,
and only in his name are we saved."

*The Word of the Lord.*

### RESPONSE: *Psalm 118*

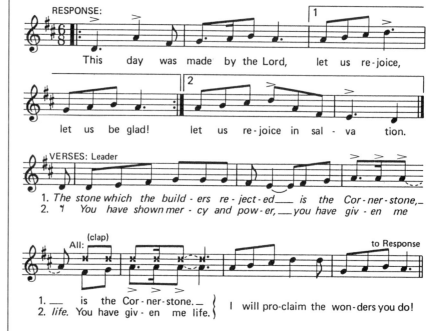

RESPONSE:
This day was made by the Lord, let us re-joice, let us be glad! let us re-joice in sal - va - tion.

VERSES: Leader
1. The stone which the build-ers re-ject-ed___ is the Cor-ner-stone,_
2. ¶ You have shown mer-cy and pow-er,___you have giv-en me

All: (clap)                                          to Response
1. ___ is the Cor-ner-stone._ }  I will pro-claim the won-ders you do!
2. life. You have giv-en me life. }

50

## GOSPEL ACCLAMATION:

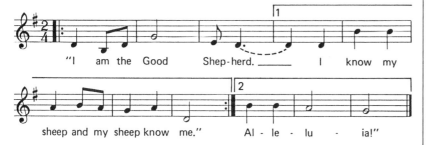

"I am the Good Shep-herd. ____ I know my
sheep and my sheep know me." Al - le - lu - ia!"

## GOSPEL: *John 10:11-18*

*This is a reading from the Gospel of John.*

Jesus said,

"I am the Good Shepherd.
The Good Shepherd
is even willing to die for the sheep.
A person who is only hired
to watch the sheep,
and doesn't own them,
runs away when a wolf comes,
and leaves the sheep to be snatched
and scattered by the wolf.
A person like that
is working only for money
and doesn't really care about the sheep.

"But I am the Good Shepherd.
God knows me, and I know God.
And in the same way,
I know my sheep and my sheep know me.
And I am willing to die for my sheep.

["I have other sheep
who aren't in this flock yet.
I must lead them too,
and they will listen to my voice.
Then there will be only one flock
with one shepherd.]
God loves me
because I am willing to die for my sheep.
No one makes me give up my life;
I give it up freely.
I have the power to raise it up again.
[This is what God commanded me to do."]

*The Gospel of the Lord.*

[ ] *Reader may omit text that appears in brackets.*

## REFLECTING ON THE READINGS WITH CHILDREN:

*After the Gospel*, ask the children to recall what they heard. Help them to recall that Jesus, like the true shepherd, will never leave us. He will always care for us even when we are in danger. Even when we are afraid, he is not afraid. He is even willing to die rather than leave us.

Ask the children what they know about sheep and shepherds. Have they ever seen sheep with a shepherd? For many children, especially those living in cities or suburbs, the image of sheep and shepherd will not be a familiar one. It is a powerful and frequently used image in both the Old and New Testaments. It will be well worth the time to familiarize the children with both the shepherding of Jesus' time and of today. Perhaps you will find pictures or even a short film on shepherding today.

The image rests on the reality of the intimacy that exists between sheep and their shepherd. Even today, where sheep are tended, they respond to the voice of the shepherd who leads them to the sheep fold at night and, in the morning, to good pastures. A true shepherd is different from a hired hand. It is this intimacy and care that Jesus speaks of here.

Jesus said that he wants everyone to listen to his voice. How do we listen to his voice today? Ask the children who tells them about Jesus: parents, teachers, priests and other ministers. Help them to see that these people are shepherds in the church today. Jesus continues to be our Good Shepherd through these people. Jesus wants everyone in the whole world to be united as sisters and brothers. Jesus called this "one flock of sheep with one shepherd."

How can we help everyone to be united as "one flock"
- at home?
- at school?
- in groups to which we belong?
- in our neighborhood?

You may wish to conclude by singing the Psalm response again.

# FIFTH SUNDAY OF EASTER

## YEAR B

### PRAYER OF THE DAY:

God, our Father,
you want
more than anything else
to share with us
all the good things
of your life.
That is why you sent Jesus
to tell us about you
and show us the way.
So when we get tired
of doing good,
make us strong
and determined again,
and help us to believe in you
more and more.
We pray this prayer
through Christ, our Lord.

### FOCUS OF THE READINGS:

The mission of the church is to give witness to the Risen Lord through preaching and by the good works that we do.

Our first reading tells us that Saul, a former persecutor of the church, has become a believer. United with Christ, he is able to preach with great power, and more and more people come to believe. The Gospel tells us that we can do this, but all good works can be accomplished only if we are united intimately with him. John uses the image of a vine and branches to show that our very life as Christians is dependent on the life of Christ. Being united to him means living by his words and doing his work.

## FIRST READING: *Acts 9:26-31*

*This is a reading from the Acts of the Apostles.*

When Saul came to Jerusalem,
he wanted to join the disciples there,
but they were afraid of him.
They didn't believe
he had really become a follower of Jesus.
So, Barnabas took him
and introduced him to the apostles.
He told them how Saul had seen the Lord
on his way to Damascus.
He told them that Jesus had spoken to Saul
and that now Saul really did believe in Jesus.
He also told the apostles
how bravely Saul was telling others about Jesus.
So Saul stayed with them in Jerusalem
and preached with great power
in the name of Jesus.

Because of Saul's preaching,
some of the people tried to kill him.
When the disciples heard
that Saul was in danger,
they took him down to Caesarea
and sent him by boat to a city called Tarsus.

With the help of the Holy Spirit,
more and more people
came to believe in the Lord
and to follow his ways.

*The Word of the Lord.*

## RESPONSE: *Psalm 134*

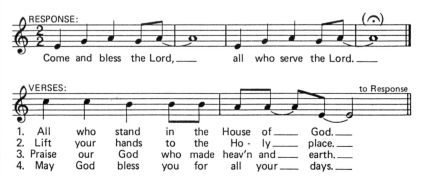

RESPONSE:
Come and bless the Lord,____ all who serve the Lord.____

VERSES: to Response
1. All who stand in the House of____ God.____
2. Lift your hands to the Ho-ly____ place.____
3. Praise our God who made heav'n and____ earth.____
4. May God bless you for all your____ days.____

# GOSPEL ACCLAMATION:

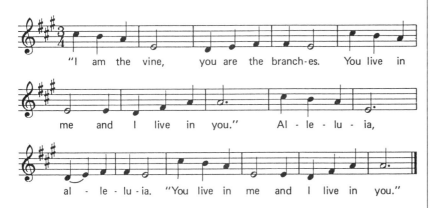

"I am the vine, you are the branch-es. You live in me and I live in you." Al-le-lu-ia, al-le-lu-ia. "You live in me and I live in you."

## GOSPEL: *John 15:5-8*

*This is a reading from the Gospel of John.*

Jesus said,

"I am the vine,
and you are the branches.
When you are a part of me
and I am living in you,
you will do great things for God.
But if you are cut off from me,
you can do nothing.
All those who do not stay part of me
are like dried up branches
that can only be gathered up and burned.
But if you are a part of me
and you live by my words,
you may ask for whatever you want,
and it will be done for you.
When you do good deeds,
you show that you are my disciples,
and you give honor and glory to God."

*The Gospel of the Lord.*

REFLECTING ON THE READINGS
WITH CHILDREN:

*After the Gospel*, ask the children to recall what they have heard.

- Why did Jesus call himself a vine and us branches?
- What did he mean?

Explore the image with the children.

Show the children a live plant, preferably a vine. Give them time to see that the branches are connected to the vine. Show them that small branches may be connected to larger branches, but all are connected to the vine.

Ask them what happens when a branch is cut off from the vine. Help them to see that the branch lives because it is connected to the vine. We know from seeing branches that are cut or fall off a tree, that soon they dry up. But the branches that remain on the tree or vine grow, and fruit can grow on them.

Help them understand that just as fruit grows on a branch that is connected to the vine or tree, we do good things when we are united with Jesus and have his life in us—when we stay close to him and live by his words.

# SIXTH SUNDAY OF EASTER

## YEAR B

### PRAYER OF THE DAY:

Lord God,
we can do nothing good
without the help
of your Spirit.
Send that Spirit to us now
so that we may be quick
to forgive those who hurt us,
ready to spread
the good news about Jesus,
and to love our neighbor
as ourself.
We ask this
through Jesus, your Son,
who lives with you,
forever and ever.

### FOCUS OF THE READINGS:

The mission of the church is to love—all people, everywhere.

The ultimate sign of the Christian believer is love. Love is not an option. It is the commandment of the one who witnessed to his love for us by giving his life. The Gospel tells us, with the clearest of focus, "You are my friends if. . .you love one another."

In our first reading Peter tells us that this love must be all inclusive. God does not have favorite people. God's Spirit is poured out on the Gentiles as well as the Jews. The Christian community is founded, not in external circumstances, but in Christ's love.

### REFLECTING ON THE READINGS WITH CHILDREN:

If you choose to reflect on the first reading, ask the children to recall the story:

- Who was there?
- Where were they?
- Why were they there?
- What happened while Peter was speaking?
- What did Peter say to the people?

Peter taught us something very special and very important in today's reading. He said, "God does not have favorite people." God loves all of us. God does not love some people more than others. We want to always remember that there isn't anyone—not anyone at all—that God loves more than you.

### FIRST READING: *Acts 10:24, 34-35, 44-48*

*This is a reading from the Acts of the Apostles.*

Peter and some of the other disciples
went to the house of Cornelius.
Cornelius had invited his relatives and friends
to hear Peter speak. Peter said to them,

"I am beginning to see now that it is true;
God does not have favorite people.
Anyone from any country
who loves God and lives in God's ways
is saved."

As Peter was speaking,
the Holy Spirit
came to all those who were listening.
They began speaking in strange languages
and praising God.
The Jewish believers who had come with Peter
were surprised that the gift of the Holy Spirit
was given to the Gentiles too. But Peter said,

"If these people have received the Holy Spirit,
just as we have,
why shouldn't they be baptized with water?"

So they were all baptized
in the name of Jesus Christ.

*The Word of the Lord.*

### RESPONSE: *Psalm 104*

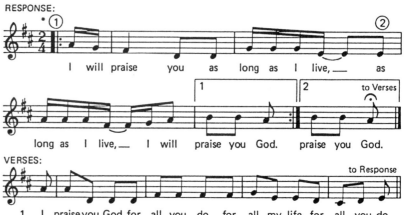

RESPONSE:

I will praise you as long as I live, ___ as long as I live, ___ I will praise you God. praise you God.

VERSES:

1. I praise you God for all you do, for all my life for all you do.
2. You give us bread to make us strong. You give us drink to make us glad.

\* Round during final response only

54

## GOSPEL ACCLAMATION:

1. Love one an-oth-er, love one an-oth-er,
2. Al - le - lu - ia, Al - le - lu - ia,

1.-2. love one an-oth-er, as I have loved you.

**GOSPEL:** *John 15:9-14, 17*

*This is a reading from the Gospel of John.*

Jesus said to his disciples,

"I love you
just as God loves me.
Live always in my love.
If you keep my commandments,
you are living in my love.
I am telling you this
so that you may be completely filled
with my joy.
This is my commandment—
love one another
just as I have loved you.
There is no greater love
than to give your life for your friends.
And you are my friends
if you do what I tell you.
The commandment I am giving you is this—
love one another."

*The Gospel of the Lord.*

During this Easter season we celebrate that Jesus loves everyone and showed his great love by dying and rising. Jesus did that for all of us: people who sin, people who try to be good, people who love him and people who don't love him, people who know him and people who don't know him, people who are in trouble, people of all races, people of all countries, people of all sizes and shapes, people who are old and people who are young and even people who aren't born yet. Let's listen to the Gospel to hear how important this love is to Jesus.

*After the Gospel,* remind the children that Jesus said he was telling us this—to love one another—so that we would have joy. Ask the children if that is their experience. Are people happier when they love one another? Perhaps they could share some examples.

Jesus tells us how he wants us to love others.

- What did he say?
- What do you think Jesus meant when he said,
  "Love one another as I
  have loved you"?

*Note: this is a crucial point in our Christian faith. Christian love is a commandment. But children can easily misunderstand this. Jesus loves with divine love. God is love. We are not commanded to love "as much as," that is, with divine love. We are commanded to love "in the way" Jesus loved. This commandment is first given in an earlier part of this last discourse of Jesus, just after he has washed the feet of his disciples in an attitude of service. And so we are commanded to love (serve) one another. The greatest love is shown by giving our lives for others—in service. Children should never feel guilty about not loving everyone equally. That is a universal love attained by few. Jesus teaches us to show loving service to anyone and everyone.*

Remind the children that Jesus said,
  "There is no greater love
  than to give your life
  for your friends."
Jesus gave his life for us when he died. But he also gave his life for others by healing them, helping them, and caring for them. How can we give our lives for others now?

Help them to see ways of doing this (things possible for children):

- including all children in games;
- talking to a child who feels alone;
- helping someone with a task;
- taking time, perhaps from play, to help someone;
- accepting people just as they are.

Jesus asks us to love this way because he loves us so much. Jesus loves everyone and wants us to love everyone too. That's what a Christian is—someone who believes Jesus is living and who lives like him.

## ASCENSION OF THE LORD

### YEAR B

### PRAYER OF THE DAY:

Lord,
just as the disciples
were happy
that Jesus returned to you,
make us happy
to know about him
and keep us always
praising you.
We ask this
through Christ, our Lord.

### FOCUS OF THE READINGS:

The mission of the church is to evangelize.

Our Gospel reading tells us that before Christ left his disciples physically, he commissioned them to preach and baptize in his name. This command is accompanied by the promise that Jesus will be with them always.

The passage from *Acts* tells us how they were able to do this. Jesus reminds the disciples of his promise to send his Spirit. Baptized in the Holy Spirit, they have the power to preach in the name of Jesus. Like love, evangelization is not an option for the church. We are commanded in today's readings, "Go; . . . you will be my witnesses. . . ."

### FIRST READING: *Acts 1:3-5, 8-11*

*This is a reading from the Acts of the Apostles.*

After Jesus died and rose,
he appeared to his apostles many times
to show them that he was really alive.
They saw him,
and he talked to them about the reign of God.
He told them not to leave Jerusalem,
but to wait for the gift of the Holy Spirit.
Jesus said,

"I have told you about this promise.
John baptized with water, but in a few days,
you will be baptized with the Holy Spirit.
The Holy Spirit will give you power
to be my witnesses in Jerusalem, in Judaea,
in Samaria and all over the world."

After he said this,
Jesus was taken up to heaven.
And even though
they couldn't see him any more,
the disciples stayed there staring into the sky.

Two men, dressed in white robes,
appeared to them and said,

"Jesus has been taken up to heaven,
but he will come back to you."

*The Word of the Lord.*

### RESPONSE: *Psalm 104*

RESPONSE: Send us your Spir-it, O Lord and re-new the face of the earth!

VERSE: May your glo-ry last for-ev-er. May you re-joice in all we do!

## GOSPEL ACCLAMATION:

"Go out to the world,___ pro-claim the Good News,___ pro-claim the Good News."___ Al - le - lu - ia!

## GOSPEL: *Mark 16:14a, 15-17, 18b-20*

*This is a reading from the Gospel of Mark.*

Jesus appeared to the apostles
and said to them,

"Go to every part of the world,
and tell everyone the Good News!
Everyone who believes and is baptized
will be saved.
Those who refuse to believe,
will be condemned.
And those who believe
will have the power to do these things:
they will destroy evil in my name,
they will speak new languages,
and they will heal those who are sick."

After saying this,
the Lord Jesus was taken up into heaven
and took his place with God.
The apostles went out
and preached everywhere.
The Lord worked with them
and proved their message was true
by the miracles they did.

*The Gospel of the Lord.*

## REFLECTING ON THE READINGS WITH CHILDREN:

*After the Gospel*, ask the children what they heard. Ask them to listen to the Gospel again, this time listening for the word they think is very important. Hopefully they will give a variety of words such as:

- go,
- tell,
- Good News,
- believe,
- baptized,
- power,
- heal,
- preached,
- message,
- miracles.

You may wish to write on newsprint the words the children say. Help them reconstruct Jesus' directions to evangelize—to tell the Good News and baptize.

Ask the children how the disciples were able to do this. Remind them of the first reading that tells us that the disciples were baptized in the Holy Spirit. With that power they were able to do many things—especially be witnesses for Jesus.

We also received the Holy Spirit when we were baptized.

"In the name of the Father, and of the Son, and of the Holy Spirit."

And so we too have the power of the Holy Spirit to be witnesses for Jesus. How can we do this?

Jesus said he wants everyone to hear the Good News that he is risen and loves them and wants them to live forever with him.

Jesus said, "Go to every part of the world and tell everyone the Good News." How can we help do that?

(As always it is important to keep the children focused on ideas truly possible for them at their ages.)

## SEVENTH SUNDAY OF EASTER

## YEAR B

### PRAYER OF THE DAY:

O God,
we belong to you
and to Jesus, your Son.
Help us to pray to you,
and as we pray,
may we get to know you
more and more each day.
We ask you this
through Jesus
who lives with you,
forever and ever.

### FOCUS OF THE READINGS:

The mission of the church is to live in unity, holiness, and fidelity.

Our Gospel reading is Jesus' prayer for his disciples—that they may remain united, that they may be holy, that they may be faithful to his Word. These are the characteristics by which the world will know who Jesus is and that he lives among his disciples. In the early church, a sign of the unity of believers was the community around the twelve apostles. The reading from *Acts* tells us that the disciples chose a man to replace Judas and thereby maintain that sign of unity. Note, however, that this man must be someone who was with them as Jesus taught them, someone who can be faithful to the Word. Note also, that before making the choice, the disciples pray. These characteristics—unity, holiness, and fidelity to the Word—remain the signs of the Christian community even today.

### FIRST READING: *Acts 1:15-17, 20-26*

*This is a reading from the Acts of the Apostles.*

One day,
when about a hundred and twenty followers
of Jesus were gathered together,
Peter said to them,

"My friends,
you know that Judas was an apostle
and shared in this ministry of ours.
But he was the one who betrayed Jesus.
It is written in the Psalms,

'Let someone else take his place.'

"So, now we must name someone
to take Judas' place and to be with us
to proclaim the resurrection.
It must be someone
who was one of our group while Jesus was with us,
from the time of John the Baptist
until the day that Jesus was taken up to heaven."

And so they suggested two men, Joseph and Matthias.
Then they prayed,

"Lord, you know the hearts of everyone.
So show us which of these two you choose
to take the place of Judas as an apostle."

Then they drew lots and Matthias was chosen,
and he became one of the apostles.

*The Word of the Lord.*

### RESPONSE: *Psalm 33*

RESPONSE:

Lord, be with us, with your love, be with us, all our hope is in you.

VERSES:

1. For your faith - ful word and all you do,
2. (♪) We are cho - sen, God, by you.

to Response

1. do, for your love we trust in you.
2. you. Bless us God, we trust in you.

58

## GOSPEL ACCLAMATION:

Sing prais-es to the Lord, al-le-lu-ia! Sing praise to greet the Word, al-le-lu-ia! The Word is God's truth and it lives in our hearts, al-le-lu-ia! Al-le-lu-ia!

**GOSPEL:** *John 17:1a, 11b-19*

*This is a reading from the Gospel of John.*

Jesus looked up to heaven and prayed,

"Most holy God,
protect these people you have given to me.
Keep them true to your name
so that they may be united as one
just as you and I are one.

"Since I have been with them,
I have taken care of them,
and I have kept them true to you.
Now I am coming to you.
But while I am still with them,
I am saying all of these things
so that they may be completely
filled with my joy.

["I taught them about you,
but the world hates them
because they believe in you.
Protect them from all evil.]

"Your Word is truth.
Make them holy
by keeping them true to your word.
[Just as you sent me into the world,
I have sent them into the world.
And now, I give myself completely for them
so that they may always be faithful to you."]

*The Gospel of the Lord.*

[ ] *Reader may omit text that appears in brackets.*

REFLECTING ON THE READINGS
WITH CHILDREN:

*After the Gospel*, ask the children
what they heard.
Jesus prayed:
• that we would be true to God,
• that we would be united as one,
• that we would share his joy,
• that we would be protected
  from evil,
• that we would be holy,
• that we would be true to
  God's word,
• that we would be faithful to God.

• What does it mean to be true to
  God? Can you give an example?
• What does it mean to be
  protected from evil? Can you
  give an example?
• What does it mean to be holy?

Help the children to relate these
to their everyday lives. Help them
see that being fair and courteous in
sports, for example, is holiness.

Remind them that Jesus prayed
this prayer for us. He truly wants
these things for us. You might, if
you have time, ask the children
which of these is most meaningful
(or important) to them now.

59

# PENTECOST SUNDAY

## YEAR B

### PRAYER OF THE DAY:

God of all people,
thank you for your gift
of the Holy Spirit
to us and the whole church.
Through the power
of your Spirit,
may we tell the whole world
about Jesus;
forgive those
who have hurt us
as we have been forgiven;
and live a happy life,
doing all
that you want us to do.
We pray this prayer
through Jesus, your Son,
who lives with you
and the Holy Spirit.

### FOCUS OF THE READINGS:

The mission of the church is to do the work of the Holy Spirit.

Jesus breathed into his disciples his own life, the Holy Spirit. By the power of that Spirit, the church is born. They are now to do what his death and resurrection were all about—forgive. Peace is the greeting of the Risen Lord and peace is his continued presence in the church.

This Spirit comes upon the disciples with power. In the name of Jesus, in every language, they are empowered to preach about the great things God has done.

## FIRST READING: *Acts 2:1-8, 11b*

*This is a reading from the Acts of the Apostles.*

On the day of Pentecost,
the believers were gathered together
in one room.
All of a sudden they heard a sound
like a strong wind
that seemed to fill the whole house.
Then they saw what looked like tongues of fire
coming and resting on each one of them.
They were all filled with the Holy Spirit,
and immediately they started to speak
in other languages.

At that time, there were visitors in Jerusalem
who had come from all over the world.
They were amazed
because they heard the believers
speaking in so many languages.
They said,

"How are they able to speak like this?
Aren't all of these people from Galilee?
Yet we can all hear them
telling in our own languages
about the great things God has done."

*The Word of the Lord.*

## RESPONSE: *Psalm 104*

RESPONSE: Send us your Spir-it, O Lord and re-new the face of the earth!

VERSE: May your glo-ry last for-ev-er. May you re-joice in all we do!

## GOSPEL ACCLAMATION:

## GOSPEL: *John 20:19-23*

*This is a reading from the Gospel of John.*

On Sunday evening
(the same day the women
had been to the tomb of Jesus),
the disciples were gathered in a room upstairs.
They had locked the doors
because they were afraid of the people
who had crucified Jesus.
Jesus came and stood in the room and said,

   "Peace be with you!"

Then he showed them his hands and his side.
The disciples were filled with joy
when they saw the Lord.
Jesus said again,

   "Peace be with you!
   As God has sent me to you,
   now I am sending you to others."

Then he breathed on the disciples
and said to them,

   "Receive the Holy Spirit.
   If you forgive the sins of anyone,
   they are forgiven.
   If you do not forgive them,
   they are not forgiven."

*The Gospel of the Lord.*

## REFLECTING ON THE READINGS WITH CHILDREN:

If you choose to reflect on the first reading, ask the children how Jesus kept the promise that he had made. Ask them how the disciples felt when they received the Holy Spirit. It is important to help them understand that the Holy Spirit is not "strong wind" and "tongues of fire." These are images used to describe an event which really cannot be put into words. We often do this. We say things such as, "She is like a cute little kitten." Or we say, "She is as strong as a rock." We are using metaphors to help us express more a feeling or a quality than a physical presence. The disciples were able to preach with clarity and so, later, when writing this account, described the event as receiving "tongues of fire." We don't know what the event was like. They (and we) knew they had received the Holy Spirit by power they had to do Christ's work, especially of preaching and healing.

Ask the children (as we have before) what words are said at a Christian baptism.

"I baptize you in the name of the Father, and of the Son, and of the Holy Spirit."

Help them to understand that we too have received the Holy Spirit. Ask them what the disciples did when they received the Holy Spirit. The emphasis here should not be on "speaking other languages" but "telling . . . about the great things God has done."

● What great things *(now)*?
● Whom can we tell?

*After the Gospel*, ask the children what they heard. What other thing (besides "telling the great things God has done") did Jesus gave us the power to do? Explore ways in which they can forgive others. Help them to see that, truly, if we (they) forgive someone, that person feels forgiven. If we refuse this, that person feels unforgiven. We have the power of the Holy Spirit to free people by being forgiving. Help them to see that when we live this way, "the face of the earth will be like new." (The Psalm refrain)

# Feasts of the Lord
## and
## Sundays in Ordinary Time

# TRINITY SUNDAY

## YEAR B

## PRAYER OF THE DAY:

God of all creation,
you embrace us
with the love
of a mother and father.
You send your own son,
Jesus, to save us.
Through the power
of your Holy Spirit,
you raise us
to life everlasting.
Your life is a mystery
that we will celebrate
and proclaim,
forever and ever.

*Note: Consistent with other specific feasts, we have chosen to keep the same readings for all three cycles. Of the readings available for this feast, these two seem to be the most easily understood by children.*

## FOCUS OF THE READINGS:

The focus of our readings is the experience of God acting in our lives in various ways. We have no adequate language for God because God is beyond any single image we may have. We experience God in Jesus Christ who shares with us his experience of God, as creator, as redeemer, and as a person of intimate relationship. Our experience of this relationship is the Spirit of God living in us.

In the first reading, Paul tells us that because we live in the Holy Spirit, and because we are brothers and sisters of Christ, we are children of God. We too can enjoy the intimate relationship that Jesus called "Abba."

In the Gospel, Jesus tells his disciples to preach, baptize and teach in the name of God—the God who is intimate like a parent (Father), who comes as Savior (Son), and who lives within us (Holy Spirit).

## FIRST READING: *Romans 8:14-17*

*This is a reading
from Paul's letter to the Romans.*

Brothers and sisters,

Everyone who is guided by the Holy Spirit
is a child of God.
We have been adopted by God,
and when we pray, "Abba, Father,"
it is the Holy Spirit and our own spirit
telling us that we truly are God's children.
And if we are God's children,
we will have eternal life like Jesus
who is God's Son.

*The Word of the Lord.*

## RESPONSE: *Psalm 104*

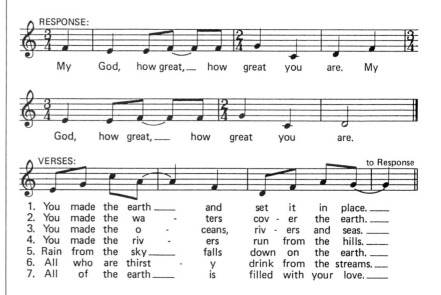

RESPONSE:
My God, how great,— how great you are. My
God, how great,— how great you are.

VERSES:
to Response
1. You made the earth ___ and set it in place. ___
2. You made the wa - ters cov - er the earth. ___
3. You made the o - ceans, riv - ers and seas. ___
4. You made the riv - ers run from the hills. ___
5. Rain from the sky ___ falls down on the earth. ___
6. All who are thirst - y drink from the streams. ___
7. All of the earth ___ is filled with your love. ___

## GOSPEL ACCLAMATION:

"Make dis-ci-ples and bap-tize them, in the name of the Fa-ther, the

name of the Son, the name of the Spir-it." Al - le - lu - ia!

## GOSPEL: *Matthew 28:16-20*

*This is a reading from the Gospel of Matthew.*

The eleven disciples
went to the mountain in Galilee
where Jesus told them to meet him.
When Jesus met them there, he said,

"God has given me
all the power and authority
of heaven and earth.
Now I am sending you out
to preach to all the nations.
I want you to make disciples
and baptize them
in the name of the Father,
and of the Son,
and of the Holy Spirit.
Teach them to keep my commandments
and do all that I have taught you.
And I promise you
that I am with you always —
yes, to the very end of the world."

*The Gospel of the Lord.*

## REFLECTING ON THE READINGS WITH CHILDREN:

As noted previously, Trinitarian language poses difficulties for children (as well as adults!) and even well-intentioned analogies serve only to confuse them more. We suggest that it is not necessary to concern ourselves with doctrinal language for Trinity, but rather with the experience of God in our lives.

*After the Gospel*, ask the children what Jesus asked the disciples to do (preach, baptize and teach). Are the disciples of Jesus still doing those things today?

Jesus said, "Preach to all nations." This might be a good time to tell the children a little about missionary work. Besides preaching in our own parishes, some people are called to go to other parts of the world.

Jesus said, "Teach them to keep my commandments." Help the children discuss the many ways the church teaches (religious education classes for children and adults, special classes on the Bible, informal teaching by parents, teachers, friends, and so forth). Draw attention especially to teaching activities in your own parish.

Jesus said, "Baptize them in the name of the Father and of the Son and of the Holy Spirit." Ask the children if they remember being at a baptism. What does the priest or deacon say? Remind them that we proclaim that we are baptized Christians every time we make the sign of the cross and say those words.

If time permits, you may wish to reflect on the first reading as well. Remind the children that Jesus often spoke of and to God using the name "Father" or even "Abba" which is like our word "Daddy." What is important here is not the masculine image of God, but rather the intimate relationship that Jesus experienced with God. St. Paul tells us that because Jesus chose us to be his brothers and sisters and gave us his Holy Spirit, we too are children of God and can call God "Abba!" The children should leave today's Liturgy of the Word knowing that God loves them and wants us to be close to them.

# BODY AND BLOOD OF CHRIST

## YEAR B

### PRAYER OF THE DAY:

God of life,
help us to know
that when we share our food,
as you do
with all who are in need,
we satisfy our hunger;
when we share our drink,
as you do
with all who are in need,
we satisfy our thirst.
We offer this prayer
as we gather
to eat the bread
and drink the wine
of your son, Jesus,
who lives with us,
now and forever.

*Note: In keeping with the* Directory for Masses With Children *(Paragraph 43), the authors have elected to use the first reading from Year C and the Gospel from Year A because they seem best suited "to the capacity of children."*

### FOCUS OF THE READINGS:

Our readings for today focus on the presence of Christ in the Eucharist. In the first reading, Paul presents what he was taught concerning the actions and words of Jesus at the Last Supper. While the words may vary in the four accounts (*Matthew, Mark, Luke* and *1 Corinthians*), what remains consistent is the belief that in the sharing of bread and wine, Christ is present.

### FIRST READING: *1 Corinthians 11:23-26*

*This is a reading
from the first letter of Paul to the Corinthians.*

Brothers and sisters,

This is what the Lord taught me
and I am now telling you.
At supper, on the night before he died,
Jesus took bread, and after he gave thanks,
he broke the bread and said,

"This is my body,
which I am giving for you.
When you eat this bread,
remember me."

After supper,
he took a cup of wine and said,

"This cup is the new covenant in my blood.
When you drink from this cup,
remember me."

For when you eat this bread
and drink from this cup,
you are proclaiming the death of the Lord
until he comes again.

*The Word of the Lord.*

### RESPONSE: *Psalm 104*

RESPONSE:
You are the one who feeds us, giv-ing us food from your hand.
You are the one who feeds us, giv-ing us all we need.

## GOSPEL ACCLAMATION:

1. "I am the Bread of Life," says the Lord.
2. Al - le - lu - ia, al - le - lu - ia!

1.-2. "All who eat this Bread will live for ev - er."

GOSPEL: *John 6:35, 51, 53, 55-56, 54*

*This is a reading from the Gospel of John.*

Jesus said to the people,

"I am the bread of life.
Anyone who comes to me
will never be hungry,
and anyone who believes in me
will never be thirsty.
I am the living bread
that came down from heaven.
Anyone who eats this bread,
which is my life, will live forever.
This bread gives life to the world.
Unless you eat this bread
and drink from this cup,
you do not have real life in you.
For I am real food and real drink for you.
Everyone who eats this bread
and drinks from this cup
lives in me,
and I live in each of them.
Those who eat this bread
and drink from this cup
have eternal life,
and I will raise them up on the last day."

*The Gospel of the Lord.*

The Gospel proclaims that Christ himself is our life. It is he who satisfies our hunger and thirst. He chose to make this concept a reality in bread and wine. Jesus invites us to share his body and blood, which in Hebrew are symbols of person and life. In these symbols we encounter the living Lord, ever present to us. To share in his life, to be one with him, is to live forever.

REFLECTING ON THE READINGS WITH CHILDREN:

Discuss with the children the many times we celebrate our unity by sharing in a special meal: Christmas, Easter, Thanksgiving, birthdays, and so forth. Are there other times? Ask the children what their family eats on these special occasions. Help them see that certain foods have become symbols of what we are celebrating. When we see and eat certain food, it makes the event real and even brings to our memory past celebrations. For example, many families have turkey for dinner every year on Christmas. It has become symbolic for the celebration of an important event. And sharing in that special dinner brings members of the family closer together.

Jesus celebrated a special meal with his disciples the night before he died. They shared bread and wine. Jesus told them that from now on, whenever his disciples share that bread and wine and remember him, he is there in a special way. When we come together for mass, we remember what Jesus said and did. We too share that bread and wine which is the very life of Jesus, and it brings us all closer together. When we eat this bread and drink from this cup, we say that we believe in Jesus, and we believe that he gives us life and that he will give us life forever.

67

# SECOND SUNDAY IN ORDINARY TIME

## YEAR B

## PRAYER OF THE DAY:

Loving God,
through Jesus
you call us to love you
and everybody in this world.
Make us wide awake
to your voice
and always prepared
to do what pleases you.
We ask this
through Jesus, your Son.

## FOCUS OF THE READINGS:

Our readings this Sunday focus on "call and response." The emphasis in the call of Samuel is on listening: "Speak to me, God, I am *listening*." Samuel is called to be a prophet—one who must constantly listen to God in order to truly speak for God. The emphasis in the Gospel is on *seeing*; "come and see." To "see" means more than to view with the physical eye. Biblically, it means "perceiving with the eye of faith." The disciples must "see" that Jesus is the Messiah and follow him in faith. Samuel hears and responds. The disciples drop everything to "come and see."

Our prayer response draws us personally into the theme:
- You ask me to listen.
- Here I am; I come to do your will.

The prophet/disciple has only one goal—to proclaim and live the will of God. This theme of "call and response" will continue through the Fifth Sunday of Ordinary Time and will recur throughout this season which presents the public life and ministry of Jesus.

## FIRST READING: *1 Samuel 3:1-11, 19*

*This is a reading from the first book of Samuel.*

A long time ago, in Jerusalem, there lived a priest
named Eli, who was very old, and he was going blind.
A young boy named Samuel looked after him
and was ministering with him in the Temple.
Samuel's ministry
was to keep the Temple light burning.

One night, when Samuel was about to go to sleep,
God called his name,

  "Samuel! Samuel!"

Samuel got up and ran to Eli and said,

  "Here I am. You called me."

But Eli said,

  "I didn't call you. Go back to sleep."

So Samuel went to sleep. But God called to him again,

  "Samuel! Samuel!"

Samuel went back to Eli and said,

  "Here I am. You called me."

Eli said,

  "I didn't call you. Go back to sleep."

Now Samuel did not know that it was God calling him.
And when God called the third time,

  "Samuel! Samuel!"

He again ran to Eli and said,

  "Here I am. You called me."

Then Eli understood that it was God
who was calling Samuel. So he said,

  "Go back to sleep. And if someone calls you again,
  answer, 'Speak to me, Lord, I am listening.' "

So Samuel went back to the Temple to go to sleep.
And again God called his name,

  "Samuel! Samuel!"

He answered,

  "Speak to me, Lord, I am listening!"

And God said to Samuel,

  "I am about to do something that will make the ears
  of everyone who hears it tingle."

As Samuel grew up, God stayed very close to him
and made him a great leader of the people.

*The Word of the Lord.*

# RESPONSE: *Psalm 40*

# GOSPEL ACCLAMATION:

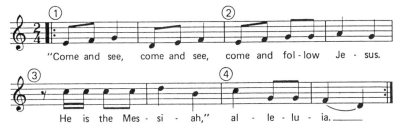

# GOSPEL: *John 1:35-42*

*This is a reading from the Gospel of John.*

When John the Baptist was in Bethany with two of his
disciples, he saw Jesus walking by, and said,

"Look! There is the Lamb of God!"

The two disciples who were with John
heard what he said and began to follow Jesus.
When Jesus turned around
and saw them following him, he asked them,

"What do you want?"

They answered, "Rabbi (this word means teacher),
where do you live?"

Jesus said, "Come and see!"

So they went with Jesus.
Now, it was about four o'clock in the afternoon,
and so they stayed with him for the rest of that day.

One of the two who followed him was Andrew,
the brother of Simon Peter.
So the next morning, the first thing Andrew did
was find his brother Simon and tell him,

"We have found the Messiah!"

When Andrew brought Simon to Jesus,
Jesus looked at him and said,

"You are Simon, the son of John.
But from now on you will be called Peter."

*The Gospel of the Lord.*

## REFLECTING ON THE READINGS WITH CHILDREN:

For this Sunday, we suggest that you
do the reflections on each of the readings
separately. The story of Samuel is long,
but it is also one that children usually
enjoy and so will be well worth separate
consideration before going on to the
Gospel.

*After the first reading*, ask the children
to recall the story of Samuel. It is always
best to give the children time to retell the
story from what they remember. If they
have difficulty recalling, you might lead
them with questions such as:

● Where was Samuel?
● What was his ministry?
● Who is Eli?
● What did Samuel hear?
● What did Eli tell Samuel to do?
● What are the words Samuel said
  when he heard the voice the third
  time?

Remind the children that Samuel was
called to be a prophet to his people.

● Why is it important for a prophet to
  "listen"?

Help the children to see that the
prophet is one who speaks for God and
therefore must always listen to God. You
may wish to sing the Psalm Response
again.

*After reading the Gospel*, ask the
children what they remember of John the
Baptist from Advent. Again, if necessary,
help them to recall what they heard in the
story.

● What did John call Jesus?
● What did Jesus ask the two disciples
  who were following him?
● When they asked "where do you
  live?" what did Jesus answer?
● What other disciples were called in
  this story?

Help the children to understand that
to "see" means more than physical sight.

● How else do we use the word "see"?
● What did Jesus mean?
● What did Andrew do after he "saw"?

Help them come to understand that as
disciples we listen, see and tell others.

*Note: If you choose to reflect on only
one of the readings, we suggest the story of
Samuel. There are very few stories
involving children in the Scriptures and
the children love to talk about them. Since
the theme is the same in both readings, the
children will profit from hearing the
Gospel proclaimed even if reflections are
not made specifically on it.*

## THIRD SUNDAY IN ORDINARY TIME

### YEAR B

PRAYER OF THE DAY:
God,
you are ready to forgive us
whenever we do wrong.
Give us the courage
to be sorry for our faults
and so open up our hearts
to your love.
We ask you this
through Jesus, the Lord.

FOCUS OF THE READINGS:

The focus of our readings is twofold: the call of the prophet/disciple and the message to be proclaimed—repent and believe.

Jonah is called and sent. Our passage for today picks up the story after the call and tells us that Jonah was sent to preach repentance to the people of Ninevah. The heart of the story is the faith response of the people of Ninevah: when they heard God's message they did in fact believe and change their lives.

In our passage from *Mark*, the first disciples are called while at their ordinary work. They change their lives immediately and follow Jesus. And as we will hear on a later Sunday, they too are eventually sent out to preach the message Jesus gives in the opening verses of this Gospel, "Change your lives and believe in the Good News."

Those who are called must first repent and believe.

FIRST READING: *Jonah 3:1-5, 10*

*This is a reading from the book of Jonah.*

God spoke to Jonah and said,

"Go to the great city of Ninevah
and give them my message.
I will tell you what to say to them."

So Jonah went to Ninevah just as God told him.
Ninevah was a very big city.
It was so big that it took three whole days
to walk from one end of it to the other.
Jonah started walking through the city,
telling the people God's message. He said,

"In just forty days from now,
the city of Ninevah will be destroyed."

The very first day
that Jonah gave this message,
all the people of Ninevah
believed God's message, and they decided
that they would change their evil ways.
They showed this by fasting and doing penance.

God saw that they were truly sorry
for all the evil they were doing
and how they really had changed their lives.
And so God did not destroy the city.

*The Word of the Lord.*

RESPONSE: *Psalm 25*

RESPONSE: 1st time: Leader; 2nd time: All

Show me your ways, O Lord. Teach me your paths. paths.

VERSES: All                                             to Response

1. You show me when I have sinned.
2. My Sav - ior, I hope in you.
3. O lead me in ways of truth.

## GOSPEL ACCLAMATION:

(Fingersnap)

"Come and fol-low__ me. __ Change your lives and

fol-low__ me."__ Al-le-lu-ia, _____ al-le-lu-ia,

1   "Change your lives and fol-low__ me."__   2   fol-low__ me."__

Leader:   All:   Leader:   All:
fol-low__ me, __   fol-low__ me, __   fol-low__ me, __   fol-low__ me. __

## GOSPEL: *Mark 1:14-20*

*This is a reading from the Gospel of Mark.*

When Jesus came to Galilee,
he proclaimed the Good News
to the people saying,

"The time you have been waiting for has come!
The reign of God is here!
Change your lives
and believe in the Good News!"

A little while later,
as Jesus was walking by the Sea of Galilee,
he saw Simon and his brother Andrew.
They were fishermen,
and they were putting their nets into the water.
Jesus called out to them,

"Come and follow me.
From now on you will be gathering people, not fish!"

Simon and Andrew left their boats
and their nets immediately
and started to follow Jesus.

Later on, Jesus saw James and his brother John.
They were in their boat taking care of their fishing nets.
Jesus called to them, and they too left their boat
and those who were working in the boat with them.
And they went to follow Jesus.

*The Gospel of the Lord.*

## REFLECTING ON THE READINGS WITH CHILDREN:

We suggest that the reflections be made only on the Gospel this Sunday. The first reading is a little difficult for children.

*Note: If the children recall last Sunday's Gospel reading, this could be a bit confusing to them. The call of the disciples here in Mark is quite different from the account given last Sunday in the Gospel of John. You may need to explain (should it come up) that the two authors, John and Mark, wrote separately, perhaps with a time span of thirty to forty years. Neither was interested in historical detail as we consider it. Their point was simply that the Lord calls. It is not of great importance in what order or manner the disciples were called.*

Ask the children to recall the story. If they have difficulty recalling you may lead them with questions such as:

- What were Simon and Andrew doing when Jesus called them?
- What did Jesus say to them?
- What other two disciples were called in this story?
- What did they do when Jesus called them?
- What does "gathering people" mean?

Spend time allowing children to share their thoughts on "change your lives and believe in the Good News."

What does it mean to follow Jesus today? (It is important that this be kept on their age level.)

71

# FOURTH SUNDAY IN ORDINARY TIME

## YEAR B

### PRAYER OF THE DAY:

God, our Guide,
you never leave us
when we are in trouble
but always send us help.
We thank you above all
for sending Jesus
to be our friend and teacher.
We want to listen to his words
and do what he asks.
Help us be true
to our promise.
We ask you this
through Jesus, our friend.

### FOCUS OF THE READINGS:

The focus of today's readings is the teaching authority of the prophet, especially Jesus.

The prophets of the Old Testament were "the voice of God" and, as such, commanded obedience. In our passage for today, God promises the people of Israel a future prophet who, like Moses, will come from among their own people. But with this promise, God issues a stern warning to obey the voice of the prophet.

The New Testament sees Jesus as that future prophet, who teaches with "real authority." He not only speaks for God but demonstrates his authority with power. The exorcism of evil spirits serves as an example of the authority of Jesus: "He teaches with real authority. . .even the evil spirits obey him."

### FIRST READING: *Deuteronomy 18:17-20*

*This is a reading
from the book of Deuteronomy.*

God said to Moses,

"Because the people have prayed for a prophet,
I will give them one like you,
one of their own people.
I myself will speak
through the voice of this prophet,
and the prophet will tell the people
everything that I say.

"I will punish anyone
who does not listen
to my teaching through the prophet.
And I will also punish any prophet
who teaches the people things in my name
that I did not really say."

*The Word of the Lord.*

### RESPONSE: *Psalm 40*

RESPONSE:
Here I am O my God. I come to do your will.

VERSES:
to Response
1. I wait-ed pa-tient-ly.__ You turned your face to me.__
2. I will tell ev'-ry-one__ how you will save us all.__
3. A new song I will sing:__ your love is won-der-ful.__

## GOSPEL ACCLAMATION:

Leader:                                        All: (sing and clap)

1. *Your Word brings us heal - ing.*    Al - le -lu - ia, al - le -lu - ia!
2. *Your Word Lord is all we need.*     Al - le -lu - ia, al - le -lu - ia!

## GOSPEL: *Mark 1:21-28*

*This is a reading from the Gospel of Mark.*

One day
while Jesus was teaching on the Sabbath,
a man who had an evil spirit in him
came into the synagogue.
The evil spirit screamed out loud,

"Why are you bothering us,
  Jesus of Nazareth?
  Did you come here to destroy us?
  I know who you are.
  You are the Holy One of God!"

Jesus spoke very sternly to the evil spirit,

"Be quiet! Come out of that man!"

The evil spirit
made the man's body
tremble and jump.
Then it screamed loudly again
and came out of the man.
Everyone who saw this happen was shocked.
They asked each other,

"What can all this mean? Who is this Jesus?
  He doesn't teach like our scribes.
  He teaches with real authority.
  When he tells the evil spirits what to do,
  even they obey him!"

From then on,
everyone around Galilee knew about Jesus!

*The Gospel of the Lord.*

## REFLECTING ON THE READINGS WITH CHILDREN:

*After the first reading,* ask the children who speaks to them about important things.

- Do they hear some people say things that they know are right?
- Do they sometimes hear people say things that they know are wrong?
- Are they sometimes confused about what they hear?
- Who teaches them the truth?

*After the Gospel,* ask them to recall the story. If they have difficulty recalling, you might lead them with questions such as:

- Where was Jesus?
- What was he doing there?
- Who came in?
- Why was the evil spirit afraid of Jesus?
- How did Jesus show that his "real authority" came from God?

The message that the children should take home is that God loves us and wants us to be free from anything that is not good for us. Jesus lives with us and is able to free us if we want him to and if we listen to him. You might ask the children if they could have Jesus free them, or the world, of something, what would it be?

- How can we help Jesus do that?

*Note: Many children have seen films such as "The Exorcist." Should the question of "possession" come up, assure the children that God does not allow the devil to take over our lives unless we choose that. We need not fear that God is going to abandon us to the devil or that the devil will "grab" us. We have the assurance of God's love, and we need not live in fear.*

# FIFTH SUNDAY IN ORDINARY TIME

## YEAR B

## PRAYER OF THE DAY:

Caring God,
to make this world happy
and peaceful as you want it
we must work hard
at loving and helping
all people.
See how weak we are;
make us strong
to do your work,
because without you
we can do nothing.
We ask you to do this
through Jesus, your Son.

## FOCUS OF THE READINGS:

The readings for this Sunday continue the theme of the past Sundays of "call and response" and preaching the message. But they also lead us into the miracle stories of Jesus. The reading from *Job* (which we have omitted because of its difficult language for children) speaks of the sufferings of the human condition. The healings in our Gospel passage respond to that. We have chosen the second reading in which Paul speaks of his call to preach the Gospel. The focus of this reading is that he *must* respond to that call and that he must respond in a way that will truly bring the Good News (of healing and salvation) to all. Paul does not mean here that he has no free will, but rather, that the call is so compelling that it takes hold of his whole being.

In the Gospel reading, Mark combines the themes of healing and preaching. Jesus, after healing many, tells his disciples he must "go to other towns to proclaim the Good News there also." In short, the focus of our call is to preach the Good News of healing and salvation which is found in Christ.

## FIRST READING: *1 Corinthians 9:16-19, 22-23*

*This is a reading
from Paul's first letter to the Corinthians.*

Brothers and sisters,

When I preach the Gospel,
I don't do it so that I can brag.
I do it because God told me to preach.

I am a free person.
But I have made myself
like a servant to everyone
so that they will accept me
and what I am preaching.
When someone is weak,
I become weak with them
so that they will accept the Gospel.
I am always ready
to accept the people I preach to
so that at least some of them
might accept the Gospel.

Everything I do, I do because of the Gospel.
And I hope that because I do this,
I will always be blessed.

*The Word of the Lord.*

## RESPONSE: *Psalm 40*

RESPONSE: Here I am O my God. I come to do your will.

VERSES: to Response
1. Speak Lord, I'm lis-ten-ing,— I wait to hear your Word.—
2. I love your law, O God,— it makes my heart re-joice.—
3. I will tell ev'-ry-one— how you will save us all. —

## GOSPEL ACCLAMATION:

Al - le - lu - ia! Praise for the Good News___ that
God is love, God cares for us so al - le - lu - ia,
praise for the Good News___ that God is love.

## GOSPEL: *Mark 1:29-39*

*This is a reading from the Gospel of Mark.*

One day Jesus went with James and John
to Simon and Andrew's house.
Simon's mother-in-law was sick in bed
with a high fever.
As soon as Jesus went into the house,
Simon and Andrew told him about her.
So Jesus went to her,
took her by the hand and helped her up.
Her fever left her immediately,
and she began to serve all those who were there.
That evening, the people of the town
brought to Jesus anyone who was sick
and those who had evil spirits in them.
And Jesus healed them.
Early the next morning,
Jesus went off to a place
where he could be alone for awhile and pray.
Simon and some of the others
went to find him, and said,

"Everyone is looking for you."

But Jesus said to them,

"We must go to other towns now so that
I can proclaim the Good News there also.
Because that is what I came to do."

So Jesus went into the synagogues
all around Galilee
and preached the Good News.

*The Gospel of the Lord.*

## REFLECTING ON THE READINGS WITH CHILDREN:

We suggest that the readings be reflected on separately this Sunday.

*After the first reading*, ask the children to share what they know about St. Paul. If they are unfamiliar with his life, tell them a little about his conversion.

St. Paul (Saul) was a Jew—a Pharisee. He was proud of his Jewish background and was a leader among his people. He was well educated and had studied the Jewish law very carefully. Because he believed so much in his Hebrew faith, he began to persecute anyone he could find who was a follower of Jesus. He thought Christians were sinning against God, and so he wanted to keep people from believing in Jesus. He even agreed with those who stoned St. Stephen to death. One day, when he was on his way to the city of Damascus to put Christians in prison, Jesus appeared to him and spoke to him. From that moment, Paul's life was completely changed. He became a believer and was baptized. He spent the rest of his life preaching about Jesus, especially how Jesus saves people even when they have sinned.

Help the children understand why St. Paul was so eager to share with others the good news about Jesus. Explain to them what Paul means by "I am always ready to accept the people I preach to. . . ." Help them understand that when we receive a gift freely, we want others to have that gift freely too.

*After the Gospel*, reflect with the children on the meaning of "Good News." Tell them that "Gospel" means "Good News." What is the Good News that Jesus went to proclaim? Help them see that Jesus prayed before he preached. And we too must pray if we want to share the Good News.

*Note: We will have many miracle stories in Year B with Mark. It may be best to concentrate on the second half of this reading. How can we share the Good News today? (Be sure that this discussion remains on a level which is truly practical for their age.)*

# SIXTH SUNDAY IN ORDINARY TIME

## YEAR B

## PRAYER OF THE DAY:

Healing God,
there are many people
who need our friendship—
sick people, lonely people,
people we do not like.
Put in our hearts
a real love for them.
We make this prayer to you
through Jesus, your Son.

### FOCUS OF THE READINGS:

The primary focus of these readings would be difficult to present to children—namely, that leprosy symbolizes sin (clearly indicated in both the Old and New Testaments) and that Jesus has the power to forgive sin. We can easily move, however, to a secondary, though not less important, focus.

All disease and illness—especially those as severe as leprosy—are dreaded by human beings. Jesus reveals that he has the power to heal these ailments and that he indeed wants to. Jesus, in his compassion, reached out and touched a man with leprosy—a man who, by the standard of the time, was untouchable. This was not a demonstration against the law. It was an act of genuine love—"I do want to." At the same time, Jesus reveals his power—"you are cured right now." This is in striking contrast to the rejection and inability to heal evident in the reading from *Deuteronomy*. This Gospel focuses on the compassion and the power of Jesus.

## FIRST READING: *Leviticus 13:1-2, 44-46*

*This is a reading from the book of Leviticus.*

It is written in the law:

> People who have a scab or an open sore
> on their skin and it becomes leprosy
> must be brought to one of the priests.
> The priest must tell them
> that they are "unclean,"
> because anyone with leprosy
> is considered unclean by the law.

> Those who have leprosy
> must wear torn clothes
> and must not wear anything on their heads.
> They must live outside the camp
> away from the other people.
> When they come into the town,
> they must shout out loud,

> "Unclean! Unclean!"

> They will be considered unclean
> as long as they have the disease of leprosy.

*The Word of the Lord.*

## RESPONSE: *Psalm 103/31*

RESPONSE:
My God, my God, have mer-cy on me, for
all my hope is in you, my God, all my hope is in you.

VERSES: to Response
1. You see I am in trou-ble, you know what makes me sad.
2. O God, you are my strength,— my life is in your hands.

## GOSPEL ACCLAMATION:

Sing prais-es to the Lord, al - le - lu - ia! Sing praise to greet the Word, al - le - lu - ia! Your Word brings us heal-ing, it brings us new life, al - le - lu - ia! Al - le - lu - ia!

## GOSPEL: *Mark 1:40-45*

*This is a reading from the Gospel of Mark.*

One day a man who had leprosy came to Jesus
because he wanted Jesus to heal him.
He knelt in front of Jesus and said,

   "If you want to, you can cure me."

Jesus felt very sorry for the man,
and so he reached out and touched him
and said,

   "I do want to cure you.
   You are cured right now."

The man was cured of his leprosy immediately.
Then Jesus warned the man, saying,

   "Now don't tell anyone about this,
   but go and show yourself to the priest
   as Moses said,
   and make an offering
   because you have been cured."

But instead, the man went away
and began to tell everyone what happened.
Because of this,
Jesus was not able to go into any town
without being noticed by everyone.
So he stayed outside of the towns,
but people still kept coming
from everywhere to see him.

*The Gospel of the Lord.*

## REFLECTING ON THE READINGS WITH CHILDREN:

It will not be necessary to dwell on "the law" with regard to leprosy. It is sufficient just to make clear to the children that leprosy was a dreaded disease and that those who had it were not permitted to live in the towns. People were afraid of lepers and certainly would not touch them. Explain to children that because the people did not understand leprosy (or most illnesses) they often thought it was a punishment for sin.

*After the Gospel*, ask the children to recall the story. In particular, help them to recall the compassion of Jesus. It is important that they recall that Jesus

- felt sorry for the leper,
- touched the leper (though to others he was an outcast),
- truly wanted to heal the leper.

Ask the children if they have ever experienced being left out or have felt alone and unwanted. Who "brought them back"? Who helped them feel better? How did that person do that? When someone forgives or tells you you are loved, does it help if they put their arms around you or if they touch you gently? Help the children see that the way Jesus treats people is as important as his miracles.

Without moralizing, we can help children see that often our gentleness, our kindness, our attention or our touch is all someone really needs or wants.

The children may have heard a great deal about AIDS. You may want to help them see the parallel— a dreaded disease that many people feel is a punishment. Jesus calls us to treat those with AIDS compassionately.

## SEVENTH SUNDAY IN ORDINARY TIME

YEAR B

### PRAYER OF THE DAY:

Dearest God,
we often do things
which do not please you.
Forgive us
for not loving you enough.
Teach us to understand
what is right
and what is wrong.
May we always follow Jesus,
the healer of our hearts,
who lives with you
forever and ever.

### FOCUS OF THE READINGS:

The focus of the readings for today is the forgiveness of sin. The first two lines of the reading from *Isaiah* may easily be misunderstood. For this reason, we have eliminated them from the children's version. The "things of the past" refer, not to sin, but to the events of the exodus—God's mighty act of salvation. God now says, in effect, "I am now going to do an even greater thing. I am going to bring you home from your exile (in Babylon)." The second paragraph of the reading explains that they were in exile because they had sinned. But God says, "I am God, and so I forgive." The Gospel reading focuses on the power of Jesus to forgive sin. Note the focus also on the faith of the community as instrumental in this forgiveness. It is the community (represented by the four men) who express faith by bringing the paralyzed man to Jesus.

"Look not on our sins, but on the faith of your church."

### FIRST READING: *Isaiah 43:21, 24-25*

*This is a reading from the prophet Isaiah.*

Our God says,

"My people, I created you for myself
so that you would give me praise.
But you did not call upon me
because you got tired of me.
You went on sinning and doing evil things.

"But I am the one who forgives your sins.
I am your God,
and so I forgive all you do wrong,
and I forget about your sins."

*The Word of the Lord.*

### RESPONSE: *Psalm 103*

### GOSPEL ACCLAMATION:

78

## GOSPEL: *Mark 2:1-12*

### *This is a reading from the Gospel of Mark.*

When Jesus came back to Capernaum,
everyone heard that he was home.
Many people came to the house where he was staying
so they could hear him speak.
The house was so crowded
that there was no room left anywhere,
even in front of the door.

While Jesus was teaching all these people,
four men carrying a man on a stretcher
came to the house.
The man was paralyzed and could not walk.
They were bringing him to see Jesus, but,
because of the huge crowd,
they could not get in through the door.
So they climbed up onto the roof
and made a hole in it.
Then they lowered the stretcher with the man on it
down through the roof to the floor in front of Jesus.

When Jesus saw how much they trusted
and believed in him, he said to the paralyzed man,

"My friend, your sins are forgiven."

Some of the people
who were there were teachers of the law
and they thought to themselves,

"How can this man say, 'Your sins are forgiven'?
Only God can forgive sins. He is making fun of
God."

Jesus knew what they were thinking,
and so he said to them,

"Which do you think is easier to do:
heal this man so he can walk again
or forgive his sins?
But I will show you
that I do have the power to forgive sins."

So Jesus said to the paralyzed man,

"Stand up! Pick up your stretcher and walk!"

The man got up at once, picked up his stretcher and
walked out in front of the crowd.
Everyone who was there saw what happened,
and they praised God, saying,

"We have never seen anything like this!"

### *The Gospel of the Lord.*

## REFLECTING ON THE READINGS WITH CHILDREN:

Hopefully, the Gospel has been proclaimed with all the joy of an exciting story. Let the children really hear the details which Mark has been so careful to include (compare *Matthew 9:1-8*). This marvelous episode teaches the loving forgiveness of God and the children will enjoy it all the more if they can picture the scene vividly.

Ask the children to recall the story. Take the details slowly:

- Jesus was at home;
- there was a large crowd;
- there was no room, even in front of the door;
- Jesus was teaching;
- four men carrying a stretcher, on which was a man who was paralyzed, looked for a way to get in;
- they climbed onto the roof and made a hole in it (by taking away tiles);
- they lowered the stretcher with the man on it to the floor in front of Jesus.
- How do you think the crowd reacted?
- What did Jesus say to the man?
- Why were the teachers of the law unhappy with this?
- How do you think the man felt during this discussion between Jesus and the teachers of the law?
- Then what did Jesus say to the man?
- How do you think the man felt then? What did he do?

*Deeper Reflection:*
- Why did Jesus say, "Your sins are forgiven"?
- Who had faith that Jesus could heal the man?

Help the children see that it was the faith of his friends that brought this man to Jesus to be healed. When others are weak, we can help them. We need each other in the church.

## EIGHTH SUNDAY IN ORDINARY TIME

## YEAR B

### PRAYER OF THE DAY:

Lord God,
we promise
to try to do your will
in hard times
as well as good.
Yet without your strength
we will fail.
Look on us in love and pity;
see how much we need you,
and be always at our side.
We ask you to do this
through Jesus, your Son.

### FOCUS OF THE READINGS:

The image of marriage is used in both of our readings. In the first reading, Hosea used his broken marriage with his wife, Gomer, as an image of the broken covenant between God and the people of Israel. Just as Hosea will take Gomer to the desert (a place alone), speak tenderly to her heart and woo her back, so will God renew the broken covenant with unfaithful Israel, and with us when we have strayed. God's fidelity is unconditional and everlasting.

The Gospel reading picks up the image of marriage, with Jesus as the bridegroom and the believers the friends of the bridegroom. Jesus is creating a new relationship. This newness of Jesus is compared with putting a patch of new cloth on old material—it is so new that the old ways cannot support it. Jesus is with us intimately—as in a marriage. This is cause, not for fasting, but for joy!

### FIRST READING:  *Hosea 2:14b, 15b, 19-20*

*This is a reading from the prophet Hosea.*

Our God says:

"I will take (Israel) with me into the desert.
We will be alone,
and I will speak to her heart.
She will speak to me
just as she did when she was young,
when I brought her out of Egypt.

"I will say to her:
I will marry you forever;
I will marry you,
and I will give you goodness and justice.
I will be faithful to you,
and you will know me as I really am.
And you will know that I am your God."

*The Word of the Lord.*

### RESPONSE:  *Psalm 118*

RESPONSE: 2nd time, All repeat

You are my help, I thank you. You are my Sav-ior, I thank you. You are my light, you are my love, O how I thank you my God.

## GOSPEL ACCLAMATION:

We lis-ten for your voice, al-le-lu-ia! We praise you and re-joice, al-le-lu-ia! Your Word is a-live and it lives in our hearts, al-le-lu-ia! Al-le-lu-ia!

## GOSPEL: *Mark 2:18-21*

*This is a reading from the Gospel of Mark.*

Some people came to Jesus and asked him,

"Why do the disciples of John the Baptist
and the disciples of the Pharisees
fast and make sacrifices,
and your disciples do not?"

Jesus said,

"During a wedding party,
the friends of the groom
are happy and celebrate.
They do not fast
while the groom is there with them.
But after a while, the groom leaves,
and then his friends will fast."

[Jesus also said to them,

"People do not sew a new piece of cloth
onto an old piece of material.
If they do, when the material is washed,
the patch will shrink
and tear away from the old material,
and it will be worse than before."]

*The Gospel of the Lord.*

[ ] *Reader may omit text that appears in brackets.*

## REFLECTING ON THE READINGS WITH CHILDREN:

Ask the children if they have ever been to a wedding.

- Who are the guests of honor?
- Why are people joyful at a wedding?
- Wouldn't it be strange if people fasted and did penance at a wedding?

A wedding is a time for dancing, eating and rejoicing.

Jesus compared himself to a bridegroom at a wedding. He says, "I am with you—be joyful."

Help the children see that while we do sometimes fast and do penance, we are joyful people because Jesus is with us. This is the point of emphasis—Jesus brings us happiness. When we are with him, we have joy. When we live like Jesus, we bring others joy. Tell the children that Jesus explained this in a parable. Ask them what they understood by the parable. You may wish to have an old garment—a shirt or blouse—that needs a patch. Have also a piece of new material. Explain to the children that if a piece of new material is sewn onto the old and then washed, the new piece will shrink and tear away. Jesus is so new—so different from anyone who came before him—that we must "throw away" our old ways and follow his ways.

## NINTH SUNDAY IN ORDINARY TIME

### YEAR B

### PRAYER OF THE DAY:

God,
you want us
always to do good
and show how
we love one another.
Keep us from not helping
others because of
what people will say.
Give us courage
and a determination
to stand up
for your Son, Jesus,
who lives with you
and the Holy Spirit,
forever and ever.

### FOCUS OF THE READINGS:

The focus of today's readings is that Jesus has fulfilled the Sabbath. The first reading tells us that the Jews kept the Sabbath as a memorial of their salvation in the Exodus. The focus therefore is not on the prohibition against working on the Sabbath, but on the reason for the Sabbath. Over the centuries, the prohibitions became the focus, and it is this, not the Sabbath, that Jesus rejected. When legalism becomes central, hardness of heart is the result. Jesus proclaims that the life (salvation) which is in him is the completion of the memorial which the Sabbath honored. He is this salvation foreshadowed and prefigured in the Exodus. Therefore, the Sabbath is a day, not for prohibition, but for celebration and rejoicing in the salvation brought to completion in Christ. Love replaces legalism; life is more than the Sabbath.

### FIRST READING: *Deuteronomy 5:12-15*

*This is a reading
from the book of Deuteronomy.*

Moses said to the people of Israel,

"Remember to keep the Sabbath day special.
Keep it holy
because your God commanded you to.
During the other six days of the week,
you may work.
But the seventh day is the Sabbath day.
It is the special day of God,
and on that day you may not work.

"No one who lives in your house
must work on that day—
not your sons and daughters,
or any visitors who are staying with you.
Your servants must also rest on that day
just as you do.
Remember that you were slaves before
when you lived in Egypt.
But God brought you away from there
with great power and strength.

"Because of this,
God has commanded you
to keep the Sabbath day special and holy."

*The Word of the Lord.*

### RESPONSE: *Psalm 25*

RESPONSE: 1st time: Leader; 2nd time: All

Show me your ways, O Lord. Teach me your paths. paths.

VERSES: All                                                          to Response

1. I        trust     you.     I        hope     in       you.
2. O        lead      me       in       ways     of       truth.
3. Your     words     bring     me       light     and      joy.

## GOSPEL ACCLAMATION:

Leader:                  All: (sing and clap)

1. Your Word brings us heal - ing.    Al - le - lu - ia, al - le - lu - ia!
2. Your Word Lord is all we need.    Al - le - lu - ia, al - le - lu - ia!

## GOSPEL: *Mark 3:1-6*

*This is a reading from the Gospel of Mark.*

It was the Sabbath day,
and Jesus went into the synagogue.
There was a man there
whose hand was crippled and all shriveled up.
Now, it was against the law
to heal anyone on the Sabbath day,
so the people who were there
kept watching Jesus
to see if they could catch him breaking the law.
Jesus said to the man with the crippled hand,

   "Come, and stand up here
   in front of everyone."

Then Jesus said to the people,

   "Does the law allow us to do good things
   for others on the Sabbath day?
   Does it allow us to save life?"

They did not answer him.
Jesus was angry with them
because they were so stubborn.
Then he said to the man,

   "Hold out your hand."

So the man held out his hand,
and it was completely healed.
The Pharisees left the synagogue
and began to make plans
to find a way to get rid of Jesus.

*The Gospel of the Lord.*

## REFLECTING ON THE READINGS WITH CHILDREN:

The goal of your reflections will be to help the children see the difference between following God's commandments and being legalistic. (This isn't always easy for adults to see!) You might want to begin with an example of when a good law must be set aside for a higher good. One example comes to mind, but you may have one that will speak more clearly to your children.

Speed limits exist in our country to help prevent accidents and save lives. These laws were made for the common good—to keep us safe. And they should be obeyed.

If you had someone in your car who had to be rushed to the hospital, would it be all right to drive a little faster than the law says if you were not endangering the lives of others?

This discussion should lead the children to understand that this law was made for the common good. But it should not prevent someone from saving a life.

Help them see that God commanded the Jewish people to keep the Sabbath day holy because it was a reminder to them of how much God loved them. It was giving honor to God because God had saved them. Jesus does not question this. He is angry with the people because they wanted him to keep a law that did not allow him to heal someone on the Sabbath. They were more concerned about the law than the man who had a crippled hand. Jesus believed that God always loves us and wants to heal us. The Sabbath day is a special day to honor God. Jesus believed that healing a person was also a way of honoring God.

What do we do today to keep a day special for God?

# TENTH SUNDAY IN ORDINARY TIME

## YEAR B

### PRAYER OF THE DAY:

God always faithful,
may we never speak evil
of what is good.
Put in our hearts
a love for everything
that is right and true,
so that through us,
other people
may come to know
and love Jesus, your Son,
who lives with you
and the Holy Spirit,
forever and ever.

### FOCUS OF THE READINGS:

The focus of our readings for today is the power of Jesus over evil. The passage from *Genesis* is the story of a man and woman who accepted the temptation of disobeying God and thus introduced the continuing struggle between humankind and evil. But the story ends with God's promise that in the struggle, humankind, not evil, will prevail.

The Gospel focuses on the power of Jesus to cast out evil spirits. Both readings tell us that evil exists but that it is subject to divine power.

## FIRST READING: *Genesis 3:9-15*

*This is a reading from the book of Genesis.*

*Adam had eaten some fruit from the tree in the middle of the garden.*

God then called to him and asked,
"Where are you?"

Adam said,
"I heard you coming through the garden,
but I was afraid.
I hid from you because I was naked."

God said to Adam,
"But who told you that you were naked?
You must have eaten the fruit
that I told you not to eat!"

Adam said,
"The woman that you put here with me
gave me some and I ate it."

God asked Eve,
"Why did you do that?"

Eve said,
"The serpent tricked me, so I ate the fruit."

[Then God said to the serpent,
"Because you did this, you will be separated
from all the other animals.
You will crawl around on your stomach
and eat dirt for the rest of your life.
I am going to make you and the woman enemies.
The child who will be born of the woman
will step on your head
and you will bite the heel of his foot."]

*The Word of the Lord.*

[ ] *Reader may omit text that appears in brackets.*

## RESPONSE: *Psalm 130*

RESPONSE:
Lis-ten to my prayer, I trust in you my God.    God.

VERSES:                                         to Response
1. In my trou-ble hear my cry, hear my cry to you for help.
2. My soul hopes in you my God. You have saved me in your love.
3. My soul waits for you my God like the night that waits for day.

## GOSPEL ACCLAMATION:

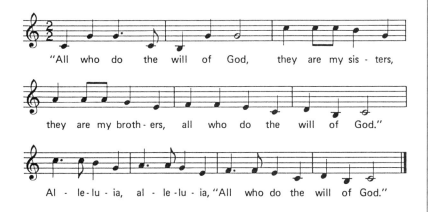

"All who do the will of God, they are my sis - ters,

they are my broth - ers, all who do the will of God."

Al - le - lu - ia, al - le - lu - ia, "All who do the will of God."

## GOSPEL: *Mark 3:20-23a, 28-35*

*This is a reading from the Gospel of Mark.*

When Jesus was home,
many people gathered to listen to him teach.
The crowd was so big that Jesus and his disciples
couldn't even take time to eat.

Some of the teachers of the law
were there from Jerusalem.
They were talking about Jesus
sending evil spirits out of people. They said,

  "He has the chief devil, Beelzebul,
    living inside of him.
    That's where he gets the power
    to drive evil spirits out of others."

So Jesus called the people together and said to them,

  "I tell you honestly, God will forgive all sins.
    But if you say evil things against the Holy Spirit,
    you will not be forgiven."

He told them this
because they said the Spirit of Jesus was evil.

Then his mother and brothers came,
and they asked someone to go inside and say to Jesus,

  "Your mother and your brothers
    are outside waiting for you."

Then Jesus looked at the people
who were sitting there listening to him and he said,

  "These people here are also my mother
    and my brothers and sisters,
    because my brothers and sisters and mother
    are people who do what God wants them to do."

*The Gospel of the Lord.*

## REFLECTING ON THE READINGS WITH CHILDREN:

The point of "the fall" section of the creation story is that indeed evil exists and that God did not intend for things to be this way. The authors of this story, like ourselves, experienced the effects of evil in the world and sought an explanation for it. It was clear to them that God created all things good (hence the earlier part of the creation story: "and God saw that it was good.") So, just as clearly, it was through the choice of human beings that sin entered the world.

Hence our passage for today. It will not serve the children particularly well to dwell on the details of the story. Rather, we will concentrate on the heart of the matter, our freedom of choice.

Help the children see that people are not evil. All people are created in the image of God. But we are created with free will and therefore can choose good or evil. God does not stop us from doing evil because God respects our freedom.

Ask the children if they see evil in the world. Help them focus on the evil and not on the persons.

Ask them if they think evil deeds can be avoided? How? Help them see that the story in *Genesis* is an example of how many people can choose to disobey God. And the story tells us how many people act when they do what they know is wrong: they hide; they blame others.

But God always promises to help us. God sent Jesus to help us, and Jesus has power over sin and evil. Jesus calls us to choose to do good and not evil, and he gives us the strength we need to do that. A note of caution: while we want to help children realize that they have the freedom to choose, and while, even at a young age, they certainly can choose to do things that are wrong, they do not participate in those choices which allow so much evil in our world. These readings, far from engendering guilt in little children, can help in their formation of making good choices. It is the matter of choice, not evil, that we must stress with them.

Your discussion with them might focus on the choices they can and do make in their everyday lives.

# ELEVENTH SUNDAY IN ORDINARY TIME

## YEAR B

### PRAYER OF THE DAY:

God,
you are full of power
and might and we are small
and not very strong.
Give us a share
in your power,
so that like a small seed,
your family may grow
all over the world
and more and more people
come to know about you
and Jesus, your Son,
who lives with you
forever and ever.

### FOCUS OF THE READINGS:

Both readings focus on the final, glorious coming of the reign of God. In the first reading, the "little branch" which God will take from a tall cedar represents the remnant, the small group of Israelites who have remained faithful throughout the exile. But small though it may be, from it will come a "strong and beautiful tree. . .where all kinds of birds will build their nests." The focus of Ezekiel is that God will bring to glorious manifestation what is *already present* in the small remnant.

The focus of the Gospel is the same. The final glorious reign of God is *already present* in Jesus and in his followers. It is often small and hidden (mustard seed) and is not always easily detected but will one day come to full growth in all its glory and splendor. God will bring to glorious manifestation what is *already present* in Jesus and his followers.

## FIRST READING: *Ezekiel 17:22-24*

*This is a reading from the prophet Ezekiel.*

Our God says,

"I will take a tiny branch
  from the very top of a cedar tree,
  and I will plant it on a high mountain.
It will become a strong and beautiful tree
  and good fruit will grow on its branches.
All kinds of animals will live in its shade,
  and birds will build their nests
  in its branches.
And all the trees of the fields
  will know that I am God.
I make high trees small and small trees high.
I dry up green trees
  and make trees that are dried up
  bloom again.

"I am God, and I will do what I have said."

*The Word of the Lord.*

## RESPONSE: *Psalm 104*

RESPONSE:
We praise you, O God, all your works are won-der-ful, won-der-ful are your works.

VERSES:
1. It is good to give thanks, to sing your
2. How wonder-ful are the things you

1. praise, sing praise for your ho-ly name!
2. do! All you do for us makes us glad.

to Response

86

## GOSPEL ACCLAMATION:

Al - le - lu - ia, al - le - lu - ia. Al - le - lu - ia, al - le - lu - ia!

Plant your Word__ in our hearts.__ Let it bear__ fruit in us!__

## GOSPEL: *Mark 4:30-34*

*This is a reading from the Gospel of Mark.*

Jesus said to his disciples,

"Here is another example
of what the kingdom of God is like:
it is like a mustard seed.
A mustard seed is the smallest of all seeds.
But when it grows, it becomes very large,
and its branches are so big
that birds can come
and make their nests in it
and be protected from the hot sun."

Jesus always taught the people
by using examples like this
so they would be able to understand.
But whenever Jesus was alone
with the twelve apostles,
he explained everything to them.

*The Gospel of the Lord.*

## REFLECTING ON THE READINGS WITH CHILDREN:

The goal of our reflections will be to help the children see that the reign of God is already present among us—but will one day be fully seen. The seed is a good image of this.

Show the children a seed. Ask them what will come of it. Will it be a daisy, a carrot, a pine tree?

Now tell them what kind of seed it is and ask them again what will become of it. If it is a carrot seed, it will become a carrot (not a daisy or a pine tree) because the carrot is already present in the seed, but we cannot see it.

You may wish to use several examples. When the children understand the concept, ask them why Jesus said the "kingdom of God is like a mustard seed."

- How is the reign (or kingdom) of God already present?

At the beginning of his public teaching, Jesus said, "The kingdom of God is here!" He meant that he brought the reign of God to earth. *It* is here among us because *he* is here among us. But sometimes we cannot see it. Why is it sometimes hard to see the reign of God already present among us? When we do not act as Jesus did, others cannot see him (the reign [or kingdom] of God.)

Help the children to understand that when we pray in the Lord's Prayer "thy kingdom come," we pray that it will be seen.

How can we help that seed—the kingdom of God—to grow and to be seen by others? How will others see the fact that the reign of God is already here among us?

It is important that the reflections end positively. Our concentration should not be on how we *hinder* the reign of God, but how we *help* reveal it.

# TWELFTH SUNDAY IN ORDINARY TIME

## YEAR B

### PRAYER OF THE DAY:

God,
you made the world
and all that is in it.
We thank you
for being good to us.
Show us
how to treat the plants
and the animals,
the people and our planet,
as your special gift to us.
By following Jesus,
may we never misuse them
but be happy
that everything tells us
something about you.
We pray to you
through Christ, our Lord.

*Note: In keeping with the* Directory for Masses With Children *(Paragraph 43), the authors have elected to use an alternate biblical excerpt instead of the first reading for the 12th Sunday of Ordinary Time because it seems best suited "to the capacity of children."*

### FOCUS OF THE READINGS:

The Gospel reading focuses on Jesus' power over nature. It is a continuation of Mark's revelation of the divine authority of Jesus. Jesus had healed the sick and cast out evil spirits. Mark tells us that "even the evil spirits obey him!" And here, "even the wind and water obey him!" The focus is not the actual calming of the storm but the power that is in Jesus because of who he is. When Jesus asks, "Why are you afraid? Don't you believe in me?" he questions their faith in him

### FIRST READING: *Genesis 1:1-2, 9-10*

*This is a reading from the book of Genesis.*

In the beginning,
God created the heavens and the earth.
There was nothing on the earth,
and it had no shape.
And the Spirit of God
was moving like a wind over the waters.

And God said,

  "Let all the waters be gathered into one place
    with dry land around it."

God called the dry land "earth"
and the waters "seas."

And God saw that it was good.

*The Word of the Lord.*

### RESPONSE: *Psalm 104*

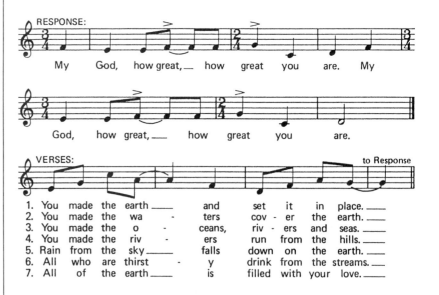

1. You made the earth _____ and set it in place. _____
2. You made the wa - ters cov - er the earth. _____
3. You made the o - ceans, riv - ers and seas. _____
4. You made the riv - ers run from the hills. _____
5. Rain from the sky _____ falls down on the earth. _____
6. All who are thirst - y drink from the streams. _____
7. All of the earth _____ is filled with your love. _____

## GOSPEL ACCLAMATION:

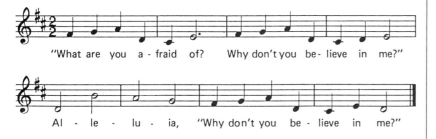

"What are you a-fraid of? Why don't you be-lieve in me?"

Al - le - lu - ia, "Why don't you be-lieve in me?"

## GOSPEL: *Mark 4:35-41*

*This is a reading from the Gospel of Mark.*

One evening while Jesus and his disciples
were near the lake, he said to them,

   "Let's go now to the other side."

While they were crossing the lake,
a bad storm came up,
and a strong wind
washed the waves over the side of the boat.
Soon the boat was nearly filled with water.

But Jesus was asleep on a pillow
in the back of the boat.
The disciples woke him and said,

   "Don't you care that we're going to drown?"

So Jesus got up and commanded the wind
and waves to stop, saying,

   "Be still!  Be quiet!"

Then Jesus said to his disciples,

   "Why are you afraid?
   Don't you believe in me?"

The disciples were shocked and amazed
at what they had just seen Jesus do.
They kept asking each other,

   "Who is this man?
   Even the wind and the water obey him!"

*The Gospel of the Lord.*

before the action of calming of the storm. Did they not trust that all would be well simply because he was there?  In other words, we are not to look to Jesus because he does miracles but because of who he is. His miracles are signs that point to a deeper reality.  Mark calls us to a belief in the person of Jesus who has divine authority over everything.  If we fail to see the deeper reality—the person of Jesus—we miss the point of his miracles.

The first reading from *Genesis* is a substitution for the reading from the book of *Job*.  *Genesis* sets the stage for the Gospel story.  (Such substitutions are in keeping with the guidelines in the *Directory for Masses with Children*.)  God is the creator of water, and it is with this same divine power that Jesus controls the wind and water.

## REFLECTING ON THE READINGS WITH CHILDREN:

This Gospel should be read with drama, emphasizing the details.  Ask the children to recall the story.  After they have retold the story, ask them again what Jesus said to his disciples after he calmed the storm.

"Why are you afraid?  Don't you believe in me?"

Ask the children if they have ever experienced a storm.  Were they afraid? Assure them that their fear is perfectly understandable but that we can learn to be less afraid when we know that Jesus will help us.

It is important that we not give children the impression that their natural fear of darkness, storms, water, or whatever, represents a lack of faith. (They are children, learning to trust in Jesus).

Lead them to see that "storm" can also mean "trouble" or "problems" in life.  Let them discuss this, and lead them to see that Jesus is always with us and has the power to calm these storms too.

You might encourage the children to ask Jesus to "calm the storm inside of me" when they have problems or are worried about things.

# THIRTEENTH SUNDAY IN ORDINARY TIME

## YEAR B

### PRAYER OF THE DAY:

God of all people who live
and of all who are dead,
look with pity on those
who are close to dying
and on those in our families
who have died.
Teach us to understand
that dying is just a doorway
to a new and better life
and that one day,
with the help of Jesus,
we will all live
together with you
in a world that will last
forever and ever.

### FOCUS OF THE READINGS:

The focus of the Gospel is the power of Jesus over death. Mark continues his revelation of the divine authority and power of Jesus—over evil spirits, over sin, over wind and water and even over death. It is a prefigurement, a hint at the Resurrection, when Jesus will be ultimately victorious over death.

The first reading focuses on the reality that we were created by God to live forever. God loves us and wants us to live. God made all things good. To do evil is a choice. Evil exists, but we choose to follow either evil or God.

The two readings together tell us that those who choose to act in faith have life. Jairus' daughter lived because Jairus believed in Jesus.

### FIRST READING: *Wisdom 1:13-15, 2:23-24*

*This is a reading from the book of Wisdom.*

God did not make death,
and God never wanted people to die.
All living things are good,
and there is no evil in them.
All people were created in God's image
so that they would live forever.

But the devil was jealous
and brought evil and death into the world.
People who choose
to follow the ways of the devil
choose death instead of a life with God.

*The Word of the Lord.*

### RESPONSE: *Psalm 16* and *Psalm 27*

RESPONSE: Have mer-cy God, have mer-cy God. I trust in you for my safe-ty. safe-ty.
1-2 to Verses  3  Fine

VERSES: to Response
1. You are my light my sav-ior; with your help I shall not be a-fraid.
2. When it is dark a-round me, noth-ing takes me a-way from your love.

### GOSPEL ACCLAMATION:

Je-sus said: "Ta-li-tha kum, lit-tle girl get up I tell you."
Al-le-lu-ia, praise the Lord, al-le-lu-ia, praise the Lord.

GOSPEL: *Mark 5:22-24, 35-43*

*This is a reading from the Gospel of Mark.*

One day a man named Jairus
came to see Jesus.
He was one of the rulers of the synagogue.
He knelt in front of Jesus
and begged him to help him.  He told Jesus,

"My little daughter is dying.
  Please come and put your hands on her
  so she will get well and live."

So Jesus went with Jairus,
and a large crowd of people followed them.
While they were on their way,
some people from Jairus' house came and said,

"Your little girl is dead.  There is no need
  to bother this Teacher now."

But Jesus said to Jairus,

"Don't be afraid.  Just have faith and believe."

Then Jesus took Peter,
James and John with him to Jairus' house.
When they got there,
many people were inside crying loudly.
Jesus went in and said to them,

"Why are you crying
  and making all this noise?
  The child is not dead.  She is asleep!"

When he said this,
the people began to laugh and make fun of him.
Jesus told them all to go outside.
Then he took the little girl's mother and father
and the three disciples and went into the room
where the little girl was in bed.
Jesus took her hand and said,

"*Talitha, kum!*"

which means, "Little girl, I say to you, get up!"

The little girl, who was twelve years old,
got up immediately and began to walk around.
Her family was amazed and filled with wonder.
Jesus told them not to tell anyone
what had happened.
Then he told them to give the little girl
something to eat.

*The Gospel of the Lord.*

REFLECTING ON THE READINGS
WITH CHILDREN:

*After the first reading*, ask the
children to recall what they heard.
This should be fairly brief—just
enough for the children to recall that
God made all things good and that
God created us to live forever.

The Gospel:  like so many stories
in *Mark*, this one should be read as a
drama, emphasizing all the details
Mark is so careful to include.

Ask the children to recall what
they heard.  Perhaps they could
share how the father felt, how Jesus
felt.  How did the little girl feel when
Jesus healed her?  Since this story is
specifically about Jesus and a child,
the children will easily relate to it.
That is why we have chosen to retain
the Aramaic "*Talitha kum.*"
Children often remember things that
are unusual or strange sounding to
their ear.

Allow the children time to discuss
Jesus' power over death.  The little
girl lived because Jesus said, "I tell
you to get up."

Remind them that we have
already seen his power over evil
spirits, over sin, over wind and water.

What Jesus did here he will do for
all of us at the end of time.  We will
be raised up and will live with him
forever.

# FOURTEENTH SUNDAY IN ORDINARY TIME

## YEAR B

### PRAYER OF THE DAY:

God,
you speak to us
through Jesus, your Son.
Do not let us ignore
what he has to say
nor think that we
know better than he.
Instead, open our ears
to your voice
and our hearts to your love,
so that we may live
as sisters and brothers
of Jesus, who is with you,
forever and ever.

### FOCUS OF THE READINGS:

The focus of both readings is the rejection of God's messengers and ultimately of God's message.

In our first reading, Ezekiel is warned at the outset that he, and his message, may be rejected because "they are stubborn and rebellious people." But he is not to change the message. When Ezekiel proclaims God's message faithfully, whether it is accepted or not, they will know that he is truly a prophet. That is the sin God has warned against— they know he is a prophet, yet they will not listen.

Jesus is rejected apparently because he is too common, too well known among his neighbors, to be a spokesperson for God. Note that this comes after a series of manifestations of the divine authority in Jesus— over evil spirits, over sin, over wind and water, and even over death.

### FIRST READING: *Ezekiel 2:2-5*

*This is a reading from the prophet Ezekiel.*

The spirit came to me, and I heard God say,

"I am sending you to speak to my people.
    They are stubborn
    and have turned away from me.
But I am sending you to them,
    and you will say,

    'Your God is speaking to you!'

"And whether they accept
    what you say or not,
(remember they are stubborn people!)
    they will know that a real prophet
    has come to them!"

*The Word of the Lord.*

### RESPONSE: *Psalm 40*

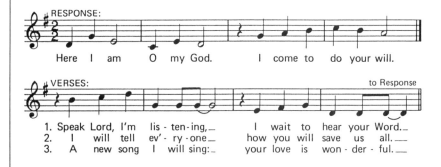

### GOSPEL ACCLAMATION:

*Use the *We Believe*, without the Alleluia, as a response for the Creed,

## GOSPEL: *Mark 6:1-6*

*This is a reading from the Gospel of Mark.*

Jesus went to his home town,
and his disciples went with him.
On the Sabbath day,
he went to the synagogue to teach.
The people there were amazed
at everything he said.
They asked,

"Where did he get all his wisdom?
And how is he able
to do the miracles he does?
Isn't he the carpenter, the son of Mary?
Isn't he the brother of James
and Joset and Judas and Simon?
And don't his sisters
live right here in our town?"

They just could not accept Jesus
as someone special.

Jesus said to them,

"Prophets are always honored
by everyone except their own people,
especially in their own home town."

And Jesus could not do many miracles there,
except to heal a few people
by laying hands on them.
He was surprised at how hard it was
for them to believe.
And he went to teach in other towns.

*The Gospel of the Lord.*

Ultimately, Mark tells us, miracles are not enough—we must believe in the person of Jesus. We are moving toward the question of faith for Mark —the question Jesus asked at Caesarea Philippi—"who do you say that I am?" (*Mark 8:29*)

REFLECTING ON THE READINGS WITH CHILDREN:

Ask the children if they have ever felt misunderstood or shunned or even rejected (perhaps made fun of) because they spoke the truth. Allow them time to relate their stories without comment. When all who wish have spoken, ask them why they think this happened—why they were shunned or made fun of. Again, allow them time to offer their ideas without comment.

*After the first reading*, you might, in very few words, relate the call of Ezekiel to what the children have shared. Then invite them to listen to the Gospel.

*After the Gospel*, ask them why Jesus was not accepted when he taught. Help them to focus on the reason given in this Gospel reading. What did he do when his home town rejected him?

This last point is important. Children, too, feel rejected or made fun of for speaking the truth. They, like adults, are tempted to think it isn't worth the effort and give up. Help them to see that it is part of the Christian life and that Jesus himself experienced it. We can learn from Jesus not to give up.

## FIFTEENTH SUNDAY IN ORDINARY TIME

### YEAR B

### PRAYER OF THE DAY:

Tender God,
we know
you want
to welcome everybody
into your family of love.
Take away from us
all that is hateful,
unkind and selfish,
and make us your disciples,
telling the whole world
about you
by the way we live and love.
We ask you this
through Jesus Christ,
your Son,
who lives with you
and the Holy Spirit,
forever and ever.

### FOCUS OF THE READINGS:

The focus of our readings for this Sunday is mission. The apostles (the word means "sent") are sent out to preach. They are warned, however, that they must be true to their mission and that for this they may be rejected. In our first reading, Amos was rejected because he preached the Word of God which was in opposition to the civil authorities. The message of God is not always in harmony with the ways of the world. What matters most is fidelity to the message. For the prophet/apostle there can be no question of watering down God's message—even in the face of rejection.

### FIRST READING: *Amos 7:12-15*

*This is a reading from the prophet Amos.*

*Amos, the prophet, was rejected in Israel.*

Amos said to the priest,

"I was not born a prophet.
I was a shepherd,
and I took care of sycamore trees.
But God called me away from my sheep
and said to me,

'Go, be my prophet. Speak to my people.'"

*The Word of the Lord.*

### RESPONSE: *Psalm 71*

I will pro-claim your pow - er. I will pro-claim your won-der-ful deeds! I will pro-claim sal - va - tion, and your faith - ful love!___

## GOSPEL ACCLAMATION:

"Go out to the world,___ pro - claim the Good News,___ pro - claim the Good News."___ Al - le - lu - ia!

## GOSPEL: *Mark 6:7-13*

*This is a reading from the Gospel of Mark.*

Jesus called the twelve apostles together
and began to send them to other places
two at a time.
He gave them power over evil spirits.
He told them not to take extra things
with them as they traveled.
He told them they could take a stick
to help them walk,
but not to take food
or a traveling bag or money.
They were to wear sandals, but he told them,

"Do not take along extra clothes.
  And when you go to a house,
  stay there until you leave that town.
  If the people will not accept you
  or listen to you, leave that town.
  And as you leave,
  shake off the dust from your feet.
  This will show them that they were wrong
  not to accept you."

So the disciples went
and preached to the people,
telling them to change their hearts
and their lives.
They also sent away evil spirits,
anointed the sick with oil,
and healed many people.

*The Gospel of the Lord.*

### REFLECTING ON THE READINGS WITH CHILDREN:

Ask the children what they remember about last Sunday's readings. Jesus, himself, was rejected as a prophet. In today's Gospel, Jesus sends his apostles to preach and warns them that they too might be rejected. Tell the children that these people were called "apostles" because that word means "a person who is sent."

- What instructions did Jesus give his apostles?
- Why do you think he gave them these instructions?

Help the children to see that an apostle must be free from a lot of possessions so that when God sends them, he or she can really be free to go and work for the Lord.

Help them see that Jesus was asking the apostles to live simply, to trust in him, and to be concerned about preaching.

Lead them to see that Christians today are also sent to preach. It might be a good time to talk about and pray for missionaries. The church is always missionary because the church must always preach the Good News. We are all called to do that. But some people are sent as missionaries as the first apostles were.

# SIXTEENTH SUNDAY IN ORDINARY TIME

## YEAR B

### PRAYER OF THE DAY:

God,
you look after us
like a loving Father.
Never let us go astray.
We do not want to do
what displeases you,
and we wish always
to be with you.
Guide us along the road
to our home with you
where we hope to live
with you, with your Son,
Jesus Christ,
and with the Holy Spirit,
forever and ever.

### FOCUS OF THE READINGS:

The focus of our readings is God's loving care for everyone, expressed in the image of a shepherd. In Israel, the concepts of king and shepherd were often related. As the shepherd bore the responsibility for the needs of the flock, so the king was responsible for the needs of the people. Jeremiah expresses anger that the recent kings of Israel have not fulfilled this responsibility well. In this particular passage he denounces them for turning the people away and scattering them. The emphasis seems to be on the failure of the king to hold them together as a people united to their God. They had become like sheep without a shepherd. God promises a future king/shepherd who will do what is right!

### FIRST READING: *Jeremiah 23:2-6*

*This is a reading from the prophet Jeremiah.*

Our God says,

"Listen, you who are shepherds of my flock!
You have not taken good care of my people.
You have turned them away
and scattered them.
But I will punish you for your evil ways.
And I, myself, will gather my flock
and bring them back from all over the world.
I will ask other shepherds
to take care of them
so that my people will be together
and not be afraid any longer.

"I will send someone from the family of David
to my people.
He will be a wise king,
and he will do what is right.
The people will be saved, and they will know
that I am their God and that I am just."

*The Word of the Lord.*

### RESPONSE: *Psalm 23*

RESPONSE:
You are my shep-herd, you are my friend. I want to fol-low you al - ways, _____ just to fol-low my friend. (Fine)

VERSES: to Response
1. I have all I need. You are my Shep-herd, your hand is with me.
2. When path-ways are dark, you are there guid-ing me, keep-ing me safe.
3. You give me to eat. You make me wel-come, you fill me with joy.
4. Your good-ness I know. Your love will be with me all of my life.

## GOSPEL ACCLAMATION:

1. Teach us Je-sus, you are our Shep-herd.
2. Al - le - lu - ia, al - le - lu - ia.

1-2. Teach us Je-sus, we are your sheep.

## GOSPEL: *Mark 6:30-34*

*This is a reading from the Gospel of Mark.*

After the disciples had been out teaching,
they came to Jesus
to tell him everything they had done
and what they had taught.
So many people were coming to be with Jesus
and his disciples
that they didn't even have time to eat.
So Jesus said to them,

  "Come with me.
    We will go to a quiet place
    where we can rest for a while."

So they went in a boat
to a place where they could be alone.
But some people saw them leaving
and told others where they were going.
So people from all around ran to the place
and got there before Jesus and his disciples.
When Jesus saw all the people waiting for him,
he felt sorry for them
because they were sheep
who didn't have a shepherd.
So Jesus stayed with them
and taught them many things.

*The Gospel of the Lord.*

Our Gospel passage picks up this theme very subtly. Jesus, though tired and in need of rest, stays with the hungry crowd and teaches them because "they are like sheep without a shepherd." This passage leads to the famous "Feeding of the 5,000," and so Mark has presented Jesus as the shepherd who feeds by teaching and feeds with bread.

Next Sunday, instead of hearing Mark's account of the "Feeding of the 5,000," however, we turn to John's account. This will begin a five-week series from the Gospel of John on the Bread of Life.

REFLECTING ON THE READINGS WITH CHILDREN:

Ask the children why Jesus invited the apostles to go away to a quiet place. (Help them recall last Sunday's Gospel: the apostles had been out preaching and have just returned, tired and in need of rest.)

● Why did so many people follow them?

Mark tells us that Jesus felt sorry for the crowd because they were like "sheep without a shepherd." Ask the children what they think that means.

Discuss with them the relationship between a shepherd and sheep. Ask the children what they remember about the first reading. (You may have to help them.)

God promised to send a good leader. Jesus is always with us as our shepherd.

Who are the people who care for us in the name of Jesus? (You may wish to consult the reflections for the 4th Sunday of Easter on the Good Shepherd.)

If there is time, you may wish to sing the Psalm Response again.

## SEVENTEENTH SUNDAY IN ORDINARY TIME

YEAR B

### PRAYER OF THE DAY:

You take good care of us, God,
always and everywhere,
and you protect us
from all harm.
Make us forever followers
of Jesus, your Son,
not worrying
about how weak we are,
but trusting in his goodness.
We make this prayer to you
through Jesus Christ,
who lives with you
and the Holy Spirit,
forever and ever.

### FOCUS OF THE READINGS:

The focus of our readings is God's loving care for us. God is able (and wants) to supply all that we need, and more.

Our two readings are stories about miraculous feedings which are alike in many ways. The outline of each story includes a special person (Elisha/Jesus), a large crowd (100/5,000), and insufficient bread (20 loaves/5 loaves). In both, the number of people and the number of loaves is relatively unimportant. What is important is the action of God. The point is not whether or not these events took place exactly as described, but rather that God did, and does, provide. Both the Jews and the Christians have consistently related this truth through stories in which God supplies food, the basic need of human life.

### FIRST READING: *2 Kings 4:42-44*

*This is a reading from the second book of Kings.*

*Elisha the prophet was in the city of Gilgal.*

A man came
and brought him twenty loaves of barley bread.
Elisha said to the man,

"Give the bread to the people to eat."

But the man said,

"There are a hundred people here.
This will never be enough bread
to feed them all."

But Elisha said again,

"Give them the twenty loaves of bread,
for God says,

'They will all have enough to eat
and will even have some left over.' "

So the man gave the loaves of bread
to the people.
They all ate and there was bread left over,
just as God had said.

*The Word of the Lord.*

### RESPONSE: *Psalm 104/145*

RESPONSE: You are the one who feeds us, giv-ing us food from your hand.__

__ You are the one who feeds us, giv-ing us all we need.___

## GOSPEL ACCLAMATION:

1. Je - sus, feed us, } Give us the Bread that brings us life.
2. Al - le - lu - ia, }

## GOSPEL: *John 6:1-12*

*This is a reading from the Gospel of John.*

*One day while Jesus was up on a mountain
with his disciples, a large crowd of people
came to see him, because they knew
he had cured some sick people.*

When Jesus saw the crowd, he said to Philip,

"Where can we buy enough bread
to feed all these people?"

Actually Jesus already knew
what he was going to do,
but he wanted to see what Philip would say.
Philip said,

"The money earned for 200 days' work
wouldn't buy enough bread
to give each person even a little piece."

Then Andrew, Simon Peter's brother, said,

"There is a young boy here
who has five loaves of barley bread
and a couple of fish.
But that won't feed all these people."

There were about five thousand people there.
But Jesus said,

"Get the people to sit down."

Then he took the loaves of bread,
and after he gave thanks,
he passed them to the people.
He also gave them the fish.
Everyone ate as much as they wanted.
When they were finished, Jesus said to his disciples,

"Gather up all the leftover pieces
so that nothing will go to waste."

When they gathered up all the leftover pieces
they had twelve baskets full.

*The Gospel of the Lord.*

## REFLECTING ON THE READINGS WITH CHILDREN:

Both of these readings should be read in storytelling form, emphasizing both detail and dialogue.

*After the first reading,* ask the children to recall the story. If they have difficulty, you might help them with questions such as:

- What is the prophet's name?
- What did the man bring to him?
- What did Elisha tell the man to do with the bread?
- How did the man respond?

Tell the children that this is a perfectly normal response. But Elisha wanted to show the people something special about God.

What happened when the man gave the bread to the people?

*After the Gospel,* again ask the children what they recall. You might ask some specific questions as before.

Be sure to ask the children *who* helped Jesus by giving some bread and fish. So much of what children hear from the Bible relates to adults. So whenever possible, it is good to highlight the role children play in the reading.

After discussing the story, ask the children what they think both of these stories tell us about God.

Help them to see that God is always with us to provide for us, even when it doesn't seem possible.

You might also relate this story with the Eucharist. Jesus gives himself as bread and is always there for everyone. He uses almost the same words in this story as he used at the last supper.

| In this story, Jesus: | At the last supper, Jesus: |
|---|---|
| • took the bread, | • took the bread, |
| • gave thanks, | • gave thanks and said, "take this all of you and eat," |
| • gave it to the people. | • gave it to them. |

# EIGHTEENTH SUNDAY IN ORDINARY TIME

## YEAR B

## PRAYER OF THE DAY:

God of all the world,
we believe in you
and in Jesus,
whom you sent to save us.
May we believe in you
more and more
and learn to put all our trust
in you.
We ask this
through Jesus Christ,
our Lord.

### FOCUS OF THE READINGS:

Both of our readings tell us that God does not simply *send* food (manna/bread) but that God really is personally present in the event. It is not so much the bread we receive but believing in the one who gives bread. Bread sustains our life for the moment. Believing in the one who gives the bread sustains our life forever.

The people in the desert complained constantly about physical needs. And God answered their cries but always with the underlying message, "Believe; trust in me."

Jesus tells the miracle-seeking crowd not to work for the bread of the moment only, but for the bread of life. "This is the work God wants you to do: believe in the one sent by God," (the Bread of Life).

Again we are called to see more than bread. We are called to see and believe in the one who gives us bread/life.

## FIRST READING: *Exodus 16:12-15*

*This is a reading from the book of Exodus.*

*When the people of Israel were in the desert, they complained to Moses and Aaron because they did not have enough food to eat.*

Then God said to Moses,

"I have heard the people complaining.
I am going to send down bread from heaven for you.
The people must gather the bread every day, but they must gather only enough for each day.
I want to see if they trust me and will follow my ways.
Say to the people,

'In the evening you will eat meat, and in the morning you will have bread.
Then you will know that I am your God!' "

That evening, many quails flew into the camp. And in the morning, the ground was covered with something like white flakes.
When the people saw it, they asked,

"What is it?"

Moses said,

"This is the bread that God has given you to eat."

*The Word of the Lord.*

## RESPONSE: *Psalm 104*

RESPONSE:

I will praise you as long as I live, ____ as long as I live, ____ I will praise you God. praise you God.

VERSES:

1. I praise you God for all you do, for all my life for all you do.
2. You give us bread to make us strong. You give us drink to make us glad.

\* Round during final response only

## GOSPEL ACCLAMATION:

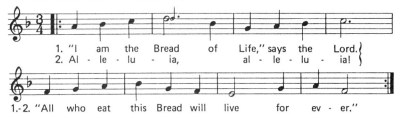

1. "I am the Bread of Life," says the Lord.
2. Al - le - lu - ia, al - le - lu - ia!

1.-2. "All who eat this Bread will live for ev - er."

## GOSPEL: *John 6:24-35*

*This is a reading from the Gospel of John.*

*The next day, the crowd of people
who had eaten the bread went looking for Jesus.*

And [when they found him, Jesus said to them,
 "You are not looking for me
  because you saw my power in miracles.
  No, you are looking for me
  because you ate all the bread you wanted.
  Don't spend your life working only for regular food.
  That doesn't last.
  Work to get the kind of food
  that will make you live forever."
Then the people asked Jesus,
 "Rabbi, what does God want us to do?
  What is the work of God?"
Jesus answered,
 "The work God wants you to do is this:
  believe in the One sent by God."
Then] the people asked Jesus,

 "What miracle can you do
  to prove that you are the One sent by God?
  Our ancestors ate manna
  when they were in the desert.
  God gave them that bread from heaven to eat."
Jesus said,
 "God is the one
  who gives the true bread from heaven.
  God's bread comes down from heaven
  and gives life to the people of the world."
The people said,
 "Give us this bread always."
Jesus told them,
 "I am the bread of life.
  Anyone who comes to me will never be hungry.
  Anyone who believes in me will never be thirsty."

*The Gospel of the Lord.*

[ ] *Reader may omit text that appears in brackets.*

## RELECTING ON THE READINGS WITH CHILDREN:

*After the first reading*, ask the children to recall what they heard. If they have difficulty recalling, ask them some specific questions to help them. Recall especially God's promise,

- "In the evening you will have meat to eat and in the morning you will have bread. Then you will know that I am your God."

Remind the children that God had already brought these people away from slavery in Egypt. And still they complained. And even after all of their complaining, God said, "If I do this, then you will know that I am your God." God wants so very much for us to be happy and to know God personally.

*After the Gospel*, ask the children what kind of bread Jesus told us we should work for. Help the children understand that Jesus is *not* saying that the food we eat every day is not important. He knows it is important to eat well to be healthy. But besides that, we should see the real value of having his life within us.

- Why do you think Jesus calls himself "bread"?

Help the children see that bread represents all food, and we need food to live. When we eat enough food, we are no longer hungry. When we drink something refreshing, we are no longer thirsty. Jesus tells us that, in the same way, when we have his life within us, we have everything we need to be truly happy and to live forever.

In the Eucharist, Jesus feeds us by giving us himself. With him, we have the strength to live as he lives.

101

## NINETEENTH SUNDAY IN ORDINARY TIME

### YEAR B

### PRAYER OF THE DAY:

Loving Lord,
how difficult it is
to do what you ask!
Thank you
for sending Jesus to us
because he is the food
that gives us the strength
and courage to carry on.
Let us never forget
he is with us always.
We ask this
through that same
Jesus Christ, our Lord.

### FOCUS OF THE READINGS:

Our focus is twofold: the bread God provides is both strength and divine presence. Elijah is told to eat the food provided by God so he will have the strength to go to Mt. Horeb where he will meet God. In the Gospel, Jesus tells the people "anyone who eats this bread will live forever." Jesus is the one sent by God, and it is in him (the Bread of Life) that we meet God.

### FIRST READING: *1 Kings 19:5-8*

*This is a reading from the first book of Kings.*

*Queen Jezabel, the wife of King Ahab,
threatened to kill the prophet Elijah.
So he went into the desert alone to hide.
After a day's journey in the desert,
he fell asleep under a tree.*

While he was sleeping,
an angel of God came
and touched him and said,
  "Elijah, get up and eat."

He got up, and when he looked around,
he saw a small cake and jug of water.
So he ate and drank.
Then he went back to sleep under the tree.
But the angel came again
and touched him and said,

  "Elijah, get up and eat
    so you will have enough strength
    for your journey."

Elijah got up and ate and drank again.
And he had enough strength
to travel for forty days and forty nights
to Horeb, the mountain of God.

*The Word of the Lord.*

### RESPONSE: *Psalm 145/104*

1. When we are hun - gry    you give us    food.
2. Each day you give __ us    all that we    need.
3. Your hand is o - pen    with gifts for    all.
4. I will sing prais - es    and bless your    name.

102

## GOSPEL ACCLAMATION:

1. Je - sus, feed us,  Give us the Bread— that brings us— life. —
2. Al - le - lu - ia,

## GOSPEL: *John 6:41-51*

*This is a reading from the Gospel of John.*

The Jews began to grumble
and complain about Jesus because he said,

"I am the bread of life
that comes down from heaven."

They said to each other,

"We know this man very well.
He is Joseph's son.
We know his father and mother.
How can he say,
'I came down from heaven?' "

Jesus said to them,

"Stop grumbling among yourselves.
God is the one who sent me.
But no one can know this without God's help.
God teaches everyone.
And those who listen to God come to me.
No one has ever seen God
except the One who came from God.
I tell you the truth;
those people who believe this
will live forever.
I will raise them up on the last day.

"I am the bread of life.
I am the bread that came down from heaven.
Anyone who eats this bread will live forever.
The bread that I will give is my body.
I will give my body
so that people can live forever."

*The Gospel of the Lord.*

REFLECTING ON THE READINGS
WITH CHILDREN:

*After the first reading*, ask the
children to retell the story of Elijah.
If they have difficulty, help them
with specific questions. Lead them
to see that God provides food to
strengthen us.

*After the Gospel*, ask the children
why the Jews had difficulty believing
that Jesus came from heaven.

Lead the children to see that in
the Gospel we learn that Jesus is
both a human being and God. This
concept is not easy for children or
adults. It remains for us a mystery
that is at the heart of our faith. We
present it as a seed planted that
continues to grow in them (and us!).
Jesus said, "No one has actually
seen God except the one who came
from God."

Help the children realize that we
know something about what God is
like because we know what Jesus is
like. Jesus came from God and
shows us who God is. What Jesus
says and does tells us what God is
like. The most important thing
Jesus tells us is that he is always
with us, especially in the Bread of
Life. We receive this Bread of Life
especially in the Eucharist. Jesus
tells us that when we receive the
Eucharist, we really receive him.
When Jesus is with us, we can be
happy and live just as Jesus wants us
to live.

# TWENTIETH SUNDAY IN ORDINARY TIME

## YEAR B

### PRAYER OF THE DAY:

Like a caring mother
and father, God,
you prepare for us
a wonderful meal,
in which the food and drink
are Jesus himself.
Make us ready for that meal
where we will be one family
with everybody
in the church,
and with you and Jesus
who lives with you
and the Holy Spirit
forever and ever.

### FOCUS OF THE READINGS:

Our focus today is the Eucharist. The readings of the past three Sundays have led us to this.

In our first reading, wisdom (an image of God) builds her house and invites all to come "eat my bread, drink my wine. . .walk in my ways and choose real life."

In the Gospel, Jesus invites us to eat and drink his body and blood and have real life.

In both of these readings, we want to focus, not so much on the physical (bread/body, wine/blood) but on its meaning—a sharing in the very life of God. In the sharing of the meal, we have real life because Jesus says, "I am living in you and you are living in me."

### FIRST READING: *Proverbs 9:1, 3-6*

*This is a reading from the book of Proverbs.*

Wisdom has built her house
and invites everyone to come.
She says to the people:

"Those who want wisdom come to my house.
  Come, eat my bread and drink my wine.
  Don't be foolish;
  come, walk in my ways and choose real life."

*The Word of the Lord.*

### RESPONSE: *Psalm 34*

Taste and see, taste and see. Taste and see that God is good.

1. I will thank you. I will praise you for all you do to make us glad.
2. Come_ chil-dren, I will teach you to hon-or God, to love_ God.
3. You are close to all the low-ly who lose_ hope. You save_ them.
4. I will nev-er-more be fear-ful, you hear me cry and help_ me.

## GOSPEL ACCLAMATION:

1. "I am the Bread of Life," says the Lord.
2. Al - le - lu - ia, al - le - lu - ia!

1.-2. "All who eat this Bread will live for ev - er."

## GOSPEL: *John 6:51-58*

*This is a reading from the Gospel of John.*

*Jesus had told the crowd that his body
is the Bread from heaven
and that anyone who eats this Bread
will live forever.*

But the people argued,

"How can this man give us his body to eat?"

Jesus said,

"I tell you the truth;
if you do not eat my body
and drink my blood,
you don't have real life in you.

"But if you eat my body and drink my blood,
you will live forever.
I will raise you up on the last day.
When you eat my body
and drink my blood,
you have real life
because I am living in you,
and you are living in me.

"I am the Bread that came down from heaven.
Anyone who eats this Bread
will live forever."

*The Gospel of the Lord.*

## REFLECTING ON THE READINGS WITH CHILDREN:

*After reading the Gospel,* ask the children about special meals they have in their homes.

- When do they have special meals?
- What do they eat?
- Who is there?
- Why do we usually celebrate special occasions at a meal: Christmas, birthdays, and so forth?
- Does it matter what we eat at these meals?
- Does it matter who is there?
- What makes a meal special?

Help the children see that what we eat at special meals *is* important. But more important is the joy of being together and sharing.

Jesus also celebrated special meals with his family and friends. Jesus celebrated Passover meals, weddings, and special times in the lives of his disciples. Jesus ate at Matthew's house and Zacchaeus' house to celebrate that they had changed their lives and followed him.

Jesus wants to be with us and share his life with us. And he chose to do this at a special meal, the Eucharist. At mass we sing, we hear from the Bible a story of God's love for us, and we share bread and wine. Jesus tells us that when we do this, he is really present with us. When we share in his life, we will live forever.

*Note: It is important to remember that the Hebraic use of the word "body" equates with person while "blood" equates with life. Such an understanding of distinct language helps us to grasp the significance of the terms "body" and "blood" of Christ. So, when we share the "body of Christ" we share in the Person; when we share his "blood," we share the life of Christ.*

## TWENTY-FIRST SUNDAY IN ORDINARY TIME

### YEAR B

### PRAYER OF THE DAY:

Lord God,
you sent Jesus to show us
the way to you.
May we always be strong
in our belief in him
and never give up
following him
until we come to our home,
where you live
with Jesus Christ
and the Holy Spirit,
forever and ever.

### FOCUS OF THE READINGS:

The focus of our readings is our freedom to choose God. We must choose whether or not we will follow Christ. God does not force anyone. If we are to be true disciples, it must be a free, loving choice. That is a profound and often overlooked revelation of God.

The Israelites are told, "You must choose whether you will serve our God or false gods."

Jesus asks his disciples, "Will you also leave me?"

Our readings today call us to reflect on whether or not we have made a conscious choice to follow Christ.

### FIRST READING: *Joshua 24:1-2, 14-17, 18b*

*This is a reading from the prophet Joshua.*

Joshua called the people of Israel
and their leaders together and said to them,

"You must make a choice.
You must choose
whether you will serve our God
or false gods.
But as for me and my family,
we will serve our God,
who is the only true God."

The people said to Joshua,

"We will never turn away from our God.
We will never serve false gods.
For it is God
who brought us away from slavery in Egypt.
It is God
who gave all those wonderful signs for us
and who protected us on our journey.
Yes, we also will serve the one true God!"

*The Word of the Lord.*

### RESPONSE: *Psalm 134*

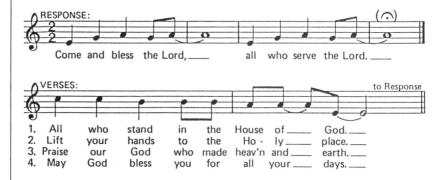

RESPONSE:
Come and bless the Lord,___ all who serve the Lord.___

VERSES:                 to Response
1. All who stand in the House of ___ God. ___
2. Lift your hands to the Ho - ly ___ place. ___
3. Praise our God who made heav'n and ___ earth. ___
4. May God bless you for all your ___ days. ___

# GOSPEL ACCLAMATION:

Al - le - lu - ia, al - le - lu - ia. We be-lieve,___

we be-lieve.___ Lord, help our un - be - lief.___

We be-lieve,_ we be-lieve,_ Lord, help our un - be-lief. _

*Use the *We Believe*, without the Alleluia, as a response for the Creed.

## GOSPEL: *John 6:60-63, 66-69*

*This is a reading from the Gospel of John.*

*The disciples heard Jesus say
that his body was bread
and that those who eat it will live forever.*

Many of the disciples said,

   "What he is saying is hard to accept.
   Who could believe it?"

Jesus knew what they were saying. So he said,

   "Are you disturbed
   and confused by what I said?
   Is this too hard for you to believe?
   I tell you the truth,
   it isn't the body that gives real life.
   It is the spirit that gives real life.
   The things I have been telling you
   are about spirit and life.
   But I know that some of you don't believe."

After Jesus had said this,
many of the disciples stopped believing in him
and went away.
So Jesus asked his twelve apostles,

   "Do you want to leave me too?"

Peter said to Jesus,

   "Lord, who else would we follow?
   You are the One who gives life forever.
   We truly believe
   that you are the Holy One sent by God."

*The Gospel of the Lord.*

## REFLECTING ON THE READINGS WITH CHILDREN:

*After the first reading*, ask the children what was the choice Joshua told the people of Israel they must make.

Explain to the children that during the time of Joshua, most people believed that there were many gods. But God told the Israelites that there is only one God and that they must not believe in or worship false gods—gods that really weren't gods at all. Some of the people continued to worship false gods. So Joshua told them, "You must make a choice between God and false gods."

   ● How did the people respond? Why?

*After reading the Gospel*, ask the children what choice the apostles had to make.

Lead the children to see that sometimes people find the teachings of Jesus hard to accept. For example, Jesus said, "Love your neighbor." Sometimes that is hard to do. Jesus told us not to be nasty to others even when they are nasty to us. Even in those difficult times, we can choose to follow Jesus. He is always present to help us. He knows that it is not easy to follow him when matters are troublesome. But he will help us.

We want to focus on the children's choice to live as Jesus lives. They are too young to be expected to make the radical choice of accepting or rejecting Christ. In these formative years, they are dependent on the choice of their parents. But they can, and do, make choices every day in their relationships with parents, brothers and sisters, friends, and so forth. They can't begin to make choices about their behavior on a conscious level.

107

# TWENTY-SECOND SUNDAY IN ORDINARY TIME

## YEAR B

## PRAYER OF THE DAY:

We love you, God,
above everything else.
Let our love
be more than just words;
let it come
from our hearts.
Teach us to be true
in all that we say and do.
We ask you to do this
through Jesus Christ,
our Lord.

## FOCUS OF THE READINGS:

The focus of our readings is twofold. First, we have the teaching (commandment) to follow God's law and not replace it with laws of our own making. Second, we have Jesus' condemnation of legalism. He insists that we not concern ourselves with the purification of objects, but rather with the purification of our lives, our intentions, and our behavior. This twofold focus draws our attention to the danger of hindering inner, thoughtful obedience to God by redirecting obedience to external laws made by humans.

## FIRST READING: *Deuteronomy 4:1-2, 6-8*

*This is a reading
from the book of Deuteronomy.*

Moses said to the people of Israel,

"Listen to the laws that I am teaching you.
Obey them, and you will have a good life
and will enter the country
which your God is giving to you.
You must not add anything to these laws
or take anything away from them.

"When you obey these laws,
all the other nations
will see that you are wise
and you know what is good.
For no other nation
has laws that are as just and fair
as the laws I am teaching you today."

*The Word of the Lord.*

## RESPONSE: *Psalm 15*

RESPONSE:
We will live with you, O God, we will live for ev-er.

VERSES 1,3 & 4:                    to Response    VERSE 2:                    to Response
1. If we speak the ___ truth.      2. If we keep our prom-ise.
3. If we do no ___ wrong.
4. If we do what is right.

# GOSPEL ACCLAMATION:

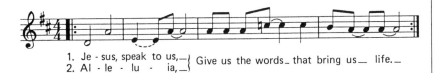

1. Je - sus, speak to us,— } Give us the words— that bring us— life.—
2. Al - le - lu - ia,—

## GOSPEL: *Mark 7:1-8, 14-15, 21-23*

*This is a reading from the Gospel of Mark.*

Some Pharisees and teachers of the Jewish law
came from Galilee to see Jesus.
They had noticed that some of Jesus' disciples
ate their food without washing their hands first.
The Jewish law says
that the Jews must never eat
without washing their hands in a special way.
And when they come home from the market,
they always wash in a special way too.
The Jewish people have many other traditions
like this which they always follow.
So the Pharisees asked Jesus,

"Why don't your disciples
follow the customs and rules of our people?
Why do they eat their food
with hands that are not clean?"

Jesus said to them,

"You are hypocrites.
You are not being really honest.
You don't follow God's laws.
You follow the laws you made up yourselves."

Then he said to the people,

"Listen to me, all of you,
and understand what I am saying.
Nothing outside of you
and nothing you eat is bad.
It is the things you do
that can make you wrong.
Stealing, murder, selfishness,
treating others unjustly, being jealous,
being disrespectful about God, bragging—
all these evil things
come from inside a person,
and these are the things that are wrong."

*The Gospel of the Lord.*

REFLECTING ON THE READINGS
WITH CHILDREN:

Ask the children if they have ever
played in a game where others kept
changing the rules or making up new
rules during the game as they went
along. What is it like to play like
that?

Explain that some people have
tried to do that with God's law. Over
the years, people changed it and
made up new laws. Sometimes they
did this because they thought it
would make the laws easier to
understand. But in the end they had
made up so many laws that it was too
complicated, and the people could no
longer keep them all. That made
people feel guilty.

The Pharisees and teachers of the
law saw that Jesus and his disciples
didn't keep all of the little laws that
had been made. Ask the children if
they remember what it was that the
disciples didn't do.

- What answer did Jesus give?

*Discuss the meaning of the word
"hypocrite." Help them to see that it
is a person who says one thing but
does something else.*

- Why did Jesus use this very
  strong word?

Reread the last paragraph. Ask
the children what they understand
about it.

Help them to see that God cares
what we think in our hearts and how
we act, especially how we treat others.

# TWENTY-THIRD SUNDAY IN ORDINARY TIME

## YEAR B

### PRAYER OF THE DAY:

Open our ears
to hear your teaching,
Lord God,
and give us the words
to tell others
about your wonderful love.
Make us strong
in doing what you command
so that others, seeing us,
may come to know
that you have saved us
through Jesus, your Son,
who lives with you,
forever and ever.

### FOCUS OF THE READINGS:

The focus of our readings is God's love and salvation expressed in physical healing. The readings show God's concern for those who have no hope apart from miraculous intervention.

Isaiah images the redemption of God's people in the wonderful, gratuitous healing of the blind, the deaf, the crippled, and the mute.

Our passage from *Mark* reveals Jesus as the fulfillment of that promise. Jesus himself is redemption. The man who is deaf and mute experiences this in his gift of hearing and speech. Like all miracle stories, it is a sign of ultimate salvation.

Just as those in physical need look to God for healing, so, too, we look to God for the free gift of salvation.

### FIRST READING: *Isaiah 35:4-6*

*This is a reading from the prophet Isaiah.*

Our God says,

"Have courage! Don't be afraid!
Your God is coming with justice
to reward and save you."

Then those who are blind will see.
Those who are deaf will hear.
Those who are crippled will jump like deer.
And those who cannot speak will sing.

*The Word of the Lord.*

### RESPONSE: *Psalm 146*

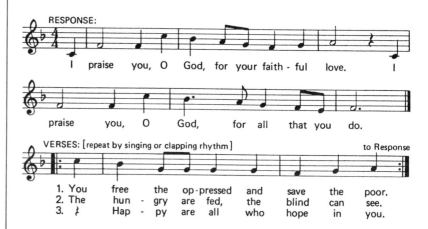

RESPONSE:
I praise you, O God, for your faith-ful love. I praise you, O God, for all that you do.

VERSES: [repeat by singing or clapping rhythm]    to Response
1. You free the op-pressed and save the poor.
2. The hun-gry are fed, the blind can see.
3. Hap-py are all who hope in you.

## GOSPEL ACCLAMATION:

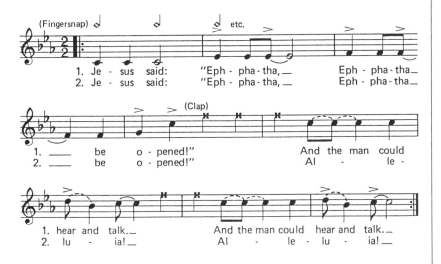

1. Je - sus said: "Eph - pha - tha,— Eph - pha - tha—
2. Je - sus said: "Eph - pha - tha,— Eph - pha - tha—

1. ___ be o - pened!" And the man could
2. ___ be o - pened!" Al - le -

1. hear and talk.— And the man could hear and talk.—
2. lu - ia!— Al - le - lu - ia! —

## GOSPEL: *Mark 7:31-37*

*This is a reading from the Gospel of Mark.*

Jesus went to the area of the Ten Cities
near the Sea of Galilee.
Some people came to him,
bringing a man who was deaf
and could not talk.
They begged Jesus to heal the man
by laying his hands on him.
Jesus took the man to a place
away from the crowd.
He touched the man's ears and tongue.
Then he looked up to heaven and prayed.
He said,

"*Ephphatha!*"

This word means "Be opened."

Immediately the man could hear and talk.
Jesus told the people
not to tell anyone what happened.
But they were filled with wonder
and amazement,
and they went around telling everyone,

"This man, Jesus, does everything well!
He can even make deaf people hear
and those who cannot talk speak."

*The Gospel of the Lord.*

## REFLECTING ON THE READINGS WITH CHILDREN:

*After the reading*, ask the children to whom God was speaking. Explain to the children that the people of Israel were in exile. They had been captured and were living a long way from their home with those who had captured them. They wanted nothing more than to be freed to return to their home. Ask the children why God spoke especially about the blind, the deaf, and so forth. Help the children understand that it is often those who are most helpless in the world who know they need God.

*After the Gospel*, ask the children to recall the story. If they have difficulty recalling, you might help them with questions such as:

- Where was Jesus?
- Who asked Jesus to cure the deaf man?
- What did Jesus do? Help them recall the details:
  - took him alone,
  - touched his ears and tongue,
  - prayed,
  - said, "*Ephphatha!*"
- What does "ephphatha" mean?
- How do you think the man felt?
- Why do you think Jesus told the people not to tell anyone? (See Introduction to the Gospel of *Mark*, pp. 170-171.)

Help the children see that there are other forms of "deafness."

We can refuse to listen to what Jesus wants to say to us.

We can ask Jesus to touch us and say "*Ephphatha!*"

111

# TWENTY-FOURTH SUNDAY IN ORDINARY TIME

## YEAR B

### PRAYER OF THE DAY:

Mighty God,
we want to be with you
and share your life.
Fill us with your courage
so that we do not
just talk about this
but really try to carry it out.
Let us be
true followers of Jesus,
giving up everything
that gets in the way
of loving you,
and so come to our home
with you and live with you
forever and ever.

### FOCUS OF THE READINGS:

Our focus today is the call to truly express our faith in Christ. It is of little use to say we believe in Christ but not in his cross, as Peter seems to have done in today's Gospel reading. Acceptance of Christ means acceptance of his cross and also of our own cross in union with him. To reject the reality of suffering is to reject the reality of the crucified Christ.

In our first reading, James tells us that it is false to say we believe in Christ if we do not live as Christ lived, namely, for others. To reject the reality of service in the Christian life is to reject the reality of Christ who came not to be served, but to serve. Further, James calls us to live with the belief that Christ died for all, and therefore we are all brothers and sisters of the same family. To deny this is to deny Christ.

Christ's death on the cross is the culmination of his life for others. For us, too, the cross and service must go together.

### FIRST READING: *James 2:8, 14-18*

*This is a reading from a letter written by James.*

My brothers and sisters,

The most important commandment is:

"Love your neighbor as yourself."

If you really keep this commandment,
you are doing what God wants you to do.
But what good is it to say we believe
if we don't do good things for other people?
That isn't real faith, is it?
For example, if a brother or a sister
doesn't have clothes or enough food to eat,
it's not enough just to say,

"Good luck to you!
I hope you are warm enough,
and I hope you find enough food to eat."

If you don't help your brother or sister
find food or clothes, what good are your words?
It's the same way with our faith.
If we don't do good things for others,
our faith isn't real faith at all. It's dead.
I show what I believe by the good things I do.

*The Word of the Lord.*

### RESPONSE: *Psalm 145/104*

RESPONSE:

All liv-ing things ___ look to you ___ look to you. ___

All liv-ing things ___ look to you ___ to help them Lord! ___

Leader:

All: All - liv-ing things ___

1. When we are hun - gry     you give us    food.
2. Each day you give ___ us   all that we   need.
3. Your hand is o - pen   with gifts for   all.
4. I will sing prais - es   and bless your   name.

*Round during final response only

## GOSPEL ACCLAMATION:

1. "If you would be my dis-ci-ples,___ ac-cept the cross and fol-low me."
2. Al - le - lu - ia, al - le - lu - ia,___"Ac-cept the cross and fol-low me."

## GOSPEL: *Mark 8:27-35*

*This is a reading from the Gospel of Mark.*

Jesus and his disciples were going to the towns
around Caesarea Philippi.
On the way, Jesus asked them,
 "Who do other people think I am?"
They told him,
 "Some think you are John the Baptist
 or one of the prophets."
Then Jesus said,
 "Who do you think I am?"
Peter said,
 "You are the Messiah, the Christ."
Jesus told his disciples not to tell that to anyone.

Then Jesus began to teach his disciples
that he was going to suffer very much.
He told them that he was going to be killed
but that he would rise again after three days.
He said all of this very clearly
so that the disciples would know
what was going to happen.

Peter took Jesus away from the group
and told him not to say those things.
Jesus looked at the disciples,
and then he scolded Peter, and said,
 "Go away from me!
 You are talking like Satan.
 You want things to be
 just as human beings want them.
 You don't care what God wants!"

Then Jesus spoke to all the disciples
and the people who were there with them. He said,
 "Those who want to be my disciples
 will not be able to have everything
 the way they want it.
 They will have to give up some things.
 My disciples must accept the cross and follow me.
 Those who live this way because of me
 and because of the Good News,
 will live with me forever."

*The Gospel of the Lord.*

## REFLECTING ON THE READINGS WITH CHILDREN:

Both of these readings are
important in our on-going formation
as Christians, and they are important
in the formation of children as well.
But we must be cautious in reflecting
on them with small children.
"Accepting one's cross" as well as the
exhortation in *James* must be
applied in suitable language and
specific examples appropriate to the
age of the children. We want to avoid
burdening them with expectations
beyond their understanding or
capacity to fulfill.

*After the first reading*, ask the
children to explain in their own
words what James is teaching us in
this passage. Ask them to give other
examples of this. You will know by
these examples if they have
understood the reading and can
apply it to their own lives. Help
them see that God wants to help the
poor, the hungry, the blind and all
those in need, and often does that by
using our hands, feet, and so forth.
We help God do this because we
believe.

*After the Gospel*, ask the children
what Jesus said about those who
want to be his disciples. (You may
have to read the last paragraph
again.)

- What does Jesus mean when
 he says that his disciples "may
 not have everything the way
 they want it"? How can this
 help others?
- What does Jesus mean when
 he says "accept the cross and
 follow me"?

Help the children understand
that to accept the cross means to live
as Jesus lived.

Jesus promises that those who do
this will live forever.

## TWENTY-FIFTH SUNDAY IN ORDINARY TIME

YEAR B

### PRAYER OF THE DAY:

Dear Lord,
you are the ruler of all things;
we are weak and
unimportant.
Yet, you love us
and sent Jesus to save us.
Take us by the hand;
protect us from all harm
and bring us
to our home with you,
where you are with Jesus
and the Holy Spirit,
forever and ever.

### FOCUS OF THE READINGS:

Our readings focus on the attitude Christians have toward each other. Christians, living by God's wisdom rather than earthly values, treat one another with respect and love.

Our first reading gives us a list of virtues to be found among those who live by wisdom. It also describes life without those virtues—when people are jealous and think only of themselves, it leads only to fights and arguments.

The Gospel passage gives us an example of this among the disciples. Jesus is quick to correct them. "If you want to be among the most important . . . , you must serve all other people." Our faith in Christ should make a difference in the way we treat others. Jesus presents a little child as a model for this simplicity and humility.

### FIRST READING: *James 3:14-18; 4:1-3, 7-8*

*This is a reading from a letter written by James.*

My brothers and sisters,

When people are jealous
and think only about themselves,
they do all kinds of evil things.
But when people live by God's wisdom,
they are honest and kind.
They are gentle and forgiving.
They live in peace
and try to make peace with everyone.

Why do you have fights and arguments?
Isn't it because
when you don't get what you want,
you are jealous,
and so you fight and argue?
You don't get what you want
because you don't ask for it
or because you ask for the wrong reasons.
You ask for what you want just to be selfish.

Give up these evil ways.
Stay near to God and God will stay near to you.

*The Word of the Lord.*

### RESPONSE: *Psalm 25*

RESPONSE: 1st time: Leader; 2nd time: All

Show me your ways, O Lord. Teach me your paths. paths.

VERSES: All                    to Response

1. You show me when I have sinned.
2. My Sav - ior, I hope in you.
3. O lead me in ways of truth.

114

## GOSPEL ACCLAMATION:

(Fingersnap)

"If you want to be the great-est you must serve my bro-thers serve my sis-ters." Al - le - lu - ia,___ al - le - lu - ia.___ "If you want to be the great-est you must serve."___

GOSPEL: *Mark 9:33-37*

*This is a reading from the Gospel of Mark.*

Jesus and his disciples went to Capernaum.
And when they were inside the house,
Jesus asked his disciples,

"What were you talking about
on the way home?"

They didn't answer him
because they had been talking
about which one of them
was the most important disciple.

Jesus sat down and called the twelve apostles
to come and sit with him.  He said to them,

"If you really want to be the most important,
you must treat everyone else
as more important than yourself.
And you must serve all other people."

Then Jesus put a little child in front of them.
He put his arms around the child
and said to the disciples,

"Those who accept a little child like this
because of me
are also accepting me.
And those who accept me
are really accepting the One who sent me."

*The Gospel of the Lord.*

REFLECTING ON THE READINGS
WITH CHILDREN:

*After reading the Gospel,* ask the
children what they heard.

Ask them why the disciples did
not want to answer Jesus when he
asked them what they were talking
about on the way home.  Help the
children see that Jesus taught the
disciples that they should not be
jealous. Jesus did not scold them for
this because he understands that
sometimes it's hard not to be jealous
of other people.  Instead, he asked
them to sit down with him so he
could explain this concept to them.

Ask the children what they
remember about the first reading.
Perhaps you will need to read it again.

Ask the children what they think
about James' statement.  Is that
their experience?  Is that why fights
and arguments happen?  Perhaps
some would share other examples.

Help them see that God will help
us when we feel jealous.  The children
should know that it is not bad to *feel*
jealous.  James is warning us about
how we *act* when we are jealous.

# TWENTY-SIXTH SUNDAY IN ORDINARY TIME

YEAR B

## PRAYER OF THE DAY:

God of love,
all that is good and right
pleases you.
Show us how to be happy
whenever people do
what is right
and show
they care for each other.
We ask you this
through Jesus Christ,
our Lord, who lives with you
and the Holy Spirit,
forever and ever.

## FOCUS OF THE READINGS:

Our readings focus on the freedom of the Spirit to blow when and where it will. The Spirit of God is not, and cannot be, limited to officially appointed positions. In both readings, we find the complaint that others outside the group are exercising ministry reserved for those officially appointed: prophecy, casting out evil spirits. This attempt to limit and guard spiritual power is corrected by both Moses and Jesus. God's Spirit, and therefore the various ministries for good works, are open to all. Any attempt to limit these ministries to officially designated people is an attempt to limit the freedom of the Spirit of God.

## FIRST READING: *Numbers 11:25-29*

*This is a reading from the book of Numbers.*

Seventy of the leaders of Israel
received the same Spirit that was in Moses.
And when the Spirit of God came upon them,
they all began to prophesy.
Now there were two men, Eldad and Medad,
who were on the list of the leaders,
but they were not in the tent with the others
when all this happened.
But the Spirit also came upon them
and they began to prophesy in the camp.
A young man from the camp
ran and told Moses,

"Eldad and Medad
are prophesying in the camp!"

Joshua, who was one of Moses' helpers, said,

"Moses, stop them from doing that!"

But Moses said,

"Do you think I am jealous?
No, I want them all to have God's spirit!
I wish all of God's people
would be prophets!"

*The Word of the Lord.*

## RESPONSE: *Psalm 19*

RESPONSE:

All that I think or say, may it please you this day.
God, my strength my Re-deem-er, may it please you this day.

## GOSPEL ACCLAMATION:

1. Je - sus, speak to us,—} Give us the words_ that bring us_ life._
2. Al - le - lu - ia,_}

## GOSPEL: *Mark 9:38-41*

*This is a reading from the Gospel of Mark.*

John, one of the twelve apostles, said to Jesus,

"Teacher,
we saw a man curing people of evil spirits
by using your name.
We told him to stop doing that
because he does not belong to our group."

Jesus said,

"Don't stop anyone from doing good.
Anyone who does miracles using my name
will never say anything bad about me.
And anyone who is not against us
is part of us.

"Anyone who gives you a drink of water
because you belong to Christ
will surely receive a reward."

*The Gospel of the Lord.*

REFLECTING ON THE READINGS
WITH CHILDREN:

*After the Gospel*, ask the children
to retell what happened.

What did Moses and Jesus say
about other people prophesying and
curing people of evil spirits?

Be sure the children understand
the meaning of the word "prophesy."

Discuss with the children how we
might have similar experiences in
our lives.

- Perhaps we have been excluded
  from a group.
- Perhaps we have excluded
  someone.
- Perhaps someone has felt they
  were better than we.
- Perhaps we have felt we are
  better than others.

Do we know people who are
almost always left out of games or
other events? Why are they left out?

Jesus teaches us that he wants
everyone to do good. We are all part
of the same group or family if we
belong to Christ. The Holy Spirit
may act in and through anyone.

# TWENTY-SEVENTH SUNDAY IN ORDINARY TIME

## YEAR B

### PRAYER OF THE DAY:

Protector God,
you show your care for us
through our families
and those who look after us.
Help all husbands and wives,
and mothers and fathers,
to be true to each other.
May our homes be filled
with your happiness
and peace.
We ask you this
through Jesus, your Son.

### FOCUS OF THE READINGS:

The focus of our readings today is the sacredness of marriage. This focus is extended to the sacredness of the family in the Gospel passage with the blessing of the children.

The description of the creation of woman (a different description from the one presented in *Genesis 1*) focuses on the common humanity of man and woman. They are made of the same bone and flesh, and they complement each other. The account tells us that for this reason men and women leave their parents and share a life together; they belong to one another. This theology was accompanied by a prohibition of divorce. It is this point that links the first reading with the Gospel. The creation stories focus on the sacredness of marriage, and Jesus, refusing to be trapped by legalism, responds to the question of divorce by reaffirming this sacredness. Children are the natural fruit of this sacred union, and Jesus here affirms their sanctity as well.

## FIRST READING: *Genesis 2:18-24*

*This is a reading from the book of Genesis.*

God said,

"It is not good for the man I have created
to live alone.
I will make a partner for him,
someone like himself."

So God made the man go to sleep.
And while he was sleeping,
God took one of his ribs out of his side
and put flesh in its place.
Then God made the rib into a woman
and took her to the man. The man said,

"This person is really part of my body.
Because she was taken out of a man,
she will be called woman."

And that is why men and women
leave their mothers and fathers
and belong to each other.

*The Word of the Lord.*

## RESPONSE: *Psalm 104*

RESPONSE:

I will praise you as long as I live,____ as long as I live____ I will praise you God. praise you God.

VERSES:

to Response

1. I praise you God for all you do, for all my life for all you do.
2. How man-y are your works O God, in wis-dom you have made them all.
3. O God may all I think please you. I sing and find my joy in you.

* Round after final verse is sung

118

## GOSPEL ACCLAMATION:

"Let the lit-tle_ chil-dren come to me." Je-sus hugged the

chil-dren, and he gave them all his bless-ing. Al-le-lu - ia.

## GOSPEL: *Mark 10:13-16*

*This is a reading from the Gospel of Mark.*

People were bringing their little children
to Jesus so he would touch them.
The disciples scolded the people
for bothering him.
But when Jesus saw this,
he became angry and said to the disciples,

"Let the little children come to me,
and don't try to stop them.
The kingdom of God belongs to people
who are like these little children.
I tell you honestly,
unless you become like a little child,
you will not enter the kingdom of God."

Then Jesus hugged the children
and blessed them.

*The Gospel of the Lord.*

REFLECTING ON THE READINGS
WITH CHILDREN:

Because children tend to be literal
and because this account of the
creation of woman differs from the
one they usually hear (*Genesis 1*)
they may be confused. It may be best
not to deal too explicitly with the
details of the first reading. The
Gospel passage picks up the main
focus of the first reading and can be
explored there.

*After the Gospel*, ask the children
to recall the reading. This may likely
be a delicate subject for discussion if
there are children present whose
parents are divorced. It may seem to
be a judgment of their parents in
light of the Gospel. Also, children
often feel they themselves are to
blame for the separation of their
parents. Furthermore, it seems
inappropriate to spend a great deal of
time on a teaching that is, practically
speaking, irrelevant to small
children. Perhaps it would be better
to simply state that Jesus blesses
marriage and indeed all of family life.
We can then concentrate on the
second part of the Gospel, the
blessing of the children. They
should see in this reading that Jesus
is never too busy for children. And
indeed, Jesus wants children to come
to him and to be with him.

You may want to have a special
ceremony for this day. If it works
well in your parish, the children
could come forward for a special
blessing at the conclusion of the
liturgy in the general assembly. If
this is not possible in your parish,
the Minister of the Word might
preside at a blessing ceremony before
the children return to the assembly.
Ideally, each child would be called by
name. This might also be an
occasion to give the children a small
picture or holy card of Jesus—
perhaps one of Jesus blessing the
children.

# TWENTY-EIGHTH SUNDAY IN ORDINARY TIME

## YEAR B

### PRAYER OF THE DAY:

We want nothing
but you, God;
you are the greatest treasure.
Do not allow us
to be greedy and selfish,
thinking we are important
because of the things we own.
Instead, let us rely
completely on you
and on the teaching
of your son, Jesus,
who lives with you
and the Holy Spirit,
forever and ever.

### FOCUS OF THE READINGS:

Both of our readings focus on the choice to be made between God and riches. In the first reading, wisdom is desired more than "all the riches I could have." Wisdom here is not knowledge, but a personification of God, an image of God. It is, therefore, God who is preferred more than riches. In our Gospel passage, Jesus challenges a man to "sell everything you have—then come follow me." When the man rejects this challenge, Jesus tells his disciples that it is harder for a rich person to enter heaven than for a camel to go through the eye of a needle. Biblically, riches seem to be an obstacle to a deep relationship with God. But the meaning of the Gospel goes beyond material wealth. It is a call to put aside anything and everything that keeps us from wholeheartedly following Jesus.

### FIRST READING: *Wisdom 7:7-11*

*This is a reading from the book of Wisdom.*

I prayed for the spirit of wisdom,
and she came to me
and helped me to understand all things.
Wisdom is more important to me
than all the riches I could have.
She is more wonderful
than the most expensive jewels.
She is more important to me
than power or even health.
And when I have true wisdom,
I have everything else that is good.

*The Word of the Lord.*

### RESPONSE: *Psalm 90*

Fill us with your gift of love. Help us find our joy in you. joy in you.

VERSES:
1. God, our God, ev-er-last - ing. May our hearts al-ways turn to you.
2. God, our God, ev-er-last - ing. Bless the work that we do to-day.

### GOSPEL ACCLAMATION:

Al - le - lu - ia. Al - le - lu - ia.
"Noth-ing is im-pos-si-ble, God can do all things."

## GOSPEL: *Mark 10:17-27*

*This is a reading from the Gospel of Mark.*

One day a man ran up to Jesus
and knelt down in front of him, and asked,

"Good teacher, what do I have to do
so that I will live with God forever?"

Jesus said,

"You know the commandments:
You must not steal. You must not kill.
You must not sin
against your husband or wife.
You must not cheat. You must not lie.
Honor your mother and father."

The man said,

"Teacher,
I have always kept these commandments,
ever since I was a little child."

Jesus looked at the young man with love
and said,

"There is still one more thing you must do.
Go and sell everything you have
and give the money to the poor.
God will reward you for doing this.
Then come and follow me."

When Jesus said this,
the young man went away very sad,
because he owned many things.
Then Jesus said to his disciples,

"It is very hard for a rich person
to enter the kingdom of God.
It is easier for a camel
to get through the eye of a needle
than for a rich person
to enter the kingdom of God."

The disciples were shocked at this and asked,

"Then how is it possible
for anyone to be saved and go to heaven?"

Jesus said,

"You cannot save yourselves. God saves you.
God can do all things,
for nothing is impossible for God."

*The Gospel of the Lord.*

REFLECTING ON THE READINGS
WITH CHILDREN:

*After the Gospel*, ask the children
to recall the story. If they have
difficulty recalling, you might ask
questions such as these:

- What did the man ask Jesus?
- Why did Jesus answer with the
  10 commandments?
- Can you remember what those
  commandments are?

But the man wanted to know what
more he could do for God.

- What did Jesus answer?
- How did the man respond to
  what Jesus said?
- Why did Jesus say,
  "It is easier for a camel to get
  through the eye of a needle
  than for a rich person to enter
  the Kingdom of heaven"?

Help the children understand
that Jesus did *not* say that rich
people are not going to heaven. It is
not money itself that Jesus asks us to
give up. It is holding onto
things—letting possessions come
between God and us. This man's
possessions meant more to him than
being a disciple of Jesus. Perhaps for
another person it would not be
money or things but holding onto a
certain idea about something or
someone. Jesus may be asking some
to give up some of their time to help
others.

You may need to develop this
point rather than eliciting it from
the children. After you have
developed it, they may be able to
offer some ideas on it.

The children should leave
understanding that the point of the
two readings is that our love for God,
and following Jesus, is more precious
than anything we could have or own.

# TWENTY-NINTH SUNDAY IN ORDINARY TIME

## YEAR B

### PRAYER OF THE DAY:

Patient God,
you wait on us
as we struggle
and often fail to do your will.
Turn us from our selfish ways
to serve each other.
May we be alive to the needs
of our families and friends,
and so be like Jesus,
the servant of us all.
We make this prayer
through Christ, our Lord.

### FOCUS OF THE READINGS:

The focus of the readings is the difficult message that suffering, willingly accepted in an attitude of service, can be a means of salvation. The servant in *Isaiah* gives his life for sins of others, and "his suffering will save many people." Jesus presents the same challenge. It is the servant, not the power-loving rulers, who image the life of Jesus. It is the servant, whose life is given willingly, who saves many people. Both readings present the profound mystery of salvation through suffering.

### FIRST READING: *Isaiah 53:10-11*

*This is a reading from the prophet Isaiah.*

If my servant gives his life
to make up for the sins of others,
he will live to see his family for many years.
He will be doing what God wants him to do.
Because he suffers, he will be given light,
and his suffering will save many people.

*The Word of the Lord.*

### RESPONSE: *Psalm 16 and Psalm 27*

RESPONSE:
Have mer-cy God, have mer-cy God. I trust in
1-2 to Verses / 3 Fine
you for my safe-ty. safe-ty.

VERSES: to Response
1. You are my light my sav-ior; with your help I shall not be a-fraid.
2. When it is dark a-round me, noth-ing takes me a-way from your love.

122

## GOSPEL ACCLAMATION:

(Fingersnap)

"If you want to be the great-est you must serve my bro-thers

serve my sis-ters." Al-le-lu - ia,___ al-le-lu-ia.___

"If you want to be the great-est you must serve."___

**GOSPEL:** *Mark 10:42-45*

*This is a reading from the Gospel of Mark.*

Jesus said to his disciples,

"You know that rulers of the Gentiles
(who don't believe in God) use their power
to take advantage of the people.
Those rulers love to feel very important
and to have other people serve them.

"But you must not be like that.
If you want to be truly great,
you must serve others.
And if you want to be the most important,
you must serve everyone.

"I did not come so that others could serve me.
I came so that I could serve everyone.
I came to give my life to save all people."

*The Gospel of the Lord.*

REFLECTING ON THE READINGS
WITH CHILDREN:

Ask the children if they have ever played in games where one or two children take charge and bully the rest of the children. Ask them how they feel when this happens and why the other children continue to play with these bullies.

- How did Jesus describe the leaders who don't believe in God?
- What did he say about being leaders among Christians?
- How did he describe Christian leaders?
- Who did Jesus say are the truly great people in Christianity?
- Do you know anyone who serves others:
    - in our parish?
    - in your school?
    - in your family?
- How are they like Jesus?

Help the children see that Jesus gave his life for others by dying, yes, but also by the way he lived.

- How can we be like him?

As always, it is important to keep the children focused on ideas appropriate and reasonable for their age level.

# THIRTIETH SUNDAY IN ORDINARY TIME

## YEAR B

### PRAYER OF THE DAY:

Heal us, God our maker;
do not let us be blind
to all the good you do for us.
We place ourselves
in your hands,
knowing you care for us
and want us to be happy.
We ask you to do this
through Jesus Christ,
our Lord.

### FOCUS OF THE READINGS:

Our readings again focus on God's loving care expressed in real terms. In the first reading, Jeremiah tells his people of the good news of their release from exile in Babylon. It is cause for joy and praise, especially for the blind, the crippled, those who are lost; all those who are weak. They will rejoice in God's loving intervention.

Jesus expresses this hope for the blind in his healing of Bartimaeus. This story reveals its theme of ultimate salvation in the words,

"Teacher, I want to see!"

"You are healed, because you believe in me."

An interesting image in both readings is the road. Jeremiah tells us that God promised a straight road on which no one would stumble and fall. Mark tells us that Bartimaeus called out for pity, as he was sitting by the side of the road. When he receives his sight, he immediately follows Jesus on the road—a biblical symbol for the way of salvation.

### FIRST READING: *Jeremiah 31:7-9*

*This is a reading from the prophet Jeremiah.*

Our God says:

Shout with joy! Sing praise!
I will bring my people back to their home.
I will gather them from all over the world
where they have been scattered.
I will bring those who are blind
and those who are crippled.
I will comfort them
and lead them to refreshing water.
I will lead them on a straight road,
so that no one will stumble and fall.
For they are my children,
and I take care of them.

*The Word of the Lord.*

### RESPONSE: *Psalm 146*

### GOSPEL ACCLAMATION:

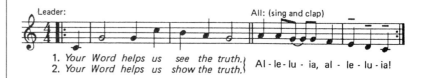

GOSPEL: *Mark 10:46-52*

*This is a reading from the Gospel of Mark.*

One day as Jesus and his disciples
were leaving the city of Jericho,
there was a blind man
sitting by the side of the road begging.
His name was Bartimaeus.
When Bartimaeus heard
that it was Jesus who was walking by,
he called out,

"Jesus, have pity on me! Help me!"

Some of the people who were there
scolded the blind man and told him to be quiet.
But he shouted even louder,

"Jesus, have pity on me! Help me!"

Jesus stopped and said,

"Tell the man to come here."

So they said to Bartimaeus,

"Have courage! Get up!
Jesus is calling you!"

So the man jumped up,
left his coat by the road, and ran to Jesus.
Jesus asked him,

"What do you want me to do for you?"

The blind man said,

"Teacher, I want to be able to see!"

Jesus said,

"You are healed because you believe in me."

Immediately the man was able to see.
And he became a disciple
and began to follow Jesus on the road.

*The Gospel of the Lord.*

REFLECTING ON THE READINGS
WITH CHILDREN:

We have this week another story
from Mark filled with wonderful
details. It should be read
dramatically, giving great attention
to both detail and dialogue.

Ask the children to recall the
story.

- Where were Jesus and his
  disciples coming from?
- Where was the blind man?
  What is his name?
- What did the blind man call out
  to Jesus? When Jesus heard
  him, what did he say?
- When Jesus asked Bartimaeus
  what he wanted, what did he
  say? What did Jesus say?
- What did Bartimaeus do after
  he could see?

Ask the children if there are other
forms of blindness besides physical.

- What are they?
- Can we sometimes not see
  because we don't understand?
- Can we refuse to see something?

Perhaps you may wish to pray a
litany with the children such as:

When we don't see the good in
  others,
    *Jesus, have pity on us. Help us.*
When we don't understand,
    *Jesus, have pity on us. Help us.*
When we don't see the truth,
    *Jesus, have pity on us. Help us.*

What is important here is that
you use examples the children gave
so that they come to "see" that when
we are "blind," we can turn to Jesus
in faith.

## THIRTY-FIRST SUNDAY IN ORDINARY TIME

### YEAR B

### PRAYER OF THE DAY:

Mighty God,
there is no one
greater than you.
Put in our hearts
a deep love for you;
teach us how to pray,
and guide us always
to do what you wish.
We ask you this
through Jesus Christ,
who is God with you
and the Holy Spirit,
forever and ever.

### FOCUS OF THE READINGS:

The focus of our readings is "love of God and neighbor." Because our society tends to trivialize the word "love," we are apt to miss the profound nature of this teaching in our two readings. The introduction to this commandment in *Deuteronomy* is a radical call to faith in one God—a notion known only to the people of Israel. Precisely because there is only one true God, they are commanded to give total, unconditional love to God. For the Hebrew, heart, mind, and soul are not three separate faculties but rather the total person. Jesus combines this total, unconditional love of God with the love of neighbor. It is with this same love of mind, heart, and soul that we are commanded to love our neighbor. The focus comes from the conclusion Jesus draws—there is no greater commandment; nothing, no sacrifice, substitutes for it.

### FIRST READING: *Deuteronomy 6:4-6*

*This is a reading from the book of Deuteronomy.*

Moses said to the people:

"People of Israel, listen!
We have only one God.
And you must love God with all your heart,
with all your soul,
and with all your strength.
This is God's commandment.
Keep these words always in your heart!"

*The Word of the Lord.*

### RESPONSE: *Psalm 18*

I love you God, for you are my strength. You are my God. I give you my praise. praise. You are my God.

126

## GOSPEL ACCLAMATION:

1. Love ___ God with all your heart:
2. Love your neigh-bor as your-self: } Al - le - lu - ia, al - le - lu - ia!

## GOSPEL: *Mark 12:28-34*

*This is a reading from the Gospel of Mark.*

One of the teachers of the Jewish law
came to Jesus and asked him,

"Which one of the commandments
is the most important?"

Jesus said,

"The most important commandment is this:
You must love God with all your heart,
with all your soul, with all your mind,
and with all your strength.
And the second most important is this:
You must love your neighbor
the same as you love yourself."

The man who asked Jesus the question said,

"Teacher, you are right.
We have only one God.
And we must love God with all our heart,
all our mind, and all our strength.
And we must love our neighbor
as we love ourselves.
Doing this is more important
than anything else we could do for God."

Jesus was pleased with what the man said,
and he told him,

"You are very close to the reign of God."

*The Gospel of the Lord.*

## REFLECTING ON THE READINGS WITH CHILDREN:

At first glance this may seem a simple Gospel to reflect on with children. But, remembering that children take our words very seriously and often literally, we will want to exercise caution. I recall a vivid experience with this very text. After hearing Sister say that we "must love God more than anyone," one little girl went home crying.

Finally that evening, after much prodding, she told her parents that she thought God didn't love her because she loved them (her parents) more than she loved God. And quite naturally so! Fortunately, the parents were very understanding and had the kindness to tell Sister what happened. When she shared this with the rest of the faculty, it was a learning experience for all of us!

With this caution in mind, let us proceed to our reflection on the Gospel. Rather than dwelling on how much we love God, we might explore with the children ways we show our love for God:

- in our prayer,
- at Mass,
- at home,
- with others,
- by telling others about the good things that happen (instead of the bad),
- by having a joyful disposition,
- by showing gratitude for God's gifts,
- by showing respect for the things God created and using them respectfully.

We might also explore how we show our love for our neighbor. The children will be able to make many suggestions. The Minister of the Word will want to keep the children focused on ways they can show love of neighbor which are truly possible for them. For example, they *cannot* feed the hungry of the world, but they *can* share their goodies generously with others. They *cannot* make global peace, but they *can* work for peace in their families and with their playmates.

# THIRTY-SECOND SUNDAY IN ORDINARY TIME

## YEAR B

## PRAYER OF THE DAY:

Lord God,
you know we are young
and cannot do for you
everything we would like.
Look on us with kindness;
accept our little prayers
and the good things
we try to do for each other.
What we can do
we do for you
and Jesus, your Son,
and the Holy Spirit—
one God, forever and ever.

## FOCUS OF THE READINGS:

The focus of our readings is giving generously—not of excess, but from our need. Underlying this giving, of course, is faith. Faith allowed the widow to give all she had to live on at the request of the prophet Elijah. She was rewarded by God's generosity. In the Gospel, Jesus praises a poor widow for giving two small coins to the temple treasury. Her gift was praised by Jesus, not for its amount, but because it was all she had to live on and thus was an expression of her faith and total gift of self. We may be assured that his praise was accompanied by salvation since the Gospel consistently assumes faith and total surrender as prerequisite for salvation.

## FIRST READING: *I Kings 17:10-16*

*This is a reading from the first book of Kings.*

When the prophet Elijah
went to the city of Zarephath,
he saw a widow gathering sticks to build a fire.
He said to her,

  "Please bring me some water to drink."

The woman was going to get the water,
and Elijah called to her and said,

  "Please bring me a little bread also."

The woman said,

  "As sure as your God lives,
    I do not have any bread baked right now.
    I have only a little bit of flour in a jar
    and a little oil.
    I was just gathering sticks to build a fire
    so that I can make some bread
    for my son and myself.
    But after we eat that,
    we have no more food, and so we will die."

Elijah said to her,

  "Go in and make the bread
    for your son and yourself.
    But first, make some for me.
    And don't be afraid, for my God says,

      'The jar of flour and the bottle of oil
        will not go empty.' "

The woman went and did
just what Elijah told her.
And she and her son and Elijah
were able to eat for a long time,
for the jar of flour and the bottle of oil
did not go empty,
just as God had said
through the prophet Elijah.

*The Word of the Lord.*

## RESPONSE: *Psalm 146*

## GOSPEL ACCLAMATION:

## GOSPEL: *Mark 12:41-44*

*This is a reading from the Gospel of Mark.*

One day as Jesus was near the temple,
he saw the people
coming to put money into the collection box.
Many rich people came
and put in a lot of money.
But a poor lady, who was a widow,
came and put in only two small coins.
It was worth only about one penny.
When Jesus saw this, he said to his disciples,

"This poor widow
has given more to the collection
than all the others.
The rich people gave money
that they didn't really need.
For them, it was extra money.
But this poor widow has very little money,
and she needs all of it to live on.
Yet she gave everything she had."

*The Gospel of the Lord.*

## REFLECTING ON THE READINGS WITH CHILDREN:

*After the first reading*, ask the children to retell this marvelous story. Help them to recall the details, the dialogue. Finish the retelling with the last line, the heart of the story,

"for the jar of flour and the bottle of oil did not go empty, just as God had said through the prophet Elijah."

*After reading the Gospel*, ask the children to retell this story. What it lacks in detail, it provides in tenderness and imagination. Though this widow is not described nor does she speak, we might imagine her. We might see her through Jesus' eyes.

- Why does Jesus praise this poor widow?
- How is she like the woman in the first reading?
- What does God promise when we give truly from our hearts?

Help the children understand that these stories teach us that God calls us to be generous—not always with money (Gospel) but in sharing what we have (first reading).

An alternative to a direct reading might be to act out this little Gospel passage. Ask several children to take the part of the rich, each putting in their offering with great flair. The poor widow is so hidden among them that she is noticed only by Jesus.

Others will be disciples with Jesus. The only words spoken are those of Jesus as he sees the widow, placing her coins in the treasury.

"This poor widow. . ."

129

# THIRTY-THIRD SUNDAY IN ORDINARY TIME

## YEAR B

### PRAYER OF THE DAY:

God of heaven and earth,
you want us all
one day to live in your home,
and you will send
Jesus Christ to take us there.
Show us
how to prepare for him
and be ready when he comes,
so that we can be with you
in happiness,
forever and ever.

### FOCUS OF THE READINGS:

The focus of our readings is much like that of the first Sunday of Advent—the coming of Christ at the end of time. Our church year begins and ends with the conviction that Christ will come again and that he will bring judgment. We are told here, as we were in Advent, that we cannot know when that time will come. In Advent, we were told to "stay awake, be ready." Now, at the close of the year, we are told to look for signs.

Our reading from *Mark* tells us what some of these signs are that will signal the end. These signs, however, are apocalyptic—that is, dealing with the future, the last days in highly symbolic language. These signs are meant to convey something which is not known for certain—the time of salvation—and are not to be taken literally. The focus is not on the signs, but on the conviction that Christ will come again. For Christians, the Second Coming is awaited with joy. The apocalyptic language appears to suggest fear, but not for those "who are wise and have helped bring about justice" — not for those who believe.

### FIRST READING: *Daniel 12:1-3*

*This is a reading from the prophet Daniel.*

The time is coming when the great prince,
Michael, will come.
He will protect you.
At that time there will be much suffering,
but you will be safe.
Everyone whose name
is written in the book of life will be safe.

Those who have already died will wake up.
Some will live forever in happiness,
but others will be punished.
The people who are wise,
and who have helped bring about justice,
will shine like beautiful stars forever.

*The Word of the Lord.*

### RESPONSE: *Psalm 27*

O God, noth-ing can take us from your love,_____

(Fine)

_____ noth-ing can take us from your love._____

VERSES: to Response

1. God, my light and my sal - va - tion,____ you are my help.____
2. You are al - ways there to love me,____ you keep me safe.____
3. And when e - vil is a - round me,____ I have no fear.____

## GOSPEL ACCLAMATION:

Your Word is a-live and it lives in our hearts. Al-le-
lu-ia to God for the Word in our hearts.

## GOSPEL: *Mark 13:22-23, 26-32*

*This is a reading from the Gospel of Mark.*

*When the time for the end of the world is near,
many things will happen.*

People will come and do great things,
even miracles.
They will claim to be Christ
or one of the great prophets.
They will try to make you stop believing in God.
I am telling you these things
so you will be careful and be on your guard.

And when the end of the world is very near,
people will see the Son of Man coming.
He will come with great power and glory.
He will send his angels all over the earth
to gather his chosen people together.

[I will explain this
by using the example of a fig tree.
When the branches of the tree
become soft and green,
and leaves begin to grow on them,
you know that summer is almost here.
It's the same way with the things
I have been telling you.
When you see the things
that I told you would happen,
you will know that the end of the world
is almost here.]

And I tell you the truth,
everything will come to an end,
even the earth and the sky.
But my Word will never end.
What I say will last forever.
No one knows exactly
when all of this will happen.
God is the only one who knows.

*The Gospel of the Lord.*

[ ] *Reader may omit text that appears in brackets.*

REFLECTING ON THE READINGS
WITH CHILDREN:

*After the Gospel*, ask the children to recall what they heard. Language of suffering and death (first reading) is sometimes frightening to children. We do not want to pretend that it isn't real. Suffering and death are part of life. But Christians, however young, gradually (very gradually) come to see this as part of the mystery of Christ and, therefore, part of our salvation. Ask the children if they remember the Psalm Response. You may wish to sing it again. That is the point we want to stress. Nothing can take us from the love of God. God has promised that to us. Ask the children if they have ever heard someone say, "I give you my word." What does that mean? Ask them if they remember what Jesus said about his word in the Gospel. "My word will never end." We have the word of Jesus that nothing can take us from the love of God. Ask the children how they feel about that.

This would be a good time to focus on the many ways we experience God's constant love for us. Ask the children to recall ways that God has shown love and protection to them.

They should leave secure in the conviction that Christ will come again and that we will live with him forever. The coming of Christ is a time of joy, not fear, for those who believe.

131

# CHRIST THE KING

## YEAR B

### PRAYER OF THE DAY:

Loving Lord God,
you have put us
in the gentle care
of Jesus Christ, your Son.
Make us faithful to him,
our leader,
and always obey
his commands with love.
We make this prayer
through the same Jesus
who lives with you
and the Holy Spirit,
one God, forever and ever.

### FOCUS OF THE READINGS:

Our readings focus on Christ as
supreme ruler of all nations and
peoples. In our readings from
*Revelation*, Christ is revealed as the
eternal God, who is, was and always
will be, the Alpha and Omega. In his
reign we have been made priests to
serve our God. The emphasis is on
Christ triumphant.

Our Gospel reading portrays
Jesus as a misunderstood king on
trial for his life. His kingship is not
denied, but he insists that it is not of
this world. He is king of truth. If he
is king of truth for us, we listen to
his voice.

### FIRST READING: *Revelation 1:5-8*

*This is a reading from the book of Revelation.*

Jesus Christ is the faithful witness,
the first to rise from the dead!
He is the ruler of the kings on earth!
Jesus loves us
and has freed us from sin by dying for us.
He has made us priests in a royal kingdom
to serve our God.
All glory and power belong to Jesus,
forever and ever,
Amen!

The Lord God says:

["I am the Alpha and Omega,
the beginning and the end.]
I am the Lord God who is, who always was,
and who will come again."

*The Word of the Lord.*

[ ] *Reader may omit text that appears in brackets.*

### RESPONSE/GOSPEL ACCLAMATION:
*Psalm 47*

RESPONSE:

To you, great King of all the earth: sing al - le - lu - ia, sing! To

you, our Lord, our God and King: sing al - le - lu - ia, sing!

GOSPEL: *John 18:33b-37*

*This is a reading from the Gospel of John.*

Pilate asked Jesus,

"Are you the King of the Jews?"

Jesus answered,

"Are you asking this because you think I am
or because others told you about me?"

Pilate said,

"I am not a Jew!
Your own people and leaders
brought you here for me to judge you!
What have you done wrong?"

Jesus said,

"My kingdom is not a kingdom of this world."

Pilate said,

"So, you are a King?"

Jesus answered,

"You say that I am a King.
I was born into this world
to give witness to the truth.
Anyone who lives by the truth
listens to my voice."

*The Gospel of the Lord.*

## REFLECTING ON THE READINGS WITH CHILDREN:

With children it will not be easy to distinguish between the concept of "king" as we know it in the world and the "kingship" of Jesus.

Nevertheless, this distinction must be made. We would advise against all comparisons to earthly kings, whether verbal or concrete. To compare Jesus to earthly kings is to miss the point of his kingship, which is spiritual. The children should see Jesus as the one—and only one—who reigns in our hearts.

We suggest the reflection be made on the first reading. The reading from *Revelation* gives a wonderful review of all we have seen and heard of Jesus during the previous Sundays. We might review this with the children so that they (and we!) may conclude that, indeed, Jesus is Lord.

He is the faithful witness; recall the stories of Jesus continuing in his prophetic mission, even when he was rejected.

He is the first to rise from the dead; recall the stories of Jesus' power over death in the raising of the little daughter of Jairus and of his own Resurrection.

He is the ruler of kings on earth; you might recall the epiphany.

He loves us and freed us from sin by dying for us; you might recall the many times Jesus said, "your sins are forgiven" and again the stories of the Resurrection.

He has made us priests in a royal kingdom to serve our God; recall the many times Jesus called us to service—you must be the servant of all, and so forth.

Yes, "all glory and power belong to Jesus forever and ever. Amen."

The Minister of the Word will be able to recall specific Sundays that highlight the above attributes of Christ. This can only serve as a wonderful review of the glory and power of Jesus in the world and in their lives.

# Holy Days,
# Feasts of the Lord,
# and
# Solemnities

## PRESENTATION OF THE LORD

### YEAR B

### PRAYER OF THE DAY:

O God,
you have shown
such love for us.
You sent
your only Son, Jesus,
to save us.
You have given us great joy.
You have given us Light,
through Jesus Christ,
your Son.

### FOCUS OF THE READINGS:

The focus of our readings is God's presence in the temple, the one to be adored. In the first reading, the prophet Malachi tells us that God will send a messenger to prepare for the one to come. The Lord of the covenant is coming to the temple and will call all people to change their lives. Christian tradition has seen in this prophecy the persons of John the Baptist and Jesus.

The Gospel recounts the day that Mary and Joseph present Jesus in the temple. There, in the temple, he is recognized by both Simeon and Anna as the fulfillment of God's promise. He is the Savior of the Israelites and the Gentiles as well. But the Gospel also forewarns that this Savior will suffer and will be a sign of contradiction among his own people.

*Jesus is the Light and Savior of the world.*

### FIRST READING: *Malachi 3:1-4*

*This is a reading from the prophet Malachi.*

Our God says:

"See, I am sending my messenger
to prepare the way for me.
The One you are waiting for is coming.
The Lord of the covenant
is coming to the temple
and will call everyone to change their lives
and do what is right.
Then the people will make offerings
that are pleasing to me,
just as they did long ago."

*The Word of the Lord.*

### RESPONSE: *Psalm 24*

RESPONSE:

O - pen the gates! O - pen the gates! Let the King of glo-ry in!

### GOSPEL ACCLAMATION:

"I have seen the Sav - ior, the light of the world.

I have seen the Sav - ior," Al - le - lu - ia!

**GOSPEL:** *Luke 2:22, 24-25, 27-36, 38-40*

*This is a reading from the Gospel of Luke.*

Mary and Joseph brought Jesus
to the temple in Jerusalem
to present him to God
and to make an offering of two turtledoves.
That same day,
a man named Simeon came to the temple.
He was a good and holy man
and was waiting for the Messiah to come.
When Simeon saw the child Jesus,
he took him in his arms and praised God.
He said,

> "Now, God, you have kept your promise.
> I have seen the Savior.
> He is the light of the Gentiles
> and the glory of your people Israel."

[Jesus' mother and father were amazed
at what Simeon said about him.
Then Simeon blessed them and said to Mary,
Jesus' mother,

> "This child will be a sign
> for all the people of Israel.
> Some people will accept him and be saved.
> Others will reject him.
> And in your heart
> you will suffer because of this."]

There was also a holy woman,
a prophetess named Anna,
who was in the temple.
When she saw the child,
she, too, began to praise God.
And she talked about him to everyone
who was waiting for the Messiah to come.

Mary and Joseph went back to Nazareth.
And the child, Jesus, grew in size and strength.
He was filled with the wisdom and grace of God.

*The Gospel of the Lord.*

[ ] *Reader may omit text that appears in brackets.*

REFLECTING ON THE READINGS
WITH CHILDREN:

Explain to the children that it was
customary to take the first child
(son) to the temple to be consecrated
to God. Since this rite was specific to
the first male child only, we will not
want to compare it to Christian
baptism. This was a Jewish ceremony
which included a rite of purification
and the offering of a sacrifice. In this
case, the offering was two turtledoves,
the offering of the poor.

Two points might be emphasized
in today's Gospel.

1) Simeon, the holy man,
recognized Jesus as the Light and
Savior of the world. *He is our Light
and our Savior.* Help the children
understand what this means in our
everyday lives.

● How is Jesus our Light?
● How is Jesus our Savior?

Remind the children that we
often use a candle as a symbol of
Christ:

● Easter candle,
● a baptism candle,
● an altar candle,
● a sanctuary lamp.

2) Anna, the prophetess, "talked
about him to everyone who was
waiting for the Messiah." Many
people today are waiting for a sign of
hope, for help, for light, for salvation.
Can we talk to them about Jesus?
*Can we, like Anna, tell others the
Good News of Jesus?*

137

# BIRTH OF JOHN THE BAPTIST

## YEAR B

### PRAYER OF THE DAY:

O God,
you are with us every day.
Each one of us
has been given special gifts.
John the Baptist
was chosen
to preach to the people.
Help each of us
to see our gifts
and to use them
to spread your Good News
through Jesus Christ,
your Son.

### FOCUS OF THE READINGS:

Our readings focus on the call of the disciples.

The first reading is one of four passages in Isaiah referred to as "Songs of the Servant." The church has normally seen these passages fulfilled in Christ. Today, this second servant song is applied to John the Baptist. The reasons are obvious. The prophet was called and named before birth. God fills him with strength and honor, and his mission is to preach.

The Gospel picks up these themes with the birth of John the Baptist. Even before the child is born, his name, John, has been determined. He lived in the desert where God filled him with strength and holiness to preach to the people, announcing the coming of the Messiah, the light.

### FIRST READING: *Isaiah 49:1, 3, 5-6*

*This is a reading from the prophet Isaiah.*

This is what the prophet Isaiah said:

"Listen to me, people everywhere!
God chose me even before I was born.
When I was still in my mother's body,
God gave me my name.
God's hand is always upon me
to give me strength.
And I am honored in God's eyes.

"God said to me,

'You are my servant.
You are the one
who will lead my people back to me.
And I will make you a light to all people
so that they may be saved.' "

*The Word of the Lord.*

### RESPONSE: *Psalm 71*

I have been yours since the day of my birth, and you have been my God.___ been my God.___

## GOSPEL ACCLAMATION:

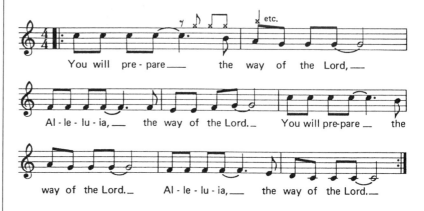

You will pre-pare___ the way of the Lord, ___ Al-le-lu-ia, ___ the way of the Lord. ___ You will pre-pare ___ the way of the Lord. _ Al-le-lu-ia, ___ the way of the Lord. _

## GOSPEL: *Luke 1:57-66, 80*

*This is a reading from the Gospel of Luke.*

When it was time
for Elizabeth to have her child,
she gave birth to a son,
and her neighbors and relatives
rejoiced with her.
When the baby was eight days old,
they came to circumcise him.
The people wanted to call him Zechariah
because that was his father's name.
But Elizabeth, his mother, said,

"No, his name will be John."

The people said,

"But no one in your family is called John."

So they asked his father, Zechariah,
what he wanted to name the baby.
Zechariah asked them
for something to write on, and he wrote,

"His name is John."

And immediately after this,
Zechariah could talk again,
and he began to praise God.
Everyone who heard about this
wondered what it all meant.
They were talking about it
all over the hill country of Judaea
where Elizabeth and Zechariah lived.
The people asked themselves,

"What is this child going to be
when he grows up?"

John grew and became strong and holy.
And he lived in the desert
until it was time for him
to preach to the people.

*The Gospel of the Lord.*

REFLECTING ON THE READINGS
WITH CHILDREN:

*Before the Gospel*, tell the children
we are going to hear the story about
the birth of John the Baptist.

- Does anyone know the name of
  his parents?
- What do you know (remember)
  about Elizabeth? about
  Zechariah?

If the children do not know the
background of these two, tell them,
so that the Gospel for today will
make sense.

- Zechariah was a priest who lost
  his speech because he didn't
  believe the message of the angel.
- Zechariah and Elizabeth were
  old and had no children.

*After the Gospel*, recall the story.
If the children have difficulty
verbalizing it, ask questions that will
help them.

- Why do we celebrate the feast of
  John the Baptist?
- What do you know about John
  the Baptist?
- Where did he live?
- What did he preach about?
- What did he do? Where?
- Who is the special person John
  baptized?

God did a very special thing for
Zechariah and Elizabeth. But the
birth of John the Baptist is special
for us too.

- What do you think makes this
  feast so special?
- What do you want to remember
  from today's celebrations?

# SS PETER AND PAUL, APOSTLES

## YEAR B

### PRAYER OF THE DAY:

You are our rock,
O God.
We know you are there
when we need you.
Help us to learn
from the strength
of Peter and Paul.
Let us never forget
your love.
We ask this
through your Son,
Jesus Christ.

### FOCUS OF THE READINGS:

The readings focus on the special
mission of two of the greatest leaders
of the church. The first reading is
somewhat of a farewell discourse.
Paul seems certain that, having gone
the limit, he will be killed for the
faith. As he approaches his
martyrdom, Paul is confident and
even joyful. The Gospel gives us the
beginning of Peter's ministry.
Having professed faith in the person
of Christ, he is assured of the
permanence of the church and his
role in it.

### FIRST READING: *2 Timothy 4:6-8, 17-18*

*This is a reading
from Paul's second letter to Timothy.*

I am sure that I am going to be killed
because I preach about Jesus.
I have done my best in the race,
and I have stayed faithful.
So I know that the Lord will give me a crown
on that special day when he comes back.
He will reward everyone who loves him
and stays faithful.
The Lord has always been with me
and made me strong
so that I could proclaim the Word of God
to people everywhere.
The Lord has always helped me,
and he will save me from every evil
and keep me safe for heaven.
May everyone give praise and glory to the Lord
forever and ever. Amen.

*The Word of the Lord.*

### RESPONSE: *Psalm 71*

RESPONSE:

I will pro-claim your pow - er. I will pro-claim your won-der-ful
deeds! I will pro-claim sal - va - tion, and your faith - ful love! ___

### GOSPEL ACCLAMATION:

Je - sus asked them: "Who am I?" 1. Pe - ter an-swered:
2. Al - le - lu - ia,
1.-2."You are ___ the Christ, you are ___ the Son of the Liv - ing God!"

GOSPEL: *Matthew 16:13-19*

*This is a reading from the Gospel of Matthew.*

When Jesus and his disciples
were in the area of Caesarea Philippi,
he asked his disciples,

   "Who do people think I am?"

They said,

   "Some people think you are John the Baptist,
      and others think you are the prophet Elijah.
   But there are others
   who say you are Jeremiah
   or some other prophet."

Jesus asked them,

   "And who do you say I am?"

Simon Peter answered,

   "You are the Christ.
   You are the Son of the living God."

Jesus·said,

   "Simon, you are blessed.
   You did not learn that
   from any human being.
   No, God told you that.
   From now on you will be called Peter,
   which means rock.
   I will build my Church on this rock,
   and it will be strong.
   Nothing will be able to destroy it.
   I will give you the keys
   to the kingdom of heaven,
   so that what you decide on earth
   will be the same in heaven."

*The Gospel of the Lord.*

REFLECTING ON THE READINGS
WITH CHILDREN:

   Since the Gospel reading appears
elsewhere in the Sunday readings
(Twenty-First Sunday in Ordinary
Time/Year A), it would seem
appropriate today to concentrate on
the two men themselves. Peter and
Paul stand out among the saints, and
even the apostles, as two giants of
the early church. Their common
feast has been celebrated in the
church since the year 258.

   There are several books for
children which contain the lives of
Peter and Paul which may be useful
for presenting the highlights of their
lives. We will want to avoid,
however, pictures and stories which
do not correspond to the Biblical
presentation. For example, many
books for both children and adults
show pictures of Paul falling from a
horse on the road to Damascus.
There is no indication in any of the
several accounts of Paul's conversion
which suggests that. The accounts of
their lives should focus on reality
and the great contribution of these
two men.

# THE TRANSFIGURATION OF THE LORD

## YEAR B

## PRAYER OF THE DAY:

O God in heaven,
you have given us
the greatest gift of all.
You sent Jesus
to live with us
and to show us how to love.
We will listen, God.
We will do our best for you
and your Son, Jesus,
our Lord.

*Note: In keeping with the* Directory for Masses With Children *(Paragraph 43), the authors have elected to use the Gospel from Year C instead of Year B because it seems best suited "to the capacity of children."*

## FOCUS OF THE READINGS:

In each cycle, the Gospel account of the Transfiguration is the same as the Gospel reading for the Second Sunday of Lent. We suggest you use the reflections for that Sunday. We reprint them here for your convenience.

## FIRST READING: *2 Peter 1:16-19*

*This is a reading from the second letter of Peter.*

Brothers and sisters,

When we told you about the power of the Lord,
Jesus Christ, and how he would come again,
we were not just telling you interesting stories
that someone made up.
No, we saw the majesty of Jesus.
We were with Jesus on the holy mountain
when God showed how special Jesus is,
and we heard the voice of God saying,

"This is my beloved Son.
I am very pleased with him."

We are sure now
that what the prophets said a long time ago
is true.
You should listen very carefully
to what they said
because it is like a lamp shining in a dark place
until the daylight comes.

*The Word of the Lord.*

## RESPONSE/ GOSPEL ACCLAMATION: *2 Peter 1:17*

A voice from heav-en said,____ "This is my be-lov-ed Son."____

____ Al-le-lu-ia. Al-le-lu-ia.____ Al-le-lu-ia. Al-le-lu-

ia.____ Al-le-lu-ia. Al-le-lu-ia. Al-le-lu-ia.

## GOSPEL: *Mark 9:2-10*

*This is a reading from the Gospel of Mark.*

Jesus took Peter, James, and John
up on a high mountain.
While they were there,
a change came over Jesus.
As they were watching him,
his clothes became a dazzling white —
whiter than anyone could wash them.
Suddenly, they saw Moses and Elijah
talking with Jesus.
Peter spoke up and said to Jesus,

> "Master, it is good for us to be here!
>   Let us make three tents:
>   one for you, one for Moses,
>   and one for Elijah."

Peter really didn't know what to say
because, like James and John,
he was amazed and frightened
by what he was seeing.
Then the shadow of a cloud came over them,
and a voice came from the cloud saying:

> "This is my beloved Son.  Listen to him."

Suddenly, they didn't see
Moses and Elijah anymore.
They only saw Jesus.
As they came down the mountain,
Jesus told them not to tell anyone
what they had seen
until he had risen from the dead.
So they didn't.
But they kept wondering what Jesus meant
when he said that he would rise from the dead.

*The Gospel of the Lord.*

REFLECTING ON THE READINGS
WITH CHILDREN:

While heeding the call of God can be understood by children, the notion of being killed for the faith may not serve as a suitable model of response.

Ask the children to recall what they heard. If they have difficulty recalling, you may wish to help them with questions such as:

- Who did Jesus take with him to the mountain?
- What happened while they were there?
- Who did Peter, James, and John see with Jesus?
- What did Peter say?  What did Peter, James, and John hear God say?

Ask the children if they have ever seen previews of coming attractions on television or in a theater. Help them understand that previews tell us about the coming attraction and help us look forward to it.

At the Transfiguration, Jesus was giving a preview of what he will be like after the Resurrection. He was also showing us that we will be like him. We will live with him in glory. As Jesus was showing this to Peter, James, and John, God told them what we must do to live with Jesus forever.

Do you remember what God said to Peter, James, and John?  God tells us, too, "This is my beloved Son, listen to him."

How do we listen to Jesus today:
- in the Bible?
- in our parents and others who teach us?
- in the good thoughts we have that encourage us to do the right thing, and so forth?

## THE ASSUMPTION OF MARY

### YEAR B

### PRAYER OF THE DAY:

O God in heaven,
you sent your only Son, Jesus,
to live among us.
You made Mary his mother.
How happy she must have been
to share in Jesus' life.
Let us learn from Mary, O God,
and from Jesus Christ,
your Son, our Lord,
forever and ever.

### FOCUS OF THE READINGS:

Both of our readings, as they are chosen and placed together for this feast, tell us something about the place of Mary in the church. The reading from *Revelation*, rich in symbolism, presents Mary in various aspects of her role in the church. She is the Mother of the Son born to be the Messiah. She is the image of the church with the 12 stars (12 tribes of Israel, 12 apostles) around her head. And the crown seems to indicate her entrance into heaven where she received the reward of those who remain faithful (*2 Tim. 4:8*).

The Gospel reading, usually called "The Visitation," indicates the real meaning of today's feast. Mary is the Mother of the Lord, and all generations will call her blessed because she believed. The feast of the Assumption places Mary among the Blessed and indeed the model of the Blessed.

### REFLECTING ON THE READINGS WITH CHILDREN:

Rather than reflecting on the readings specifically, it may be appropriate to reflect on the meaning of the feast.

### FIRST READING: *Revelation 12:1-2, 5-6, 10a*

*This is a reading from the book of Revelation.*

I, John, had a vision.
I saw a woman with the sun shining on her,
and the moon was under her feet.
She was wearing a crown on her head,
and it was made of twelve stars.
The woman was expecting a child,
and she was crying in pain.
She had a baby boy,
and he immediately
was taken up to God's throne
because this child
was to become the ruler of the world.
And the woman went to the desert
where God had prepared a place for her.

Then I heard a voice in heaven say,

"Christ has come with all the power
    and authority of God's kingdom.
    Now salvation is here."

*The Word of the Lord.*

### RESPONSE: *Psalm 24*

RESPONSE:

O - pen the gates! O - pen the gates! Let the King of glo-ry in!

### GOSPEL ACCLAMATION:

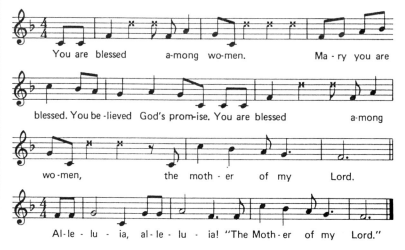

You are blessed a-mong wo-men. Ma - ry you are blessed. You be-lieved God's prom-ise. You are blessed a-mong wo-men, the moth - er of my Lord.

Al-le - lu - ia, al-le - lu - ia! "The Moth-er of my Lord."

144

## GOSPEL: *Luke 1:39-56*

*This is a reading from the Gospel of Luke.*

When the angel Gabriel told Mary
that her cousin, Elizabeth,
was also going to have a baby,
Mary went as quickly as she could to the town
where Zechariah and Elizabeth lived,
up in the hill country of Judah.
As soon as Elizabeth heard Mary's voice,
the baby inside her began to move.
Elizabeth was filled with the Holy Spirit,
and she said to Mary,

"Of all the women on earth,
you are most blessed.
And the baby in your womb is also blessed.
I am so honored because you,
the mother of my Lord,
have come to visit me!
You are blessed, Mary,
because you believed in the promise
that God made to you."

And Mary said,

"I sing with praise the greatness of the Lord,
and my heart finds joy in my Savior.
The Lord has chosen me, a humble servant;
now all people will say I am blessed.
The Lord, who is mighty,
has done great things for me.
Holy is God's name.
God has destroyed the power
of people who are proud,
and honored those who are poor and humble.
God has given good food to hungry people
and sent the rich away with nothing.
God has come to help the people of Israel
because of the promise
made to Abraham and Sarah
and their family forever."

Mary stayed with Elizabeth about three months
and then returned to her home in Nazareth.

*The Gospel of the Lord.*

The feast celebrates Mary's entrance into heaven. It tells us that human beings are destined to live, like Mary, in heaven, in the presence of God. But why was Mary taken to heaven? Why has the church celebrated this feast centuries before it was proclaimed as dogma in 1950? This would be a good time to help the children see the "blessedness" of Mary as she is presented in Scripture.

Ask the children what they remember about Mary. The obvious is that she gave birth to Jesus. Help the children recall the main features of Luke's story of the Annunciation.

- What does this tell us about Mary? *She was a woman of faith.*

Mary at Bethlehem

- What does this tell us about Mary? *She was a wife and mother.*

Mary at the Temple

- What does this tell us about Mary? *She was a woman who followed her religion.*

Mary at Cana

- What does this tell us about Mary? *She was a woman who cared for the needs of others.*

Mary at the foot of the Cross

- What does this tell us about Mary? *She remained faithful to the end.*

Mary at Pentecost

- What does this tell us about Mary? *She was a woman of prayer.*

Help the children see that these qualities are what makes Mary special and why we know she is in heaven. Mary is a human being, a woman of great faith to be imitated by all believers. And we too, when we live that way, will be in heaven.

*Note: This may be an occasion to give the children a small picture or holy card of Mary.*

# TRIUMPH OF THE CROSS

## YEAR B

### PRAYER OF THE DAY:

Praise you, O God,
for loving us enough
to send your only Son
among us.
Your love is never ending.
Your love lives on
with Jesus Christ,
your Son,
forever and ever.

### FOCUS OF THE READINGS:

Our readings focus on the entire
life of Christ. It would be a mistake
to see the cross, the death, and
resurrection as the total message of
today. Both of our readings put the
Triumph of the Cross as the climax
of a total life given for us, beginning
with the Incarnation.

The first stanza of the first
reading tells us that Jesus was always
God. At a point in history, he
became a human being and lived in
every way like us. Because, as a
human being, he obeyed God in
everything, even though it meant he
would be killed, God raised him to a
new life after he died. Death on a
cross has become the sign of God's
power over death.

The Gospel gives us the reason for
Jesus' coming to earth. "God loved
the world so much." Jesus is the
visible expression of God's
unconditional love for us. Everyone
who believes that Jesus came, lived
and died for us, and was raised to
new life, will live forever.

### FIRST READING: *Philippians 2:5-11*

*This is a reading
from Paul's letter to the Philippians.*

You must think and live like Christ.
Even though he was always God,
Jesus did not try to hold onto that.
Instead, he became a human being just like us.

As a human being, he lived a humble life.
Jesus obeyed God in everything,
even though it meant he would die on a cross.
Because Jesus obeyed God in everything,
God raised him up and gave him the name
which is above every other name,
so that at the name of Jesus
everyone should kneel and worship him.
Everyone in heaven,
on earth and everywhere
should give glory to God
by proclaiming, "Jesus Christ is Lord!"

*The Word of the Lord.*

### RESPONSE: *Psalm 34*

Glo-ri-fy God, glo-ri-fy God, glo-ri-fy God with me. Let us praise God's ho-ly name. Glo-ri-fy God glo-ri-fy God's ho-ly name!

## GOSPEL ACCLAMATION:

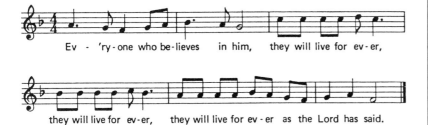

Ev - 'ry-one who be-lieves in him, they will live for ev-er,

they will live for ev-er, they will live for ev-er as the Lord has said.

## GOSPEL: *John 3:14-18a*

*This is a reading from the Gospel of John.*

Jesus said to Nicodemus,

"God's Chosen One must be lifted up
so that everyone who believes in him
will live forever.

"Yes, God loved the world so much
that God sent the only Son into the world
so that everyone who believes in him
will live forever.

"God did not send the Son
to judge the world,
but to save it.
And everyone who believes in him
will live forever."

*The Gospel of the Lord.*

## REFLECTING ON THE READINGS WITH CHILDREN:

Neither of our readings has a "story line" which will be easy for children to follow, understand and retain.

You might ask the children to recall what they heard in the first reading. It might be helpful to read the text slowly, stopping after each stanza. Ask the children what they think is the most important line in each stanza. Perhaps you could help them arrive at the following and write these on a large poster.

- He became a human being just like us.
- He obeyed God in everything.
- God raised him up.
- Jesus Christ is Lord.

We, like Jesus, want to obey God in everything. And we, like Jesus, will be raised up after we die.

- Why do you think God sent Jesus?

Let's listen to the Gospel and hear what St. John tells us.

*After the Gospel*, ask the children what John tells us about why Jesus came into the world. God loved the world (us) so much.

Ask the children what sentence was repeated three times. Add this to the large poster.

- Everyone who believes in him will live forever.

Note: As there are no leaflets for the feasts, you may wish to have the important lines of the first reading already prepared on a paper which the children can take home, decorate and put in their room. (You might change the pronoun He to Jesus.)

## ALL SAINTS

## YEAR B

## PRAYER OF THE DAY:

We love you, God.
As members
of your family,
we want to show you
our love by living
as Jesus did,
in your name,
forever and ever.

### FOCUS OF THE READINGS:

The feast of All Saints focuses attention on two of our fundamental beliefs as Christians: we are baptized into a community and we will live forever. We celebrate today our union with all those believers, children of God, who have been "rewarded in heaven," and now see God.

The first reading focuses on our life as Christians here and now. *We are children of God now!* As such, we must try to be good and pure as we wait for the day when Jesus will come again, and we will see him as he is and be like him. And so, the reading also pulls us into the future. We live a life of "already/not yet." We are *already* children of God, but we are *not yet* perfect like Jesus.

The Gospel too focuses on the already/not yet, but with an emphasis on the future. We are assured of reward in heaven, the blessing to come, when we live the life of Jesus. It is this assurance of seeing God and eternal life of blessing that motivates us to live the beatitudes here and now. Combined, these readings present the Christian view of both present and future.

*The saints are those children of God who have lived the beatitudes.*

## FIRST READING: *1 John 3:1-3*

*This is a reading from the first letter of John.*

Brothers and sisters,

See how much God loves us!
We are called children of God.
And that is who we really are, God's children.
We know that when Jesus comes again,
we will be like him
because we will see him as he really is.
Everyone who believes this
tries to be good and pure,
just as Jesus is good and pure.

*The Word of the Lord.*

## RESPONSE: *Psalm 15*

RESPONSE:

Those who seek your face, Lord, with a pure heart shall stand in your Holy Place!

# GOSPEL ACCLAMATION:

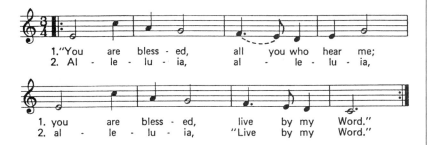

1. "You are bless - ed, all you who hear me;
2. Al - le - lu - ia, al - le - lu - ia,

1. you are bless - ed, live by my Word."
2. al - le - lu - ia, "Live by my Word."

## GOSPEL: *Matthew 5:1-12*

*This is a reading from the Gospel of Matthew.*

Jesus and his disciples went up on a mountain, and they sat down so Jesus could teach them. Jesus said to his disciples,

> "Blessed are people who know they need God,
>   for the kingdom of heaven belongs to them.
> Blessed are people who are sad now,
>   for later God will comfort them.
> Blessed are people who are humble,
>   for God will give them everything.
> Blessed are people who work for justice,
>   for God will give them all they need.
> Blessed are people who give mercy to others,
>   for God will have mercy on them.
> Blessed are people
>   who have hearts that are pure,
>   for they will see God.
> Blessed are people who make peace,
>   for they will be called children of God.
> Blessed are people who suffer
>   for doing what is right,
>   for the kingdom of heaven belongs to them.

["And you are blessed when people hurt you
  and say bad things about you
  because you believe in me.
  Be happy and glad,
  for God will reward you in heaven."]

*The Gospel of the Lord.*

[ ] *Reader may omit text that appears in brackets.*

REFLECTING ON THE READINGS
WITH CHILDREN:

We want to emphasize with the children that we live the beatitudes because we are children of God. The beatitudes are, for Christians, a way of life. We do not need to earn our relationship with God by living the beatitudes; we are already children of God.

You might compare this to family relationships. Members of a loving family do not need to earn the love of one another by being good and kind. They are good and kind because they already love one another.

We belong to the family of God. We are truly God's children and so we live as children of God. We know that we are not perfect, but one day we will see Jesus, our brother, as he really is and we will be like him. The beatitudes tell us how we should live until that day.

The saints are people who did that. They live forever with God. Today would be an ideal time to share the lives of some saints who are special to your parish or city.

# ALL SOULS

## YEAR B

## PRAYER OF THE DAY:

Your love is strong,
O God.
Nothing can stop you
from loving us.
Help us be strong too,
O God,
strong enough to live
as Jesus lived,
in your name.
Amen.

*Note: In keeping with the* Directory for Masses With Children *(Paragraph 43), the authors have elected to use readings from selections offered for* Masses for the Dead *instead of the All Souls readings because they seem better suited "to the capacity of children."*

## FOCUS OF THE READINGS:

Our readings focus on death and eternal life. The first reading assures us that nothing, not even death, can separate us from the love of God. God intended us to live forever and revealed that explicitly in Jesus Christ. We have God's promise, and nothing can take that from us.

The Gospel gives us the image of the seed which must die in order to bear fruit. The grain of wheat, when buried, becomes hidden. Only this burial will allow it to grow into what God intended it to become. Jesus himself was the example of this for us. Only by dying could he rise to new life. Death, then, becomes the process through which we become the person God intended us to become, to be lifted up by Christ, and to live with him forever. We come to this new life not only through physical death, but by being willing in our daily lives to give up our lives for others.

## FIRST READING: *Romans 8:31-34, 38-39*

*This is a reading
from Paul's letter to the Romans.*

If God is on our side,
who will be against us?
Surely not God,
who was willing to give up even Jesus
for our sake.
God has saved us through Jesus.
No one can take that away from us.

If God is on our side,
who will reject us?
Surely not Christ Jesus,
who died and was raised to life
and is now with God to help us.
I am sure that nothing
will ever take us away
from the love of God.
Not death, not anything in life,
nothing now or in the future —
nothing will ever take us away from God's love,
which is in Christ Jesus, our Lord!

*The Word of the Lord.*

## RESPONSE: *Psalm 27*

RESPONSE: *Gently*

O God, noth-ing can take us from your love, _____
noth - ing can take us from your love. _____

VERSES: to Response

1. I be-lieve that I will see you. __ Keep my heart strong. __
2. And when e - vil is a - round me, __ I have no fear. _____

## GOSPEL ACCLAMATION:

"Those who give up their lives for me, they will live for ev-er,

they will live for ev-er, they will live for ev-er," as the Lord has said.

**GOSPEL:** *John 12:24-25, 32-33*

*This is a reading from the Gospel of John.*

Jesus said to Philip and Andrew,

"You know that if you do not bury
  a grain of wheat,
  it stays just one grain of wheat.
  But if you do bury it in the ground,
  it grows and becomes many grains.

"In the same way,
  those who try to hold onto their lives
  will lose them.
  But those who are willing
  to give up their lives
  will live forever.
  And when I am lifted up,
  I will bring all people to me."

When he said this,
Jesus was telling them how he was going to die.

*The Gospel of the Lord.*

REFLECTING ON THE READINGS
WITH CHILDREN:

Let the sung response be the reflection on the first reading. Through the gentleness and memorable quality of the refrain, the children will conclude that nothing can take us from God's love.

*After the Gospel,* show the children a seed. Ask them what a seed will become if it stays on the table or in an envelope. Most children will know that a seed must be planted in order to grow. It must be buried in the earth. Discuss this process with them. After it is buried, we no longer see it. It seems like nothing is happening to it. Then one day, we see a sprout. It's growing. That means it's really alive. Now it doesn't look like a grain, but wheat.

Jesus tells us that our death is like that. When people die, it looks like the end. But, like the grain of wheat, they are alive and one day will be raised to a new kind of life. We don't know what we will look like or be like, but we will be alive. Jesus showed us that this is true because he died and was raised to a new life, and he is now alive and with us.

# DEDICATION OF ST. JOHN LATERAN

## YEAR B

## PRAYER OF THE DAY:

Loving God,
you have given each of us
a place to call our own—
a home in your own House.
Thank you, God,
for the love
you share with us,
forever and ever.

*Note: In keeping with the* Directory for Masses With Children *(Paragraph 43), the authors have elected to use the Gospel from the 31st Sunday in Ordinary Time, Year C because it seems better suited "to the capacity of children."*

### FOCUS OF THE READINGS:

Today's feast focuses on the church. The particular church, St. John Lateran in Rome, is the cathedral church of the Bishop of Rome and is also therefore the symbol of the universal church. Several choices for readings are permissible for this feast, all of which point to the true nature of the church.

In the first reading, Paul tells us that we are the temple of God. Since the word "you" is in the plural in Greek, it is clear that Paul speaks of the Christian community as the church.

The Gospel is good news for sinners! The church, the presence of Christ, is for sinners! Christ is the church, and he says to Zacchaeus, "I want to stay at your house." The church is the gathering of sinners—those who are lost—around the Lord.

### REFLECTING ON THE READINGS WITH CHILDREN:

The concept of church as Body of Christ or Presence of Christ will be too abstract for most children. Children will naturally associate church with the building. However we can at least plant the seeds.

*After the first reading,* ask the children to recall the image Paul used. A

## FIRST READING: *1 Corinthians 3:9b-11, 16-17*

*This is a reading
from Paul's first letter to the Corinthians.*

You are like a building that belongs to God.
God asked me to begin forming you,
and I used all my talent
to build a good foundation for you.
And that foundation is Jesus Christ.
So, really, you are God's temple,
and God's Spirit lives in you.
God will punish anyone
who tries to destroy that temple.
For God's temple is holy,
and you are God's temple!

*The Word of the Lord.*

## RESPONSE: *Psalm 122*

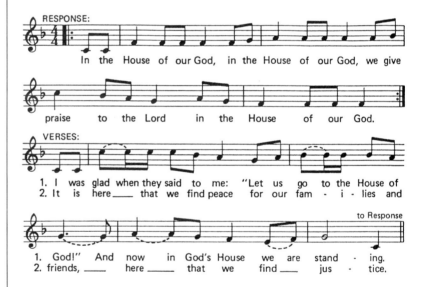

In the House of our God, in the House of our God, we give praise to the Lord in the House of our God.

VERSES:
1. I was glad when they said to me: "Let us go to the House of God!" And now in God's House we are stand-ing.
2. It is here that we find peace for our fam-i-lies and friends, here that we find jus-tice.

## GOSPEL ACCLAMATION:

1. Je-sus said: "Zac-che-us come down for I want to stay with you."
2. Al-le-lu-ia, al-le-lu-ia! "For I want to stay with you."

## GOSPEL: *Luke 19:1-10*

*This is a reading from the Gospel of Luke.*

Jesus was going through the city of Jericho,
and lots of people came out to see him.
There was a man there, named Zacchaeus,
who was the head of all the tax collectors
and was very rich.
Zacchaeus also wanted to see Jesus
and find out who he was.
But Zacchaeus was a very short man
and couldn't see Jesus through the crowd.
So he ran ahead
and climbed up into a sycamore tree
and waited for Jesus to pass by.

When Jesus came to that place,
he looked up and said,

> "Zacchaeus, come down!  Hurry!
>   I want to stay at your house today!"

Zacchaeus was so excited that he hurried down
and welcomed Jesus into his home.
The people who saw this were angry and said,

> "Look, this man Jesus
>   is staying in the home of a sinner!"

But Zacchaeus said to Jesus,

> "Lord, I am going to give
>   half of everything I have to the poor.
>   And if I have ever cheated anyone
>   out of money,
>   I am going to pay them back
>   four times as much."

Then Jesus said to Zacchaeus,

> "Today you have been saved
>   because you, too,
>   are one of the family of Abraham.
>   For I have come to seek
>   and to save the people who are lost."

*The Gospel of the Lord.*

building is a place where people live or work.

- What special "building" are we?

Try to help the children see that we use the word "church" in two ways.  It is the building but also the group of Christians who go there.  You might suggest this as a comparison.  If we have a Christian gathering—for example, a mass in the park—that is also the church.  If a group of Christians gather to prepare food for the poor, that is also the church.  Whenever we do things in the name of Christ, that's the church.  When we say we belong to the church, we don't mean the building; we mean the Christian community.

The children will relate much more easily to the story of Zacchaeus.  If you feel it appropriate, reflect only on the Gospel.  The encounter between Jesus and Zacchaeus is joyful and easy to enter into.  Perhaps there is a little Zacchaeus in all of us!

We suggest you follow the same reflections given for the Thirty-first Sunday in Ordinary Time, Year C.  They are reprinted here for your convenience.

This Gospel story will almost always appeal to children.  There is a light heartedness to it that makes of the encounter between Zacchaeus and Jesus an event we naturally want to applaud to show our joy.

Invite the children to recall and visualize.  Help them to imagine the scene.

- The crowds,
- Jesus and those with him,
- Zacchaeus scurrying along, looking for an open space, and finally running to climb the sycamore tree.
- What might the crowd have been like?
- Why did everyone want to see Jesus?
- Who was Zacchaeus?
- Why did he want to see Jesus?
- How did Jesus and Zacchaeus meet? (It is important that the children see that Jesus spoke first to a sinner. Jesus sought him out.)
- What did Jesus say to Zacchaeus? (Emphasize that he *ate* in Zacchaeus' house.)
- How did Zacchaeus respond?

Two points should be emphasized:

1.  Jesus came to look for sinners so he could save them.

2.  When we truly meet Jesus, we change our lives.

# PART TWO

# 1. Introduction to the Sunday Readings

*"What we have heard, and what we have seen with our own eyes; what we have watched and touched with our own hands, we proclaim to you so that you may be in union with us, as we are in union with God and with the Son, Jesus Christ. And we are writing this to you so that our joy may be complete"* (1 John 1:1, 3, 4).

The first disciples, filled with the joy of the Resurrection, were consumed with the desire to proclaim the Good News! This Good News of God's faithful and unconditional love continues to be proclaimed in the church today, especially in the liturgy. In a special way, this saving word is embodied in the sacred scriptures. The Second Vatican Council reminds us that God is truly present to us in the scriptures, and that this word reveals God's saving love and also nourishes us on our journey of faith. For this reason, the church teaches that all the Christian faithful should have easy access to the sacred scriptures and that translations and versions should be prepared which could more easily be read and understood by the people of God. (Paragraphs 22 and 25, *Constitution on Divine Revelation.)*

The church is also concerned with the availability and understanding of the scriptures for children, who, as members of God's family, have their rightful place in the church.

*"Jesus said, 'Let the little children come to me; do not stop them; for it is to such as these that the kingdom of God belongs.' Then he put his arms around them, laid his hands on them, and gave them his blessing"* (Mark 10:14, 16).

Jesus made a special point of welcoming children. In his great love for them, he put his arms around them and gave them his blessing. The scripture readings in SUNDAY have been adapted so that children may more easily understand the word of God, and through that word, be touched and blessed by this same Jesus who is ever present in his word.

These children have the right to hear God's word, and God wants them to hear it. We are all aware, however, of the difficulty they have in understanding the word since the scriptures were written in a language for adults which is beyond the capacity of little children.

Happily, the Congregation for Divine Worship recognized this difficulty and provided a means for solving it. The *Directory for Masses With Children*, issued on November 1, 1973 opens the door for realizing the dream of parents, catechists and priests to make the word of God accessible and understood by children. This challenging document calls us to use *"words and signs"* in our liturgies which are *"sufficiently adapted to the capacity of children"* (Par. 2). The challenge to provide such adaptation, especially of the scripture readings, is aided by the prudent and useful guidelines provided within the document itself where ministers of the word with children are encouraged to make selections and adaptations of texts guided primarily by the *"spiritual advantage which the readings can offer children"* (Par. 44).

All those who minister to children in a formal capacity, as well as parents who long to share their faith with their own children, are aware of the necessity for such adaptation. It is to assist in this important ministry that we have prepared scripture readings for each Sunday. Our selection and adaptation of these readings has been guided by four principles.

*1. Retain the Sunday Readings of the Liturgical Year.*

The Bible, a collection of seventy-three books, was written over a period of some 1800 years, in various places by a myriad of authors. Through these books, we come to see that each human being neither receives nor transmits God's revelation in exactly the same way. The various authors wrote on different topics using a variety of literary forms such as poetry, prose, narration, epic story, letter, etc. By recognizing the variety of the readings, we are open to more of God's revelation to us.

The church has spread these readings over the course of a three-year cycle during which we hear selections from both the Old and New Testaments, including nearly every book in the Bible. Through them we are in touch with the faith community throughout the ages and we hear God's call for a response in our own time.

In the Liturgy of the Word, children, too, receive God's wonderful revelation through the readings and are invited to respond in their daily lives. In almost all circumstances, therefore, the choice of readings already assigned for each Sunday has been preserved. In this way, the children may experience the mystery of God's love for them as it is unfolded during the liturgical year.

There are, however, some readings which are particularly problematic for children. In these instances, an alternative reading has been selected in accordance with the *Directory for Masses With Children.*

*"If all the readings assigned to the day seem to be unsuited to the capacity of children, it is permissible to choose readings or a reading from the Lectionary for Mass or directly from the Bible, taking into account the liturgical seasons"* (Par. 43).

Young children often have difficulty being attentive to three readings within one liturgical celebration. With this in mind, we have presented two readings for each Sunday.

Because of the harmony which usually exists between the first reading, from the Old Testament, and the reading from the gospel, we have generally adapted these two. On occasion, however, when deemed more suitable for children, the second reading replaces the Old Testament reading. It remains for the minister of the word to determine the suitability of reading only the gospel or using the two readings presented.

*"If three or even two readings on Sundays and weekdays can be understood by children only with difficulty, it is permissible to read two or one of them, but the reading of the gospel should never be omitted"* ( Par. 42).

*2. Remain Faithful to the Meaning of the Text.*

Since Christ himself is present in his word and in the assembly of the faithful, the scriptures, as the inspired word of God, always speak to us on some level. While not all of the meaning of each text is clear to adults, and certainly not to children, it is true for both adults and children that frequent reading of the scriptures reveals more and more of the meaning of that which was received initially as a seed to be nurtured. It is often through unfamiliar parables and images that God's message is revealed, and it is our prayerful meditation of these parables and images that cultivates in us a profound sense of the mystery of God's presence and unconditional love for us.

Children, who are especially open to wonder and mystery, are often easily led to a deeper level of faith and a desire to respond to God through the proclamation of the word. Any adaptation of the readings must, therefore, remain faithful to the rich images and literary forms used by the sacred writers to reveal God's love and saving power. In order that this fidelity be safeguarded, the *Directory* insists that adaptations *"should be done cautiously and in such a way that the meaning of the texts or the sense and, as it were, style of the scriptures are not mutilated"* (Par. 43). And further: *"Paraphrases of scripture should, therefore, be avoided"* (Par. 45).

In all cases, the authentic meaning of the text has clearly been preserved, even when this meaning will not be immediately evident to all children.

### 3. Use Language That is Intelligible to Children.

It is evident that children sometimes fail to understand the word simply because it is couched in words beyond their learning. If children are to understand the scriptures and be nourished by them, every effort must be made to make adaptations using a language appropriate to their capacity of comprehension. There is no question here of watering down the word of God or of rendering it in current colloquialisms. It is, rather, a question of being familiar with the vocabulary level and language structure of the age range for which the adaptation is being made. Often the meaning of an entire passage will be made clear to children by reducing multisyllabic words to a simpler vocabulary or by rearranging the order of the words in a sentence. In instances where sentences are unusually long or contain a number of clauses, we have separated these into shorter, more direct sentences.

Some exceptions to the principle of simpler vocabulary have been made. Frequently, the names of cities and the use of words or phrases in Hebrew or Aramaic have been retained. For example, in *Mark* 5:21-43 (Thirteenth Sunday of Ordinary Time, Year B*)*, we have kept the phrase *"Talitha kum"* which means "Little girl, get up, I tell you." And in *Mark* 7:31-37 (Twenty-third Sunday of Ordinary Time, Year B*)*, we retain the word *"Ephphatha"* which means "be opened." These words and phrases are as foreign to adults as they are to children, yet they have become part of our scriptural heritage and do not pose a problem for us. In fact, these bits and pieces of the original language seem to make a particular passage come alive for us. By retaining these, we hope to enlarge the biblical vocabulary of the children and at the same time expose them to some of the flavor of the time in which the scriptures were written.

Apart from these few exceptions, there has been a consistent effort to present the readings in a simple, direct language which should be easily understood by children between the ages of seven and twelve. Recognizing that children's comprehension levels may vary greatly, even within a two year span, we have concentrated on the vocabulary level of the seven- and eight-year-old. In this way, the readings will be easily understood by older children and by some younger children. Many catechists and ministers of the word will have children much younger, perhaps three to six years old. Until such time when readings are prepared specifically for these children, we encourage ministers of the word to freely adapt these readings still further. Again, we call upon the guideline given in the *Directory for Masses With Children* which tells us that the primary goal is *"the spiritual advantage the readings can offer the children."*

### 4. Use a Language Which is Inclusive of All God's People.

Since the renewal of the liturgy, which made possible the use of the vernacular, the Christian community has become more aware of the language used in liturgical celebrations, especially the Eucharist. While this language has been almost exclusively masculine, many now recognize that whatever the origins of this practice, both historical and grammatical, the use of exclusive language does not represent the true meaning of the sacred scriptures or the true nature of the church and should, therefore, be avoided in revisions of liturgical texts and translations of the Bible.

Because children relate more easily with concrete terms than with abstract concepts, the need for inclusive language is particularly important. The use of exclusively masculine or feminine language at liturgical celebrations may develop for them a limited image of God, God's people and ministry in the church. The readings in liturgical celebrations proclaim God's saving word for all people and it is important that children hear and understand this. We have, therefore, adapted the readings using a language which is inclusive of both men and women when this is clearly the intention of the sacred writer.

In presenting these Sunday readings adapted for children, we wish to encourage all ministers of the Word, the professionals, the volunteers, and especially the newcomers, to continue in their important ministry in the church. As a further aid, we have included this background information on the Sunday readings and liturgical seasons. This Weekly Leader Guide includes suggestions for reflecting on the word with the children, background materials for the minister of the word, dramatizations, music, responses, gospel acclamations, seasonal reflections and a prayer for each Sunday.

With SUNDAY, we wish to affirm and support those who desire to share the word of God with children, of whom Jesus said, *"The kingdom of God belongs to such as these"* (Mark 10:14).

## 2. Introduction to the Liturgical Seasons

Most people enjoy celebrations. Birthdays, weddings, graduations, football victories, centennials, ship launchings are just a few of the occasions people celebrate, sometimes quietly and intimately, sometimes loudly and with great gusto.

The church, for all its seriousness of purpose, is no laggard when it comes to celebrating. Indeed, the liturgy, the heartbeat of the church, is celebration. We do not say or read the liturgy, we celebrate it. Every time we come together for the liturgy we celebrate an event, a happening in the long history of God's dealings with men and women down the ages. Liturgy is the unfolding of the story of our salvation through, with, and in Jesus Christ.

This celebration takes place within two inter-linked cycles: one which we call the seasons and the other, the saints. The cycle of seasonal liturgies (Advent, Christmas, Lent, Easter and Ordinary Time) commemorates the principal events of our redemption, while the sanctoral

cycle, as it is called, commemorates particular men and women who have lived out that redemption in a special way.

Liturgical celebrations are important because the church assembles not just to look back to long-past events, but to participate fully in those same saving events. Through the liturgy, the full effects of the work of our salvation are made present: we become part of them, they become part of us. The unfolding in the liturgical seasons of the life and times of Jesus Christ is at the same time an invitation to us to actively participate in that life. Each liturgy presents us not with a faded memory or a lesson from the past, but with the grace-filled effects of that event, made present in the proclamation of God's Word and the celebration of the sacrament by a people called by God. To celebrate the liturgy is as effective for our redemption as if we had been personally present on the historical occasion commemorated. So, celebrating Christmas is more than a pleasant memory; it is involvement with the incarnation of our Savior, Jesus Christ.

Sunday is central to the church's annual cycle of celebrations. It is a journey on which we follow in the path of Christ, fully and really. By so doing we are caught up in his great journey, the victory over sin and death, which we call the paschal mystery.

A final word. The events of our salvation in Christ were, on his part, acts of worship of the God who sent him. Our participation in the unfolding history of our redemption—celebrated in the church's year and in the power of the Spirit—is, therefore, a participation in the greatest possible act of worship. What could be more important than the church's liturgy?

## 3. Season of Advent

Advent is a time of expectation, a time of preparing for the coming of the Lord. Expectation and preparation are part of the Christian way of life. We are on a journey of faith, pressing forward with greater or lesser zeal, toward the kingdom. In one breath we can say, "The Lord has come," and in the next, "He will come again." To celebrate the future hope of Christians is to celebrate that element which makes faith complete.

The Advent liturgy keeps this expectation alive. The gospel readings in all three cycles of the lectionary begin the season on the First Sunday of Advent with Jesus' warning about the unexpectedness of the end of all things and our need to be prepared for it, at whatever time it should come. The Second and Third Sundays of Advent throw a spotlight on the person and teaching of John the Baptist. This emphasis might appear at first sight to place John in the role of prophet of the imminent birth of the Savior at Bethlehem, until we remember that, according to the gospels, John exercised his ministry long after Jesus' birth, directly before his public ministry.

It is only on the Fourth Sunday of Advent that the gospel readings unequivocally turn their attention to the events leading up to Jesus' birth to Mary. It would help our understanding of the full meaning of Advent if we were to remain more faithful to the pattern laid down by the season's gospels. Commercial pressures and pre-Christmas Nativity plays, not to mention Christmas parties in early December, diminish the meaning of the preparation of Advent.

Consequently, long before the season begins, children will have been looking forward to the actual celebration of Christmas and the gifts which will accompany it. This is a pity. Such early anticipation of the climax diminishes the force and meaning of the time of preparation.

We should perhaps recognize more clearly other liturgical signs of the season and point them out to the children. First, there is the omission of the *Glory to God*, a hymn of joy, at all eucharistic celebrations of the season, though it is doubtful that a young child will notice this anyway. More noticeable is the use of liturgical colors for vestments and, in some churches, the

absence of flowers. Once upon a time, Advent was invested with many more signs of penance, and perhaps the attempt to make it into a mini-Lent was going too far, but at least we should not treat Christmas as if it were already here.

What the liturgy of Advent does, and what we should help the children to begin to understand, is fill us with expectation and an attitude of hope. The readings tell us that we should be on the watch, always ready, not only for the celebration of the birthday of Jesus, but also for his second coming, which puts the first one into perspective. Christianity is a faith for the future.

# 4. *Introduction to the Prophet Isaiah*

During cycle A, all of the Old Testament readings for the liturgy come from the book of *Isaiah*, and in cycle B three come from *Isaiah*; cycle C presents passages from four different prophets. Throughout the Advent season, even the gospel readings are heavily laced with quotations from the book of *Isaiah*. Because this book plays such an important part in our Advent readings, we will give a brief, general introduction to it as a backdrop for the more specific, liturgical introductions for the individual Sundays.

It is generally agreed by biblical scholars today that the sixty-six chapters of the book of *Isaiah* are not the work of a single prophet, but rather the work of two, or possibly three writers. While many theories about this have been presented by various scholars, it is commonly thought that the book can be divided into two major sections: chapters 1-39 being the work of the eighth century prophet, Isaiah, and chapters 40-66 the work of a prophet who lived after the Babylonian exile, perhaps in the fourth century B.C. The major reason for dividing the book into these two sections is that the content, style of writing, and audience are clearly different after chapter 39. Accordingly, chapters 1-39 are called *First Isaiah*, and chapters 40-66 are called *Second Isaiah*. (You may also find them called "Proto-Isaiah" and " Deutero-Isaiah." ) The readings for cycle A come from *First Isaiah* and in cycle B from *Second Isaiah*.

*First Isaiah (Chapters 1-39)*

Isaiah identifies himself in the opening verse of the book, and throughout the early chapters, gives us some of the details of his life. He speaks of his call and his fear of responding to that call. In chapter six he tells of his conversion from this fear to a willingness to be the spokesperson of God. From his writing we know also that Isaiah was married to a prophetess and that they had at least two children. He was an educated man who had easy access to the kings of his time, and to other members of the royalty. He tells us that he prophesied during the reigns of "Uzziah, Jotham, Ahaz, and Hezekiah, kings of Judah" (1:1). This places Isaiah in Jerusalem during the eighth century B.C.

Isaiah's task was to guide his nation through a critical period. The people were rooted in the tradition of King David and longed for a return to that golden period in their history. During the eighth century, God's promise of a "lasting dynasty in the House of David" seemed doomed. The prosperity and glory of Judah as a leading nation were fading, and the Assyrians were a constant threat to their security and independence.

From Isaiah's prophecies, it seems that God's people responded to these events by yielding to the temptation of compromising with foreign nations and, as it were, bargaining for their security rather than trusting in God. Coupled with this was the arrogant attitude that if God were truly on their side, they could do as they pleased and God would come through in the end. For Isaiah, both of these attitudes were sins of pride against the very holiness of God.

At this same time, the nation was changing from an agricultural society to a more stratified society with a class structure. Isaiah witnessed the increasing gap between the rich and the poor and the injustices that resulted from it. Those who were prosperous soon forgot the communal nature of God's chosen people!

These sins of pride and blatant injustices reflected the neglect of the moral standards expected in the covenant and resulted in a breakdown of national strength and security. Isaiah preached that God, who is holy and faithful, would surely save Israel, but would also surely punish them for their sins. Hence, Isaiah consistently proclaimed that the fall of Israel and Judah would be the punishment of their infidelity, and at the same time, he gives a constant call to return to the covenant, to live justly and to trust in the God who would forgive and redeem them.

*Second Isaiah (Chapters 40-66)*

Whereas the prophet of *First Isaiah* clearly identifies himself, the prophet of *Second Isaiah* remains anonymous. From his writing, however, we can say that he lived during the time of the Babylonian exile. Throughout his prophecy, the destruction of the city of Jerusalem and the temple, the suffering of the people in exile are presumed. His is a message of comfort and hope (40:1). He assures the people that God will restore Israel through Cyrus, the King of Persia.

*Second Isaiah*'s writing is highly liturgical, using psalms and hymns as a primary literary form. His attention is focused on the restoration of Jerusalem and the temple, the place of worship. God's people will be brought back from the desert (40:3) and will be made secure in Jerusalem.

*Second Isaiah* speaks of God in a language that seems to take on a more personal dimension. He speaks of God's intimate relationship with the people of Israel and describes God's fidelity and salvation in personal, relational images of mother, father and shepherd. The time of redemption also seems to take a more personal shape. Primarily, redemption or salvation meant freedom from oppression and a time when Israel would again be a secure, powerful nation. It was a time when God would restore strength and power to Israel. This time was called messianic time which means "the time of anointing." From this we have our word "Messiah," which means "the anointed one."

During the time of *Second Isaiah*, this messianic hope became focused on a person who would be God's anointed one. This Messiah is described as the servant of God who will proclaim truth and will atone for the sins of the people. Though he will suffer greatly, God will vindicate him. Quite obviously, Christianity has seen in these passages the foreshadowing of Jesus. These passages which describe the servant are called the "songs of the suffering servant." The notion of a person being the redeemer, the savior, and who embodies the suffering of the people distinguishes *Second Isaiah* from all former prophecy, including *First Isaiah*.

Above all, *Second Isaiah*, while exposing again the sins of Israel, proclaims the message that salvation is sure. God is our Redeemer.

# 5. *Introduction to Jeremiah, Baruch, Zephania & Micah*

The prophets of the Old Testament provide us with the backdrop for the New Testament and prepare us for the coming of Christ. As we read the prophets in the context of liturgy, we must always remember the nature of their ministry. They worked in and through the political and social order of their day, challenging and exhorting the people, especially the leaders, to return to the covenant and remain faithful to the ways of God.

During cycles A and B, we hear from the prophet Isaiah. In cycle C, we hear the message of four different prophets from the 7th and 8th century BC.

## *Jeremiah*

Jeremiah appears as perhaps the most human of the prophets. Often reluctant to fulfill his role, his writing reveals the pain and agony he experienced in being faithful. Yet, as a public figure, Jeremiah maintained uncompromising fidelity, though he was often commanded to present God's message through rather strange signs. For example, he was commanded not to marry or have children as a sign to the people that they were not living in harmony with God and that a complete restoration was in order. Jeremiah lived a life of hope and despair; he was loved and hated, ridiculed and respected. Through it all, his message was consistent: return to the covenant. Live in justice and God will save you.

## *Baruch*

Baruch is best known as the secretary to Jeremiah. What we know of him is gleaned from the book of *Jeremiah* rather than from the book which bears his name. Much of the book of *Jeremiah* was either dictated to Baruch or written by him, and he sometimes delivered the messages to the people in Jeremiah's name. The last ten chapters contain a lengthy biography of Jeremiah, written by his faithful servant, Baruch.

## *Zephania*

Zephania was a man of great conviction who spoke out fearlessly against the infidelities of his people. Though he issues strong warnings, he speaks of the "Anawim," the faithful remnant who will enjoy salvation. Of his personal life, we know almost nothing, except that he was descended from Hezekiah, who may be the King Hezekiah so often mentioned in the Old Testament.

## *Micah*

Micah came from the small village of Morsheth in Southwest Judah. Coming from a peasant background, he was familiar with the injustices suffered by the poor at the hands of the rich. In unpolished and often blunt language, he spoke out against every kind of injustice; those of the leaders, the priests and prophets, as well as the common people. Because of his constant demand for justice as the true worship of God, Micah is known as the prophet of social justice.

# 6. The Season of Christmas

That the Son of God should have taken upon himself our human nature is the most astounding and incomprehensible truth we can imagine. Indeed, it is beyond all imagining: for we know the truth only because it has been revealed to us by the power of the Holy Spirit. The joy and excitement which permeates this season is not misplaced.

The exchange of gifts which marks this entire season is thoroughly appropriate as an active symbol of God's gift to us, sinners as we are. But should we be carried away by emotion and excitement, the liturgy firmly stresses the seriousness and, if you will, the practicality of the gift. *". . . The child born today is the Savior of the world"* (prayer after communion), *". . . all the ends of the earth shall see the salvation of our God"* (first reading). *"Today in the town of David, a Savior has been born to you"* (Gospel). The child born in the stable has come not just to be among us, but to save us from our sins.

Soon after Christmas Day, we celebrate the feast of the Holy Family. Less than helpful artistic representations of what the life of Jesus, Mary and Joseph was thought to be like, and moralizing meditations of Christian family life, have tended to obscure the truth of this feast. As the gospel for cycle B tells us: *"Meanwhile, the child grew to maturity, and he was filled with wisdom; and God's favor was with him."* Jesus was truly a human being, like us in all things but sin. He lived, learned, loved and laughed like any other child of his time. He was one of us. Yet, even in the midst of the joys of Christmas, a more sombre note is struck. All three gospels of the lectionary cycle for the Holy Family speak of tension, threat, perplexity, like distant thunder announcing an impending storm. The flight from Herod's persecution, Simon's prophecy of the piercing sword, and the loss of the child in Jerusalem warn us of a mission to be accomplished.

The epiphany sheds a sharper light on that aspect of the season. *"Today you revealed in Christ your eternal plan of salvation and showed him as the light of all peoples"* (Preface of the Epiphany). He is not a passive Emmanuel, a God-among-us with no function. On the contrary, he is the Savior of all, sent by God to proclaim the Good News and lead all peoples to the peace and joy of the kingdom. That this is God's will is made abundantly clear at the very end of the Christmas season when, at the Baptism of the Lord, we hear a voice from heaven, *"This is my Son, the Beloved; my favor rests on him."*

Savior, Son, beloved though he is, Jesus seeks our free cooperation. For his mission to succeed, we must respond with a constant "yes!" The first and most complete "yes" was uttered by Mary. The solemnity of Mary is celebrated on January 1st and is a reminder of the humility and love with which we must match—that of Jesus himself. *"Let it be done to me according to your word!"* is echoed by *"your will be done"* as Jesus prayed in Gethsemane.

# 7. Introduction to the Infancy Narratives

All of our gospel readings for the Christmas season, as well as the last Sunday of Advent, come from the Infancy Narratives of Matthew and Luke. These wonderful stories tell us, in vivid images, of the unique Son of God who was born of a young virgin, and the virgin's name was Mary. They present Jesus as the One of whom the prophets spoke, the One who fulfills the expectations and desires of the people of Israel. He is Messiah and Savior, Light to the Gentiles and Lord of all.

The Infancy Narratives are a witness to all that the early Christians believed about Christ. But, in reading, praying and proclaiming the Infancy Narratives, we need to guard against two extremes. The first is to assume that these events were meant to be presented literally and are, therefore, historically accurate in every detail. On the other hand, we want to avoid rejecting the narratives as not historical and, therefore, regard them as pure legend. The purpose of the Infancy Narratives, in the view of most scripture scholars, may best be summarized in the words of the Jerome Biblical Commentary: *"The details of the narratives are symbolic and Biblical. They communicate the mystery of redemption, not a diary of early events."*

We have, perhaps, become accustomed to the Christmas story with all the details of the shepherds, the star, magi, angels, manger, etc. seen together. Yet, when we look at the two narratives separately, we find two stories that are entirely different in their presentation, both in the telling of events and in mood. For example, Matthew speaks of the star guiding the magi to Bethlehem where they adore the newborn King. Luke, on the other hand, tells us of the shepherds who, at the word of the angels, came to Bethlehem to find the child, lying in a manger.

Matthew, a Jew writing for Jewish converts, presents Jesus as one who experiences the struggles of his people, even from his birth. Throughout the narrative, we read of fear, suspicion, danger and concern for the survival of the infant. In Matthew's narrative, Jesus shares in the struggles of his Jewish ancestors and, at the same time, fulfills their hopes for salvation.

Matthew uses the language and images familiar to his Jewish audience. His narrative is written within a patriarchal context. The annunciation is made to Joseph. Joseph is to name the child. Joseph leads the family to safety, and when they return from Egypt, he settles in Nazareth.

Luke, too, used the language and images which would speak to his people. But he and his Christian community were not primarily Jewish, but Gentile in origin, with a variety of backgrounds. So his narrative is one which appeals to a more universal audience. His narrative is written around a whole host of characters, Jewish and non-Jewish, rich and poor, men and women. His audience was not part of the struggle common to Matthew's community; so his narrative is filled not with struggle but with songs of joy, sung by Zachariah, Mary, the angels, and Simeon.

Nor is Luke's community a patriarchal society. In his gospel, the annunciation is made to Mary. Mary is to name the child. Mary takes the good news to the hill country of Judea. Mary is addressed by Simeon and Anna in the temple, and Mary treasures all these things in her heart.

Whatever the differences in detail, both Matthew and Luke present the central mystery: Jesus was conceived by the power of the Holy Spirit and was born of the Virgin Mary. We are invited through their vivid and varied images to read the story of the birth of this child and, in faith, to see "more than meets the eye."

# 8. *Season of Lent*

Lent is the season with the strongest liturgy. Ashes, palms, purple vestments, omission of alleluia—all intertwined with finely tuned texts—contribute to a liturgy which makes a deep impression on all who take part in it.

Lent is a time of preparation. First and foremost, the church is concerned with the preparation of the catechumens who are to be initiated into the Christian community at the Easter Vigil services. On the First Sunday of Lent they appear before the community which gives its assent to them becoming elect, and so may embark on the final period of prayer and purification.

Lent is a time of reflection and celebration in which, especially on the third, fourth and fifth Sundays, the community prays with the men and women who are soon to become their brothers and sisters in the Lord. As the gospel stories of Jesus' encounter with the Samaritan woman at the well (third Sunday), of the healing of the man born blind (fourth Sunday) and the raising of Lazarus (fifth Sunday) unfold, all those assembled for worship are plunged once again into a renewed understanding of what it is that happens to us when we are initiated into the community which is Christ.

Lent is also a time of renewal. If the baptismal waters beckon the initiates onward, the ashes are a spur to those who have long since been members of the Christian community but have lost something of their first innocence. As the baptized accompany the soon-to-be-baptized on their journey of faith, they enter a period of prayer and fasting which must be a constant feature of the Christian way of life.

This is brought home to us graphically on the first Sunday in all three cycles when we hear the account of Jesus' time of prayer, fasting, and temptation in the desert. As he sets out on his journey to Jerusalem and his passover, we are reminded that our own journey will not reach its destination if it is not accompanied by the rejection of sin and a renewed adherence to the will of God.

That there is a destination of glory is emphasized in the account of the Transfiguration of Jesus, presented in the gospel of the second Sunday in all three cycles. Thereafter, cycle B continues the theme of dying and rising, particularly exemplified in Jesus' words that: *"unless a grain of wheat falls on the ground and dies, it remains a single grain; but if it dies, it yields a rich harvest"* (fifth Sunday).

Cycle C is more concerned with repentance and forgiveness. The moving and mysterious story of the adulterous woman (fifth Sunday) underlines the truth that if we turn from sin, the Lord will more than match our conversion with his loving forgiveness. On the preceding Sunday, we listen to the parable of the prodigal son, which perhaps best sums up our relationship with God. While we witness the catechumenal journey, we are reminded that we, too, share fully in a loving relationship with God. We have fallen away. But still, like the father of the prodigal son, God anxiously awaits our return so that we can be restored to our true home.

Passion Sunday, with its blessing and procession of palms and the reading of the accounts of the Passion by Matthew, Mark and Luke, launches us into the final period of Lent. Paradox, as always, is there: a triumphal entry into Jerusalem, only to end in Jesus' ignominious death. But, of course, we know that death is not really the end.

# 9. *Introduction to the Gospel of John*

*Who is John?*

The disciple who wrote the fourth Gospel tells in the last verses: *"This is the disciple who is bearing witness to these things, and who has written these things. And we know that his testimony is true."* This eyewitness to the life of Jesus is the "beloved disciple," the apostle John. He is one of the first to be called by Jesus. While fishing with his brother, James, and his father, Zebedee, he *"left everything and followed him."* John, unlike the other three evangelists, was with Jesus on some rather privileged occasions: the wedding feast at Cana, the healing of Peter's mother-in-law, the healing of Jairus' daughter, the Transfiguration, and he was seated next to Jesus at the Last Supper. His gospel reveals the closeness of their relationship.

*When and why did John write and for whom?*

John's gospel, composed near the end of the first century (90-100), was written for Christians who had never known the earthly Jesus. For John, Christians living in the second century and beyond have the same intimacy with the Lord as did those who were privileged to walk with him on earth. He sees Jesus as living among us in a sacramental way.

As a Palestinian Jew, John explains for his audience many of the things that would not be understood either by non-Jews or by those who lived after the events had taken place. For example, he explains why it would be unusual for Jesus to be speaking with the Samaritan woman (*John* 4) and why the parents of the blind man refused to speak (*John* 9).

*What are the special characteristics of John's gospel?*

There are many unique characteristics of the fourth gospel that make it quite different from the other three: his emphasis on the sacramental life of the church, his highly symbolic language and his emphasis on discipleship rather than a hierarchical church based on the apostles.

John presents the divinity of Christ through the signs that Jesus gives. Rather than concentrating on the miracles themselves, John sees in them the signs of who Jesus is. So, for example, at the wedding feast of Cana, John concludes by saying, *"this was the first of his signs, and his disciples believed in him."*

There are seven such signs in John's gospel. There are seven *"I am"* sayings: *"I am the bread, the light, the door, the shepherd, the Resurrection, the way, the vine."* When we recall that *"I am"* is the name of God revealed to Moses, we see in these *"I am"* sayings the revelation of Christ's divinity. This revelation reaches its climax in the confession of Thomas, *"My Lord and my God."* John's sacramental presentation is climaxed in the response of Jesus, *"Blessed are those who do not see (me) and have believed."*

It is for us, those who have not seen Jesus with our eyes, that John has written about the *"signs Jesus did in the presence of the disciples,"* that we *"might believe that Jesus is the Christ, the Son of God, and that believing, we may have life in his name."*

# 10. *Easter Season*

For fifty days, up to the celebration of the Spirit at Pentecost, the church rejoices in a special way in the risen Lord and in the life which he gave to his people. Yet the Resurrection is incomprehensible without the dying which goes before it. So Easter season begins with what we call the Easter Triduum. This starts with the celebration of the evening mass of the Lord's Supper, continues through the Good Friday Passion celebration, and so to the excitement of the Easter Vigil—three celebrations making the summit of the church's year.

Yet, not three celebrations, but one. The Triduum celebrates in word, song, silence and ritual the paschal mystery of Jesus Christ, his passing over from death to life, from this world to the reign of God. The entire life of Jesus may be seen as a journey, and it is in the last three days of Holy Week that we see and experience the journey reaching its conclusion. At the evening mass on Holy Thursday, we commemorate the passover meal which Jesus had longed to eat with his disciples (*Luke* 22:15). On Friday, we contemplate the moment when Jesus gave himself as the sacrificial victim of the new passover. Then, at the vigil service, Jesus' passover journey is completed, and we celebrate the Resurrection.

Others have also been on a journey, a passover. For some time past, the catechumens have been journeying in faith, and the Easter Vigil is that moment when, through the initiation sacraments of baptism, confirmation and Eucharist, their journey is united with Christ's. They participate in his dying and rising and become fully one with the Christian community. Thereafter, Easter season is the welcoming of the new members into the community and a continuing celebration of the Resurrection event.

With the feast of the Ascension of the Lord, we focus more sharply on the fact that Jesus' mission must become ours. We are to be his witnesses to the world. Even as Jesus is taken up into heaven "to sit at the right hand of God," where he reigns in glory, he promises that he will send his Spirit to be with us in carrying out this mission.

The Easter season is completed at Pentecost as we celebrate the coming of the Holy Spirit upon the church, which, transformed and empowered, proclaims God's word to the nations.

# 11. Introduction to the Acts of the Apostles

In all three cycles, the first reading throughout the Easter season comes from the *Acts of the Apostles*. It might be helpful, therefore, to have a short introduction to this exciting book.

*Who wrote the Acts of the Apostles?*

The introductions to the third gospel and the *Acts of the Apostles* indicate that they were written by the same author. From earliest times, it has been accepted that both were written by Luke as a single, two-volume work and were later separated in the canon of the New Testament.

Luke was a companion of St. Paul on at least one of his missionary journeys. In his letters, Paul refers to Luke as the beloved physician and twice mentions that Luke is with him as a co-worker. Luke describes himself as a careful writer who researches well before committing his story to writing.

*What is the purpose of the Acts of the Apostles?*

Luke tells us that in his first book, the gospel, he *"dealt with all that Jesus did and taught before he was taken up."* His purpose in *Acts* is to show the development of the church after Pentecost. *"When the Holy Spirit comes upon you, you are to be my witnesses in Jerusalem, throughout Judea and Samaria and to the ends of the earth"* (*Acts* 1:8). The rest of the book unfolds this mission, beginning with the speech of Peter on Pentecost in Jerusalem and concluding with the arrival of Paul in Rome, the city which symbolized *"the end of the earth."*

Through the speeches and activities of the disciples, but principally those of Peter and Paul, Luke stresses two main ideas. First, Jerusalem is the mother church, the place of its birth and the seat of its teaching. Second, through the power of the Holy Spirit, the church reaches out from Jerusalem to embrace the entire Gentile world. Luke recounts in vivid detail the missionary journeys of Paul which take him all over the known world. Throughout these journeys, Paul looks to the twelve apostles in Jerusalem for approval of his teaching. After telling us that Paul was taken to Rome and put under house arrest, Luke abruptly ends his book. His mission has been accomplished. Peter had proclaimed the Good News in Jerusalem and Paul had carried it to the ends of the earth.

*Why is this book so appropriate for the Easter season?*

Through the activities of the early disciples, we learn of the struggles and persecutions as well as the joys and successes of the early church. Under the guidance of the Holy Spirit, the first Christians lived in community, witnessed to the risen Lord, taught his message, preached his word, healed in his name, baptized converts and endured persecutions. From Jerusalem, the disciples proclaimed, in word and deed, the Good News of the Easter message: He is risen!

# 12. Sundays of the Year

Advent, Christmas season, Lent, and Easter season are the times of calling. In those seasons we celebrate the Incarnation and all the other events which made up Jesus' life on earth. It is a time of calling because it broadly commemorates the calling together of the community. "Come, follow me" is the key phrase.

A call is no use without a response. The Spirit has been sent upon the church so that we may make that response. The Sundays which follow Pentecost (the "green" Sundays) are, in a certain sense, the time of the Spirit in which the church sets forth to proclaim the living word of God. There is no imposed thematic structure for the 33 Sundays. They follow a pattern whereby the gospel of Matthew is proclaimed in cycle A, Mark in cycle B, and Luke in cycle C. The first reading from the Old Testament is selected to match some particular truth contained in the gospel of the day.

The season is concluded by the celebration of Christ the King. It is as if we are saying, *"The humble infant who grew to adulthood, preached the good news of reconciliation, brought it about in his death on the cross and rising from the dead, who sent his Spirit upon the church to complete his work, he is the King of all creation. Glory to him forevermore. Alleluia! Amen!"*

## 13. Formation of the Gospels

Over the course of the three-year cycle, we hear from each of the four evangelists and so receive the Good News of Jesus Christ from four united, yet quite distinct, sources. During cycle A, the gospel of Matthew is read; during cycle B, we have the gospel of Mark; cycle C presents the gospel of Luke. The gospel of John is read for most of the Sundays of the Easter season in all three cycles.

Each of these evangelists has a unique portrait of Jesus to present. As we prepare to enter into their gospels during the liturgy, we might ask ourselves what factors might account for four different portraits of the same person, Jesus the Christ?

In searching for our answer, it is important to realize that the gospel, the Good News, was handed on orally for over thirty years before it was written down in any organized way. Thus, the four written gospels, as we have them today, represent not the beginning but the final step in their formation. In a document issued by the Pontifical Biblical Commission in 1964, the three stages in the formation of the gospels are clearly outlined.

The *first stage* of the gospels is, of course, the actual ministry of Jesus. The Good News, from which we get our word "gospel," was first proclaimed by the life, death and resurrection of Jesus himself. In his preaching, his miracles, his encounters with others, he proclaimed the Good News of salvation. It is, therefore, the words and deeds of Jesus during his earthly ministry that are the source for all Christian tradition, both oral and written and, hence, the first stage in the formation of the gospels.

Traditionally, we say that this first stage lasted about three years, that is, from the baptism of Jesus until his crucifixion.

The *second stage* in the formation of the gospels is the ministry of Jesus as it was understood and preached orally by the disciples between the Resurrection of Jesus and the actual writing of the Gospels. This stage is very important in the formation of the Gospels, because it is here that the various portraits of Jesus begin to emerge. The early disciples had only one goal in preaching the Good News: to bring all people to the saving power of Jesus Christ, the Lord.

Obviously, Jesus did and said more than we find in the written Gospels. And so, even as we do today, the early preachers recounted those stories, deeds and words of Jesus which they found most appropriate for their local community in a particular time and in a particular place. Also, as is true today, no two preachers had the same style. Hence, the gospel came to take a slightly different shape in the various communities where the disciples went to preach. Some stories, deeds and words took on prominence in one area, others in another area. This second stage, which we might call "the oral gospel," became the substance for the gospels as we have them today.

The *third stage* in the process of the formation of the gospels spans a great number of years, perhaps from 65 to 110 AD. After years of handing on the gospel through oral preaching, disciples of those earlier eyewitnesses, the apostles, began the process of putting it into writing. Mark was the first to undertake this task sometime between 65 and 70 AD. The gospels of Matthew and Luke were written between 80 and 90 AD, using much of Mark's gospel as well as material from other sources, including the oral tradition in their local areas. The gospel of John, written between 90 and 110 AD, seems to be dependent on entirely separate sources. His gospel departs radically from the style and content of the first three. The individual style and content of each of the four will be discussed in separate introductions to each of the gospels.

All four, however, gathered their primary material from the oral tradition known to them. Each evangelist sought to bring the Good News to his contemporary community and so selected the material needed for his purpose and arranged it in the order and style best suited to his audience.

Some stories or incidents in the life of Jesus appear in only one of the four gospels. For example, the "Pearl of Great Price" appears only in *Matthew*, the parable of the Good Samaritan is found only in *Luke*, the story of the woman at the well is told only by John. Sometimes the same story will be found in two or more of the gospels but in a different order of events, with different details, and perhaps even a different meaning. In other words, the evangelists used the deeds and sayings of Jesus differently according to their audiences and their own understandings of the meaning of Jesus. The result of this is that we now have four accounts of the gospel, each with its unique presentation of the life, death and resurrection of Christ.

In reading the four gospels separately, allowing for the intention of each evangelist, we experience the richness of the early church as it sought to live and proclaim the meaning of the risen Lord. This is precisely why the church presents them separately in the three-year cycle.

# 14. Introduction to the Gospel of Matthew

*"As Jesus was walking, he saw a man named Matthew sitting by the customs house, and he said to him, 'Follow me.' And he got up and followed him"* (*Matthew*, 9:9).

*Who is Matthew?*

In the list of apostles, he is identified as "Matthew, the tax collector" (*Matthew* 10:3). Is Matthew, the tax collector and apostle, the author of the gospel which bears his name?

Given the situation of the gospel, which dates it near the end of the first century, around 80-90

AD, this seems unlikely. However, we may say that the author of this gospel is a disciple of the apostle and that he relies on the oral tradition that comes from Matthew's eyewitness account.

It was not at all unusual at that time to attach the name of an important person to one's work, either to give it prominence or to honor the person so named. It would seem that the author of this gospel has done so here. As is traditional, however, we continue to refer to the author as Matthew. Of all four evangelists, Matthew is the most clearly Jewish.

*Why and when did Matthew write?*

The gospel of Matthew was written near the end of the first century. His community had experienced a separation from the synagogue, the center of their relationship with God. The Jewish authorities had agreed that anyone who acknowledged Jesus as the Christ should be expelled (*John* 9:22). Accustomed to the rituals and ways of the synagogue, these Jewish Christians needed the assurance that Jesus himself was the Messiah and was now the center of their relationship with God. The primary purpose of Matthew's gospel, therefore, is to show Jesus as the Messiah.

*What are the specific characteristics of Matthew's gospel?*

Writing for a community of Jewish converts, he uses images, stories, references and literary techniques that are well-known to Jewish people. Matthew uses more Old Testament passages than the other three gospels combined. He frequently frames the teachings of Jesus in a dialogue with the Jewish teaching authorities, to whom he is superior.

Matthew appeals to the background of his audience. He does this by comparing Jesus to the figures of Jewish history who represented all that was ideal, all that looked forward to salvation. Jesus is the new Moses, the liberator par excellence. As Moses led the people from slavery in Egypt, so Jesus liberates us from the slavery of sin. As Moses gave the Ten Commandments on Mt. Sinai, so Jesus gives the fulfillment of this law in his sermon on the

Mount. Jesus is the new David. Just as David, the ideal king, was promised an everlasting kingdom, so Jesus is the Son of David, the king who inaugurates the kingdom of heaven here among us. This identification between Jesus and the Old Testament figures is seen clearly in Matthew's presentation of Jesus' family tree (*Matthew* 1:1-17). Whereas Luke traces the geneology to *"Adam, son of God"* (*Luke* 3:23-38), Matthew begins with *"Jesus Christ, son of David, son of Abraham."*

At the same time, this Jewish community was faced with an influx of Gentile converts. How does a people, who thought of themselves as the sole inheritors of God's salvation, come to accept the possibility of universal salvation? Matthew's Jesus reveals the fulfillment of God's promise to the Jews and the unfolding of a more universal plan of the same God. He insists that Jesus could be recognized as Messiah but was rejected by the Jews. This rejection has turned the mission of Jesus to the Gentiles. Matthew, at the end of the first century, wants his contemporary Jewish Christian community to avoid the blindness of earlier Jews. He calls them to faith in Jesus—the new Moses, the Son of David—who brings the old law to fulfillment in the reign of heaven, a reign which includes the Gentiles as well as the chosen people.

*The portrait of Jesus* that emerges from Matthew's gospel is Messiah, in the person of Emmanuel—God with us.

# 15. Introduction to the Gospel of Mark

## Who is Mark?

While we know very little about the actual person of Mark, some hints within his gospel allow us to make at least some attempt at a description. His careful attention to details and his vivid accounts may indicate that he was an eyewitness to the life of Jesus. Traditionally, it has been thought that Mark was a disciple and secretary to Peter. Some have suggested that he is the young man described in 14:51-52.

Here, Mark tells us that during the arrest of Jesus, a young man, wearing only a linen cloth, followed him at a distance. Fearful that he, too, might be arrested, the young man ran off naked, leaving the linen cloth in their grasping hands. Still others have suggested that he is the John Mark who traveled with Paul during his first missionary journey (*Acts* 13:14). Having deserted Paul, the two were later reconciled (*2 Timothy* 3:11-12).

## Why and when did Mark write and for whom?

It is generally agreed by scholars that Mark's gospel was the first to be written. Perhaps the most consistent opinion is that Mark, a Jew, wrote for Gentile Christians in Rome, sometime in the late 60s or early 70s. It seems clear from his emphasis on the suffering of Jesus that Mark is writing for people who themselves are undergoing persecution and who need to be encouraged by the example of the suffering Christ. During this time of persecution, they may have been tempted to doubt the viability of Christianity or to abandon it altogether out of fear of suffering or even death.

## What are the special characteristics of Mark's gospel?

As the first of the evangelists, Mark has truly invented a unique literary form, which has come to be known as "gospel." Certainly, before the writing of the first gospel, there existed the oral preaching of the disciples and the letters of St. Paul. But here, for the first time, the deeds and sayings of Jesus were collected in a single narrative in an attempt to present the meaning of Christ in the lives of believers at the time of the writing. Mark, taking into account the needs of his audience, selected the events and sayings from the life of Jesus and arranged them in such a way that this audience would understand their meaning in their own lives. Later, Matthew and Luke organized their gospels around the material found in *Mark*.

Mark's gospel is clearly divided into two parts. In the first half of the gospel, Jesus reveals great power and authority, both in action (miracles) and in teaching. Great emphasis is placed on the authority of Jesus—a constant source of misunderstanding. Often it is the demons who recognize him rather than those who should be his disciples. This leads to his frequent command to keep silent about his miracles. This messianic secret, so characteristic in *Mark*, is the evangelist's way of insisting that the authority and power of Jesus are not to be identified only in his miracles, but also in his death and resurrection. Until he is recognized for who he truly is, he does not want his name or his actions revealed.

The second part begins with the focal point of the gospel. This comes in 8:29 when Jesus asks the disciples, *"Who do you say that I am?"* The answer to his question (*"the Son of man who must suffer many things, and be rejected by the elders and the chief priests and the scribes, and be killed, and after three days rise again"*) leads us into the second part of the gospel. From this point on, Mark will insist that fidelity to this Christ is the hallmark of discipleship. The disciple is one who, like Jesus, suffers what is necessary for the mission. Only if one truly understands the cross will one understand resurrection. Mark's is a message of victory through suffering.

*The portrait of Jesus* that emerges in Mark's gospel is Jesus—Son of God, Son of Man—who suffered the human condition and invites us to follow him. We are called to resurrection. But the journey there is by way of the cross.

# 16. Introduction to the Gospel of Luke

## Who is Luke?

The New Testament tells us more about Luke than any other evangelist. He was the companion to St. Paul on his missionary journeys and remained his "dear friend," "co-worker," and "beloved physician." He himself tells us that he was a careful writer (*Luke* 1:1-4) who wrote both the life of Jesus and the early life of the church (*Luke* 1:1). Luke was a convert from paganism who was familiar with both Jewish and Gentile customs.

*When and why did Luke write and for whom?*

The gospel of Luke, written perhaps between 75 and 90 AD, emphasizes the universal salvation of all people, Jew and Gentile alike. Luke's primary purpose in writing seems to be to renew the faith and fidelity of Christian converts living outside of Palestine who had lost some of their earlier zeal. They had allowed community factions to occupy their attention and Luke reminds them that true discipleship means responding to the gospel in concrete, daily situations within the community. Their very community life is to be a witness.

*What are the specific characteristics of Luke's gospel?*

Luke presents the story of Jesus within the framework of a long journey. As Jesus presses on toward Jerusalem to his death, resurrection and ascension, he teaches, exhorts, and manifests his power as Lord. To those who follow him on this journey, he reveals his mission, a mission which, for Luke, has four specific characteristics: the prominence of the Holy Spirit, the importance of prayer, an attitude of joy and a special concern for marginal people such as foreigners, women and social outcasts.

He recounts stories of such people which are found only in his gospel: the Good Samaritan, the sinful woman, the ten lepers, the widow at Nain, the good thief, the pharisee and the publican, and the prodigal son. And Luke includes more women in his gospel than the other three combined. To all people, and especially to those without status, Luke gives the assurance of the tender mercy of God.

More than either Matthew or Mark, Luke presents the Holy Spirit as the creative power of God: in the Incarnation, in the mission of Jesus, and in the lives of the disciples. Jesus announces his mission on earth with a quotation from the prophet Isaiah, *"The Spirit of God is upon me"* (*Luke* 4:18). It is this same Spirit that works in and through the disciples as a sign of God's saving power on earth.

God's saving power is cause for joy and Luke's gospel abounds with this attitude. His Infancy Narrative contains four songs of joy sung by Zachariah, the angels, Mary and Simeon. And Luke tells us that there will be great joy in heaven over each sinner who repents.

The mission of Jesus and, therefore, of his disciples, is accomplished through prayer. Unlike the accounts of Matthew and Mark, Luke tells us specifically that Jesus was at prayer when he was baptized, at the Transfiguration, before choosing the twelve apostles, and before teaching the Lord's prayer. Frequently, Luke introduces a teaching or a healing story with the phrase, "while he was at prayer."

*The portrait of Jesus* that emerges from Luke's gospel is the Lord of all, whose Spirit enlivens the disciples, and who calls us to live out his mission in daily, real-life situations within the Christian community.

*"And the Word was made flesh and dwells among us . . . ."*
*John* 1:14

# PLANNING AND EVALUATION

Centering song or music _____

Welcome: *(Inspired by focus of readings)*


Readings:

First _____    Reader _____

Responsorial Psalm_____    Singer _____

Gospel Acclamation_____    Reader _____

Gospel _____    Reader _____


Reflections on Readings: *(Personal notes)*


Special Activities: *(Dramatization, reading in parts, environment, etc.)*


Symbolic Actions: *(Including special rites, gestures, banner, etc.)*


Prayers: *(Creed, prayer of the faithful)*


Evaluation of the Celebration of the Word:

*What went well:*


*What needs improvement:*


*Please duplicate this form for your leaders. Use it every week.*

# Appendix

*Supporting the vital role of parents . . .*

# BRINGING GOD'S WORD INTO THE HOME

The celebration of the word with children offers parishes a natural way of involving parents in the Christian initiation and formation of their children at home. The vision of the *Directory for Masses With Children* and the *Order for the Christian Initiation of Adults* as it applies to children brings a new focus on parents and significant adults in the lives of children. This involvement of parents means more than simply organizing religious education programs to which parents bring their children. It means adults (parents) are responsible for personally sharing their faith with those children who are part of their lives.

We can support adults in this Christian duty by the kind of material we give them to use at home. Something as simple as a weekly children's leaflet with the Sunday scriptures adapted in language children understand can make the difference in whether or not this sharing of Christian faith actually happens.

Don't misunderstand. The medium, as the expression goes, is still the message. This is not to say that children's leaflets are the message. *God's Word made flesh in us is the message.* The way we live and how we respond to God's word is a primary source of influence on children. That is why we need to reflect with children on what God is saying to us when we gather each week to celebrate God's presence in the word.

Children's leaflets help make this happen. Sending leaflets home with God's word illustrated for children to see and reflect upon through the week is a vital part of the SUNDAY celebration series. So often, parishes invest only in materials for leaders to use when children gather—and fail to provide parents with the help they need to nurture the faith of their children at home. Parents and children need this simple support. The SUNDAY leaflets for parents and children have been carefully thought out and designed to keep in focus on God's word—not on what someone else tells parents and children to hear *about* God's word.

## Should children's leaflets have lots of activities?

The function of children's leaflets is to put into the hands of parents and children God's word in language and illustrations children understand. No more and no less. Attempts are often made by publishers to give children things to do—crossword puzzles and fill-in-the-blanks kind of learning activities. Often these activities distract children from focusing on God's word and responding in prayer or quiet reflection.

Leaflets filled with learning activities and gospel applications often reveal a lack of faith in the power of God's word to initiate in children their own original and creative response. Children's leaflets, such as those in the SUNDAY series, can successfully focus the child on God's word by providing illustrations—conceived to embrace the message of the scriptures—that the child can color or paint as a reflective activity. Or, the child might be invited to create a prayer in response to the readings. We facilitate. God's word creates.

## Should children's leaflets be graded?

There is a notion carried over from the sacramental preparation (or classroom) model that raises this question about grading children's leaflets, liturgies and the scripture readings. The Christian initiation model sees older children as companions on the journey; their interaction with younger children is formative of the entire community. In other words, Christian initiation has less to do with age than it does with disposition of the heart. Also, in the home, parents do not relate to their children as a graded system but as a family sharing common experiences.

Furthermore, the lectionary is not a textbook of God's word. Though we learn from the readings, the lectionary is not a book for education but for celebration—designed to facilitate children's participation in the liturgical experience of God's presence in the word. While some parishes may feel a need to gather the very young children (3 to 5 years old) for a greatly simplified celebration, older children can gather in a mixed age group and be enriched by their varied responses to God's word. Children's leaflets that include picture-story illustrations, such as those in the SUNDAY series, help even very young children grasp enough understanding of the scriptures to

feel they are part of the celebration. Leaflets such as MY SUNDAY SHEPHERD provide a special service to parents with children 3 to 5 years old. They include an illustration and a prayer guide parents can follow through the week, enabling them to pray in a way that their children can pray with them.

## Do families really use the leaflets at home?

This question often masks another concern, parish finances, for good reason—parish budgets are usually tight. We want to be sure money is well spent. We get uneasy when we can't see someone using something for which we have paid good money. A leaflet blowing across the empty parking lot makes one wonder, not only about what's happening at home, but also about what support we give parents from the pulpit and the quality of our liturgies.

Experience has shown that the children's leaflets are not only used, but families have complained when they didn't get theirs. Experience has also shown that when the use of leaflets is encouraged from the pulpit, parents respond positively. Admonitions may reduce parking lot litter but will accomplish little toward an intelligent use of the leaflets at home.

We need to keep focused on what we're about— enriching the community's response to God's word. If our liturgies provide adults and children with a rich experience of God's presence in the celebration of the word, families will value God's word and carry that sense of presence into the home. Although we may not see to verify and measure it, the adapted readings carried home in the children's leaflets will help families sustain the spirit of God's presence in the word at home. This happens in simple ways: at mealtime conversations, at bedtime prayer, when the children are coloring or painting the scripture illustrations.

Even in the best of parish worlds, we cannot be certain that families will not occasionally leave leaflets behind. We can be certain, however, that if we do *not* provide parents with leaflets, then *none* of the families will take them home. That may give us control, but it does not give families the support for which they hunger.

*When is the best time to distribute the children's leaflets?*

The best time is after mass. It seems obvious, but some communities give leaflets to the children during their celebration of the word. Children's leaflets that contain the readings adapted for children are not to be used as some parishes use missalettes. (Nor should children's leaflets that contain activities and paraphrases of the readings be used at the celebration.) A basic liturgical principle is involved here: God's word is to be proclaimed and heard in a dramatic ritual style. (Those who cannot hear may want to read from a book.) Also, the celebration of the word is not the time for learning activities. It is the time to celebrate God's presence in song and prayer and shared reflections.

Other parishes distribute children's leaflets at the end of their celebration when they return to the adult assembly. Such use invites distractions during the celebration of the eucharist. Again, this practice should be avoided.

The most suitable time to distribute leaflets is after mass. Then the leaders of the celebration of the word have a chance to make contact with the families. The children are excited about receiving the leaflets and begin to look at them during the ride (walk) home. Their interest provides an opportunity for family members to share their responses to God's word.

There is no more natural way in which to involve parents in the Christian initiation of their children than through sharing the celebration of the word throughout the liturgical year. Such sharing draws children into the heart of the Christian community and invites us all to grow up in Christ.

*Gerard A. Pottebaum*

177

# Resources

*Note:* This listing includes basic materials that will help you nurture the spiritual life of children. Please order through:

Treehaus Communications, Inc.
P. O. Box 249   Loveland, Ohio 45140
(800) 638-4287     Fax: (513) 683-2882
Website: www.treehaus1.com
E-mail: treehaus@treehaus1.com

### SUNDAY BOOK OF READINGS
*The Lectionary Adapted for Children*

The Sunday lectionary adapted for children, endorsed for liturgical use by the Canadian Conference of Catholic Bishops, features: inclusive language, large type, lines of text end to complement natural speaking breaks, adapted in keeping with the *Directory for Masses With Children*, handsomely bound for use in celebrations of the word. Year A, B, and C in separate volumes. Developed under the direction of Christiane Brusselmans with Sr. Paule Freeburg, D.C., Rev. Edward Matthews, Christopher Walker.
ISBN 0-929496-38-8 (Year A) $29.95;
ISBN 0-929496-57-4 (Year B) $29.95;
ISBN 0-929496-91-4 (Year C) $29.95

### SUNDAY WEEKLY LEADER GUIDE

Each volume covers 52 Sundays and special feasts.Each celebration features: 1) Focus of the Readings;2) Ideas for Reflecting on the Readings with Children; 3) the Sunday readings adapted for children; 4) Music for Responses and Gospel Acclamations; 5) Prayer of the Day. Also features Background to the Sunday Readings and Liturgical Seasons. By Christiane Brusselmans, Sr. Paule Freeburg, D.C., Rev. Edward Matthews, Christopher Walker. 178 pp. Treehaus  ISBN 0-929496-93-0 (Year A);  ISBN 0-929496-58-2 (Year B);  ISBN 0-929496-92-2 (Year C) $29.95 each; subsequent volumes: $19.95 each.

### SUNDAY SCRIPTURE LEAFLETS

These four-page and six-page weekly leaflets are for use at home or school after the Sunday celebration. They feature: the Sunday readings adapted for children ages 5 to 12 years; picture-story illustrations of the readings; prayers; and description of biblical people and places. Essential for family involvement and continued reflection on the word at home.  Weekly / Treehaus. Call (800) 638-4287 for bulk discounts.

### SUNDAY SCRIPTURE RESPONSE POSTERS

A complete series of 53 beautiful posters (17 x 22 inches), designed to be decorated or colored by leaders, helpers, or parents, for use during the celebration of the word. Each poster features the enlarged text of Responses and Gospel Acclamations and a large picture-story illustration of the Sunday scriptures. Especially helpful for younger children. Available for all three cycles, Year A, B, and C. Weekly / Treehaus / Call (800) 638-4287 for discounts.

### SING GOD A SIMPLE SONG / *Volumes 1 & 2*

Singing together provides this experience of belonging as profoundly as does sharing food. So does our parish music serve to initiate our children into the ritual life of our parish assembly. The *Sing God A Simple Song* volumes provide a selection of music children can sing—music drawn from the parish assembly's repertoire. The accompanying CD recording with each volume provides the melody of each song, sung by children, to help those who cannot play an instrument learn or recall the tune. Volume 1 is a selection of 52 hymns, psalms and acclamations from GIA hymnals. Volume 2 is drawn from OCP hymnals.Compiled by Diana Kodner.  128 pp. Treehaus/1995 & 1997   Each Set: $29.95 per volume.  Additional Books: $14.95 each.

### SONGS OF LOVE *(3 to 6 Years Old)*
### SING WITH JOY *(6 to 12 Years Old)*
*Annotated by Catherine Maresca*

These songs embody a small musical tradition. They are widely sung by children in the *Catechesis of the Good Shepherd*, a pioneer work of Sofia Cavalletti and Gianna Gobbi. They celebrate the *essentials* of our faith — and, as such, are equally suitable for any catechetical or liturgical setting. These songs are, in a sense, the choice of the children. They nurture the child's natural sense of joy when encountering the sacred or engaged with mystery. Parents and catechists too will find here music for the soul.

Each book includes music and suggestions for when and how to sing each song, and a CD of children singing the songs.

*Songs of Love / 6-12 years old.* ISBN 1-886510-60-1 Bk/CD 29.95
*Sing with Joy / 3-6 years old.* ISBN 1-886510-55-5 Bk/CD 29.95

## OUR FAMILY SPIRITUAL LIFE JOURNALS

These journals follow the same reflection process as found in the *SUNDAY Liturgy of the Word* materials. Each journal includes the Sunday gospel adapted for the entire family, reflection suggestions, simple family rituals and prayers—with ample space for your family's journal entries. Generous parish discounts for bulk purchases. 160 pp. ea. Treehaus / $12.95 (less bulk discount) Titles:
LIGHT OF THE WORLD / *Year A* / *The Gospel of Matthew.*
WORD MADE FLESH / *Year B* / *The Gospel* of Mark.
BREAD OF LIFE / *Year C* / *The Gospel of Luke.*

## PERSONAL SPIRITUAL LIFE JOURNALS

These journals follow the same reflection process as found in the *SUNDAY Liturgy of the Word* materials. For young adults and adults, each journal includes the Sunday gospel adapted to facilitate understanding and meditation, reflection suggestions, and a psalm prayer verse—with ample space for journal entries. Generous parish discounts for bulk purchases. 160 pp. ea. Treehaus / $12.95 (less bulk discount) Titles:
I AM THE WAY / *Year A* / *The Gospel of Matthew.*
I AM THE TRUTH / *Year B* / *The Gospel of Mark.*
I AM THE LIFE / *Year C* / *The Gospel of Luke.*

## TO WALK WITH A CHILD

*A TRAINING PROGRAM FOR LITURGY LEADERS, CATECHISTS & PARENTS*

*PowerPoint CD & Book by Gerard Pottebaum*

"I love the presentation! I would use it to spark conversation and awareness of the natural spirituality of children and how to help them 'theologize' about life by giving them a language through Scripture, symbol and ritual." — *Joyce M. Kelleher, Director of Office of Catechetical Services / Cleveland*

What training have your liturgy leaders and catechists had in reflecting on the Scriptures with children? When your children hear God's Word, do they feel they are part of the story of God's love? Or do they feel left out? Is your children's Liturgy of the Word prayerful worship? Or has it become more like a religion class or a Bible study session? How aware are parents of their child's innate relationship with God?

*To Walk With a Child* helps you serve these needs. It is timely, graphic, and user-friendly. It provides enough material for either a one- or two-session workshop that parish leaders can conduct for children's liturgy leaders, catechists and parents. Participants learn to reflect with children on their lives in light of God's Word — in a liturgical or catechetical setting, or at home.

The book provides comprehensive background and discussion aids. Additional copies of the book are available for participants. The PowerPoint CD itself includes notes that the facilitator can follow while leading the workshop.

"Excellent pastoral guide. . . Belongs in the hands of every committee who prepares or presider who leads children in liturgical worship."
— *Elizabeth Jeep / Worship*

*$24.95 per set / 2+ sets: $19.95 each*

## A CHILD SHALL LEAD THEM:
*A Guide to Celebrating the Word With Children*

This has become the basic guide throughout the country for celebrating the Word with children. It is a companion to *TO WALK WITH A CHILD* book and CD. It captures the vision and sensitively applies the guidelines of *The Directory for Masses With Children.* This Guide follows the celebration step-by-step, giving detailed reflections and ideas on each step as the ritual unfolds. An indispensable resource for anyone who celebrates the Word with children.
Editor/Contributing Author: Gerard A. Pottebaum / Contributing Authors: Sister Paule Freeburg, D.C. & Joyce M. Kelleher. 144 pp. Treehaus / $11.95

## TURNING POINTS
*Rethinking Conventional Catechetics*

*A Parish Dialogue Handbook*

*Joyce M. Kelleher Director of the Office of Catechetical Formation, Diocese of Cleveland*

"I am so happy to see a simple process offered that any parish group can use in what they are already doing. No add-ons or extra activities. This is the right book for all pastoral ministers who try to engage the whole parish community in reflecting on their lives in light of the Scriptures. " — *Kate Dooley, O.P. The Catholic University of America*

"Rich with citations from catechetical documents. A delightful feature which makes the book 'interactive' is a series of dialogue questions on each page. They force us to consider practical applications to respond to our baptismal call." — *Bishop A. Bosco, Greensburg, PA*

"Its simplicity and readability belie the depth of the content (Joyce Kelleher) so effortlessly weaves together to fashion a tool for adult parishioners to reflect upon personally and dialogue about in their journey together in faith." — *Most Rev. Anthony M. Pilla, Diocese of Cleveland*

This *Handbook for Parish Dialogue* helps you engage the entire parish in faith formation — community style. With solid footing on catechetical documents, *TURNING POINTS* describes how to draw the entire community into a simple process that makes reflecting on the Sunday Gospel the focal point of every parish gathering, meeting, and event. "If all parish groups adopted this idea, there would bound to be a change," Kate Dooley, O.P., observed. "I am going to ask our pastor to read that section."

$12.95 / 2-5: $9.95 / 6-19: $8.95 / 20+: $8.50

## DOUBLE*CLOSE*

*The Young Child's Knowledge of God*

*Catherine Maresca*
*Director of the Center for Children and Theology*

Help parents and catechists recognize the young child's original "double close" relationship with God. *Part One* explores characteristics of young children, their potential for a rich relationship with God, and how young children know God and communicate that knowledge to observant adults. *Part Two* features responses of young children to the Word or the Liturgy, followed by a reflection designed to nurture the reader's own relationship with God.

"The voices of children — whispering, singing, exclaiming, and even pausing in silence — rise from the pages of this treasure of a book. It gives us another opportunity to enjoy children. . . . Catherine's careful exposition shines a light on words and actions that we might otherwise overlook." — *Tina Lillig, National Director, Catechesis of the Good Shepherd*

"A wonderful book! The author guides readers into the imagination, creative world and play of children, a place where a teacher, mother, and keen observer of children finds herself as learner and as one introduced once again to sacred space. DOUBLE*CLOSE* is an invaluable resource for all of us who care about education and formation. After reading the book I gave thanks again for my children and grandchildren and the gifts they have given to me . . ." — *Rev. Bud Holland, Coordinator, Office of Ministry Development, The Episcopal Church Center, New York*

$14.95 / 2-5: $11.95 / 6-19: $10.95 / 20+: $10.50

## *THE SPIRIT OF THE CHILD*

*David Hay with Rebecca Nye*

What is the nature of children's spirituality? What kinds of spiritual experience do children have? This book explains the fascinating results of a three-year investigation of children's spirituality. David Hay, director of the project, argues for greater attention to abe given to nurturing children's spirituality as the true source of social and moral cohesion for the future. Treehaus / Paperback: $19.95

## *LISTENING TO GOD WITH CHILDREN*
*The Montessori Method Applied to the Catechesis of Children*

Gianna Gobbi draws on a lifetime of experience with children, having worked personally at the side of Maria Montessori and in collaboration with Sofia Cavalletti in the development of the Catechesis of the Good Shepherd. Here Gobbi presents a rare balance of the theory and the application of Montessori principles. "The result," writes Sofia Cavalletti in her introduction, "is a rich, living work." 148 pp. Treehaus / $12.95

## *NURTURING YOUR CHILD'S SPIRIT*
*A Montessorian Approach*

Jeannine Schmid is a pioneer in the Montessori movement. In *Nurturing Your Child's Spirit,* she provides a wealth of ideas, insights and specific suggestions to help parents and teachers present basic biblical images and symbols to children in a way that nurtures the child's natural sense of the sacred. Anyone involved with the very young child will find this work a basic resource. $12.95

## *JESUS AND THE CHILDREN*

Author/scholar Hans-Ruedi Weber explores the often quoted — and often misunderstood — references to children in the Gospel. Just what was Jesus' relationship with children? What was the place of children in Jewish culture and Graeco-Roman society? Complete with study outlines, helpful comparisons of texts from four Gospel accounts. For catechists, parents, anyone who wants to gain a new insight into the Gospel through the metaphor of children. $12.95

## *EXPLORING THE SPIRITUALITY OF CHILDHOOD*
*Proceedings of the First National Conference on the Spiritual Life of Children*

*Authors: Vivian Gussin Paley, Wade Clark Roof, Jane P. Ward*
*Editor: Gerard A. Pottebaum*

This is a rare resource not only for teachers, social workers, professional childcare-givers, but also for individuals who want to better understand the influence of childhood experiences on their own spiritual lives as adults. These proceedings provide a unique chance to enter an interfaith, intercultural dialogue that explores the significance of childhood experiences of the sacred and the influences of society, family, and institutional religion on the child's original experiences of God. Lively reading and a rich resource, the work provides the thoughts of representatives from every major religious tradition and culture. $14.95

### *HOW TO CELEBRATE THE WORD WITH CHILDREN... AND WHY*
*Video*

Features a demonstration celebration with commentary by Father Edward Matthews, one of the primary authors of the *Directory for Masses With Children.* 30 minutes with guide / Treehaus $19.95

### *SUNDAY: A BASIC CELEBRATION RESOURCE*
*Video*

A video "dictionary" for the SUNDAY Celebration of the Word material, hosted by Christiane Brusselmans and Gerard A. Pottebaum. Each element of the SUNDAY Celebration of the Word material is defined, with its uses. An important tool for any parish developing liturgies that respect the spiritual life of children. 21 Minutes / Treehaus / $19.95

### *HOW PARISHES ARE CELEBRATING THE WORD WITH CHILDREN*
*Video*

This video visits four different parishes to see how they celebrate the Word with children. The purpose is to learn from these efforts, not to show the ideal. Includes Anglo, Hispanic, and African-American parishes. Settings include: classroom, special worship space, convent chapel, and a sacristy. A discussion guide aids reflecting on what is or is not appropriate liturgical practice. Running times: 10, 19, 10, and 19 minutes. Purchase: $19.95.

*Visit the Treehaus website for sample pages of SUNDAY materials.*

**www.treehaus1.com**

*E-mail:*

**treehaus@treehaus1.com**

# Index

# Index of Scripture Readings